MANAGING YOUR INVESTMENT MANAGER
The complete guide to selection, measurement, and control

MARSHA Z.

MANAGING YOUR INVESTMENT MANAGER

The complete guide to selection, measurement, and control

ARTHUR WILLIAMS III

DOW JONES-IRWIN Homewood, Illinois 60430

ISBN 0-87094-187-9
Library of Congress Catalog Card No. 79–56084

Printed in the United States of America

3 4 5 6 7 8 9 0 K 7 6 5

For Sandra, Art, Mindy, and Tom without whose patience, understanding and support this book could not have been completed.

Foreword

At last a handy and valuable reference book for pension, profit sharing, and savings plan sponsors—large, medium or small—has become available. In this much needed volume, Art Williams draws upon his years of "hands-on" experience in the investment business and points out the very real risk reward trade-offs facing plan sponsors as they go about the difficult tasks of selecting, measuring, controlling, and—most of all—managing their investment managers.

This book will be of considerable assistance to experienced pension fund professionals on both the sponsor and investment manager sides of the fence as well as to those individuals who have only recently become confronted with their fiduciary responsibilities.

In this book, Art Williams covers the investment waterfront and provides clear and concise information concerning subjects of interest to all plan sponsors. From asset allocation to international investing to the alphabet soup of modern portfolio theory, the author carefully defines his terms, explains the rationale behind the theories, and provides the reader with the information required to implement or reject the myriad of approaches to successful fund management.

I was particularly impressed with the way the author emphasized the need for risk management on the part of plan sponsors. In this post-ERISA era, plan sponsors must take an active role in managing their managers. Doing so requires a thorough understanding of the elements of risk management, which is ably provided in this book.

Finally, author Williams deserves our thanks for including what he graciously refers to as a "mathematics refresher." For those of us who have allowed the passage of years to diminish our quantitative skills, this refresher section is worth more than the book's cost. And in gently reminding us of the importance of "The Art of Being a Good Client," the author lists the do's and don'ts which all plan sponsors should periodically review.

Speaking for plan sponsors generally, *Managing Your Investment Manager* will, I feel, be a frequently referred to desk-top consultant as we plan investment strategies for the 1980s and beyond. I am grateful to Art Williams for putting so much valuable information in one easy-to-understand volume. And as you read and use Art's book, I think you will share my assessment of it.

John W. English
Director, Pension Fund Administration
American Telephone and Telegraph Company
New York, N.Y.

Preface

Anyone browsing through the financial section of a book store will be impressed by the seemingly endless number of books describing ways to invest profitably. At the same time, any trustee or fund administrator who wishes to learn how to structure and operate a large pool of assets will be frustrated by the lack of information on the subject. This is truly amazing, given the staggering sums of money flowing into public and private pension funds, the increase in fiduciary awareness engendered by ERISA, and the poor investment results achieved over the last decade, such that virtually every pension fund will require greater contributions than planned and almost every endowment fund has witnessed a deterioration in its ability to meet the long-run financial needs of its sponsoring institution. It seems clear that a whole new management system is needed to deal with this huge but frequently inadequate pool of assets and the attendant problems and opportunities. The principal components needed are a management framework for establishing goals, trained managers for implementing the goals, and an information system which provides the necessary feedback so that corrective action can be taken when actual results stray beyond predetermined limits from acceptable results.

This book has two purposes. The first purpose is to contribute to the creation and development of a management system in all three areas by presenting in a logical format the relevant issues, discussing potential solutions and the pros and cons of each, analyzing measurement techniques, and presenting a bibliography for use when further investigation is required. The book is about investing, but from the viewpoint of the trustee or the fiduciary who works with investment managers rather than from the viewpoint of the investment manager buying and selling securities.

The second purpose of the book is to build a communications bridge between fund sponsors and investment managers. Unless the two groups understand the goals of the organization and its fund, the personalities involved, and the terminology of the game, it is unlikely that the goals of the organization or of the investment manager will be met.

The book is designed both to be read and to be referred to. It is organized in the way the president of a corporation, union, or college, or the governor of a state, might look at the problem of how to operate a fund by discussing:

What are the goals of our fund?

Who in the organization should have the primary responsibility for the fund?

How do we choose an investment strategy?

How do we choose asset types?

How do we choose investment managers?

How do we work with our investment managers?

How do we evaluate our investment managers?

How do we control multiple managers?

The text of the book is followed by two appendixes, a mathematics refresher, a discussion of the tax implications of timing of contributions, and an annotated bibliography.

Acknowledgments

I wish to express my sincere thanks to the many people who provided comments and insights which assisted me in writing this book. Included are: Franklin Hendler, Laura Levine, Herbert E. Gernert, Jr., John J. Targia, Richard E. Dahab,

Arthur Carlson, Sumner Levine, Don L. Horwitz, John B. Rofrano, Arthur J. Fenton, James T. McComsey, John F. Condon, Arthur Zeikel, Robert J. Farrell, Philip R. Rettew, Jr., James J. Bohan, Adrian Wesson, Dimitri Raftopoulos, Heidi Church, Philip R. Sloan, Michael K. Polysius, William J. Rahal, Lawrence Fisher, James H. Lorie, John English, Marshall Blume, Charles Ellis, Donald E. Rossi, Henry James, Bonnie R. Cohen, Robert Angelica, Peter O. Dietz, Russell Fogler, Dennis Tito, Wayne Wagner, and Dr. Martin Liebowitz.

A special note of thanks is due Dorene C. Prinzo whose extensive efforts in preparing and editing the manuscript were vital to the publication of this book.

February 1980   Arthur Williams III

Contents

1

Establishing goals for the fund

Even though much of the subject matter of this book relates to investing, it is really not investing that we are most concerned with. Our efforts are directed at providing a rational framework within which representatives of sponsoring organizations can deal with their funds. In order to do this we will start at the very beginning by asking the question "What are we trying to accomplish?" The answer, of course, is that we are trying to help our organization through proper management of its fund. But in order to understand the goals of the fund it is first necessary to examine the goals of the organization. Second, we must ask in general terms how the fund can further those goals. Finally, we must ask how the fund can be structured to maximize the chances that goals will be met. Since the answers vary considerably, depending on the type of organization, it is well to break down the analysis by organization types. Throughout the book four types of organizations will be considered—corporations, labor unions, state and local governments, and charitable organizations.

1

CORPORATIONS

It is traditional to state that the goal of a corporation, whether publicly or privately held, is to maximize the long-run wealth of shareholders. Although this is still the goal, it is nonetheless necessary to consider three other "constituencies": employees, government, and consumers. The role of consumers, though clearly important to the corporation's success, is not particularly relevant to the subject of managing the investment manager. The significance to this subject of employees and government is, on the other hand, crucial. Employees' interests are directly related to the success of the corporation, and retirement plans are directly related to the interests of employees. Government, of course, has become greatly involved in retirement plans with the giant step known as ERISA (Employee Retirement Security Act of 1974). Because of ERISA every act taken or even contemplated by a fund sponsor or an investment manager must be considered in light of its ERISA implications.

It therefore seems appropriate for our purposes to define the corporation's goal as maximizing the long-run wealth of shareholders while giving full recognition to the needs of employees and the presence of government regulation. It can be argued that maximizing the wealth of shareholders requires consideration of employees' needs and the omnipresence of government regulators. Although this view will not be denied, it appears that the explicit recognition of employee and government interests will enhance the corporation's chances of achieving its primary profit-making function.

Although the subject of maximizing shareholders' wealth is a book in itself, suffice it to say that shareholders' wealth is composed of the stock price plus dividends received and that increases in the stock price and dividends are a function of *growth* and *risk*. Obviously growth is to be maximized and risk minimized. (These two factors, growth and risk, are analogous to *return* and *risk*, the two basic considerations in any investment.) Part of the fund's objective, therefore, is to increase the company's earnings and to decrease their volatility. These are reasonable goals, though applying them is not easy, especially since they may conflict with the goals of giving full recognition to the needs of employees and to the presence of government regulation.

The retirement fund can have an important impact on the corporation's goal of serving the needs of employees. Every employee must consider the economic effects of becoming too old to work. Many employees look forward to a less demanding retirement lifestyle. To the extent that a retirement plan can guarantee income so that employees will have financial security in their later years, the plan is important to the corporation goal of giving recognition to the needs of employees.

There appears to be a conflict between the goal of keeping employees content by providing them with high-cost fringe benefits and the primary corporate goal, maximizing the wealth of shareholders. This conflict is certainly real in the short run, since a dollar put into a retirement plan is a dollar less (before taxes) for dividends or reinvestment. In the long run, however, an optimal balance is possible, since the welfare of the corporation is intimately related to the productivity of the work force *and* the welfare of the work force is intimately related to the success of the corporation.

While attempting to operate its retirement funds so as to maximize the wealth of shareholders, the corporation must deal with the growing presence of the federal government. An interesting paradox develops, since ERISA clearly states that retirement funds "must be operated solely for the benefit" of their participants. It also seems clear that to some extent ERISA was passed because companies pursued the wealth of shareholders at the expense of employee benefits. There are well-known horror stories about employees who worked for many years in the expectation of receiving a pension, but then were denied it because of a corporate merger, a plant closing, or some other unexpected event. The conflict between maximizing the wealth of shareholders and operating a plan "solely for the benefits of participants" is real, complex, and unresolved. Yet corporate management must deal with this problem in setting policies on plan benefits and investing.

The exact steps to ensure that the goals of the fund maximize long-run shareholders' wealth by contributing to the growth and stability of sales, earnings, and dividends are explored in

Chapter 3. These steps depend on the financial needs of the corporation and the fund and on their ability to bear risk.

The effect of the stability and growth of the earnings for a *defined benefit* plan can be viewed in the context of whether the plan benefits are growing or static, although the basic outcome is similar in either case. If the benefits are *static*, the way to contribute to stability and growth is by seeing that the fund assets earn at least the assumed rate of return. This would ensure that no actuarial losses are incurred. Such losses must be amortized, through increased contributions, over no more than 15 years.

Of course, since markets decline as well as rise, and since they seem to be able to stay down longer than most of us expected them to, it would be nice to have a cushion over and above the assets needed to meet actuarial requirements. Therefore, fund sponsors tend to favor policies producing higher returns. It is a simple, logical step to recognize that if the cushion becomes large enough, an actuarial *gain* results. This gain can eventually be amortized, in which case the corporate contributions will decrease.

If plan benefits are likely to *increase*, a corporation whose fund achieves only its actuarial objective will suffer earnings decreases whenever benefits rise. This is because the higher benefits apply to all employees (even those about to retire) and no provision has been made for money to pay the higher benefits. Thus "unfunded past service costs" immediately appear, and these must be amortized over no more than 40 years, with an ensuing drop in earnings. Corporations expecting to increase benefits (and this seems to include almost all of them) thus have a strong incentive to achieve investment returns beyond those dictated by their actuarial assumptions.

Plans with *nondefined benefits,* such as profit-sharing plans, should have a minimal impact on the growth and stability of sales, earnings, and dividends. Plans of this type are usually adopted in lieu of some other form of compensating or encouraging the loyalty of employees. Consequently the cost of such plans is borne by the corporation in lieu of a similar cost for another form of compensation.

A corporation can take a number of steps to operate a retirement plan so that it gives full recognition to the needs of employees while maximizing the wealth of shareholders. A plan with assets in excess of actuarially established levels is a source of comfort to employees. It provides a greater probability that benefits will be paid and that they can be increased. Thus the corporation and its employees both have a strong interest in seeing the plan's assets enhanced through investment gain.

The next question is, "What is the attitude toward risk that each of these parties holds?" To the corporation, an investment dollar lost is a dollar that must someday be replaced (with interest at the assumed rate), and the reverse is true for a dollar gained from investment. To employees, a dollar lost by the fund is a dollar less security and a dollar less of potential gain in benefits. However, it is not a dollar in lost benefits. The corporation must still pay the defined benefit, and, presumably, if the corporation does not, the Pension Benefit Guaranty Corporation (PBGC) will. Thus the employee can be more tolerant of risk than is the corporation sponsoring the fund. However, where a fund is extremely underfunded, the corporation may feel that it will probably be required to surrender the maximum 30 percent of its net worth to the PBGC, and hence it can speculate with pension assets without regard to loss in the hopes of making a sufficient "killing" to decrease its liability to PBGC to less than 30 percent of its net worth. In this situation the employee bears no risk and the corporation bears no incremental risk beyond 30 percent of its net worth.

In order to understand how a fund can be operated in such a way as to pursue the goal of maximizing the wealth of shareholders while giving full recognition to government regulation, a brief summary of the applicable laws is required.

Prior to ERISA, trust law was the major body of law applying to corporate retirement plans (though it is less than clear that national and multinational corporations paid much attention to it). Two types of trust law prevailed: legal lists and "prudent man." Under the legal list concept state legislation listed the criteria for allowable investments in trusts. The prudent man doctrine indicated that a trustee "shall conduct himself faithfully and exercise a sound discretion. He is to observe how men of prudence, discretion and intelligence manage their own affairs, not in regard to speculation, but in regard to the permanent disposition of their funds, considering the probable income, as well as the probable safety of the capital to be invested."[1]

The Employee Retirement Income Security Act of 1974 is now the dominant legislative influence on private retirement plans. Although the act is hopelessly complex in its details, its aim is elegantly simple. A corporation does not need to provide its employees with a retirement plan, but if it does, it must tell the employees in simple terms the whole truth about the plan. It must put aside sufficient money so that the plan can pay the promised benefits, and the plan and its assets must be administered carefully and honestly by competent people with the sole objective of serving the interests of plan beneficiaries.

Relevant portions of the SEC Act of 1975 (Williams Amendment) describe the conditions under which the investment managers of a fund can also act as brokers for the fund and the conditions under which brokerage commissions can be utilized to pay for services to the fund and to the investment manager.

An appropriate approach to successful operation in a regulated environment is:

1. Be knowledgeable about the relevant law.
2. Be conscious of the relevant law whenever a significant decision is being made.
3. Be conscientious in carrying out legal responsibilities.
4. See that the necessary legal documents are prepared, and be ready to present a legally acceptable rationale for significant decisions.

LABOR UNIONS

We will now examine the goals of labor organizations, how pension funds can support those goals, and the specific steps that can be taken to further the goals.

Jointly trusteed (Taft-Hartley) funds, as the name implies, have two sets of sponsors. Typically, a union representing a group of employees secures agreement from a group of employers to contribute a certain amount of money for each hour worked by each employee. This money is then contributed

---

[1] Quoted from Harvey E. Bines, *The Law of Investment Management* (Boston: Warren, Gorham & Lamont, 1978), p. 1–3.

monthly to a common pool which is invested on behalf of the participants. An important distinction must be drawn between jointly trusteed and other pension funds; namely, that in a jointly trusteed fund the only assets (excluding government insurance) available to meet pension payments are those of the fund. No corporation, church group, or state or local government has guaranteed the fund. Thus, if the assets of a jointly trusteed fund are inadequate, retirees will eventually find that their benefits cannot be met. A second distinction is that labor unions are political organizations whose members/beneficiaries elect their officers/trustees. This condition does not exist for corporations, other private organizations, or even public funds. A governor is elected by the people of the state, not just by those state employees who are covered by a fund.

These two distinctions can lead to a marked impact on the investment philosophy of jointly trusteed funds. The lack of a sponsor which guarantees benefits clearly gives rise to the need for a conservative investment philosophy. The political nature of the organization is likely to have a varied effect. Following long periods in which the stock market has performed well, pressure is exerted on incumbents by candidates to increase return (by increasing risk). In periods when the stock market has performed poorly, the opposite will occur. Although this problem is apparent to some extent in both public and non-union private funds, it is most evident in jointly trusteed funds.

Given this background, analysis of the goals of the organization and of jointly trusteed funds is greatly simplified. The goals of the organization are to promote the economic and physical welfare of members and their families. Clearly, an important part of the members' financial and security package is their pensions. The pension fund can solve part of the members' financial needs by maintaining sufficient assets to meet benefits. A secondary but related objective is to increase fund assets at a rate greater than the fund's assumed rate of return. Like corporate employees, Taft-Hartley fund participants want to have a cushion of assets above the actuarial requirements. Further, they hope for additional asset enhancement as a source of additional benefits. However, since there is no fund sponsor to guarantee pension benefits, they are much more risk averse than are the employees of a corporation or a public body.

STATE AND LOCAL GOVERNMENTS

The factors affecting public funds are surprisingly similar to those affecting corporate funds. In both cases the sponsoring organization provides services to "customers." In order to provide the services efficiently a productive and loyal work force is needed.

The sponsor guarantees benefits to its employees, bearing the risk associated with the guarantee, in order to strengthen productivity and loyalty. Thus the goals of the two organizational types and the ways in which their funds can help meet those goals are similar. Four important distinctions should be noted. First, there are statutory restrictions (typically limiting the fund's percentage in equities) to which corporate funds are not subject. Second, many public funds are contributory, with a large percentage of their assets coming from direct employee contributions. Third, public funds are subject to much greater scrutiny than are private funds. These three factors all contribute to the tendency to establish conservative policies in operating public funds. Fourth, public funds are not subject to ERISA. However, this probably does not have a significant effect on the prudence of investments, since at some point ERISA-type legislation will probably govern public funds and in any event the standards of prudence dictated by ERISA are already having an important impact on public officials.

CHARITABLE ORGANIZATIONS

Frequently, two types of asset pools are supervised by the trustees of the endowments of charitable organizations— pension funds for employees and endowment funds which support the charitable organizations themselves. The pension funds are similar to the corporate and public funds. The endowment fund is different in that its obligation is difficult to measure. Unlike a pension fund, which is obligated to pay certain fairly predictable benefits, an endowment fund is normally obligated to support the purposes of the charitable organization. Since the importance of this support can be great, it is well to examine the goals of charitable organizations and how the endowment fund furthers those goals.

Charitable organizations seek to further specific socially beneficial activities. Obviously, money is required to pursue almost any activity, so the maintenance and enhancement of the endowment fund's assets can spell the difference between success and failure for the charitable organization. To ensure that the endowment fund supports the goals of a charitable organization, a complete assessment must be made of the timing and magnitude of the organization's financial needs. An investment portfolio must then be established which meets those financial needs. Chapter 3 addresses this complex but vital subject.

2

Assigning responsibility for operating the fund

"The simplest organization structure that will do the job is the best one."[1]

Once an understanding has been achieved of the organization's goals and how the fund can support them, a series of practical questions must be answered. Among these are:

1. Who will set policies and guidelines, including the written statement of purpose and the appropriate risk/return policy?
2. Who at the organization will have day-to-day responsibility for the fund?
3. Who will make investment decisions?
4. What other services are required, and who will provide them?
5. How will fund activities be monitored?

---

[1] Peter F. Drucker, *Management: Tasks, Responsibilities, Practices* (New York: Harper & Row, 1974), p. 601.

11

The answers to these questions depend on the type and size of the organization, the size of the fund, the importance of the fund to the success of the organization, and the availability of experienced personnel within the organization. Therefore, each of these decisions must be made in light of the characteristics and needs of the specific organization. However, before we discuss how these decisions can be made, it will be useful to summarize the services required to operate a fund.

THE SERVICES REQUIRED

The basic services required to operate a fund are investment management, safekeeping (custodial), record-keeping, monitoring, legal, and accounting services. For pension funds, actuarial services are also required.

Investment management services. These activities involve choosing the specific securities that will be used to achieve a fund's investment aims. They include economic analyses and decisions to purchase and sell individual securities. Chapter 5 analyzes in detail the need for investment management services and the available types of services.

Safekeeping (custodial) services If a fund owns securities directly, rather than through a commingled fund, it is necessary to have custodial facilities for physically maintaining possession of the securities and for collecting dividends and interest, redeeming matured securities, and effecting receipts and deliveries following purchases and sales. The custodian is also in an excellent position to account for all cash and securities movements in the fund and to provide other information on the fund.

Record-keeping services. Among the basic records required are cash or transaction statements and valuations.

Cash or transaction statements list all transactions affecting the cash balance (contributions and withdrawals, purchases and sales, and dividends and interest), as well as any contributions or distributions "in kind." Endowment funds are frequent recipients of gifts of securities since the donors avoid paying capital gains taxes on any appreciation. Corporations may contribute company stock to pension plans in order to save cash, or to profit-sharing plans in order to fulfill obligations to the plans. Such gifts in kind must be properly identified and accounted for to permit correct measurements of fund performance.

Cash statements should also contain beginning and ending cash balances. These statements should be produced quarterly or monthly. Typically the statements are in chronological order by transaction, though some custodians sort alphabetically by security. The latter system makes it easier to locate transactions in or income from particular securities, but they are more difficult to use when the history of a fund is being traced. Cash statements are normally provided on a *settlement date* basis by banks and brokers and on a *trade date* basis by investment advisers. This distinction arises because industry practice calls for a period of time (usually five business days) between the time that a stock or a corporate bond is sold and the time that payment and delivery are made, and custodians usually view their obligation in terms of cash settlement, whereas investment advisers typically think in terms of the time when securities are purchased and sold.

A *valuation* is a listing of each asset in the portfolio, along with its market value, as of a point in time. The cash balance on the valuation should agree with the cash balance on the cash statement.

Additional statements include summaries of contributions and withdrawals, dividends, interest, purchases and sales (either by asset category, such as cash equivalents, bonds, and stocks, or in aggregate), and administrative fees. Private retirement funds also need to track brokerage fees paid (for party in interest reporting) and purchases and sales by security (to report transactions under the "3 percent rule"). This information may be provided by the custodian.

Monitoring services. In order to be sure that a fund is operating as it should, the sponsoring organization must monitor investment results, risk policies, the effect of the investment manager's discretionary activities on the fund, and the effectiveness of the custodial process. Chapters 6 to 13 discuss these activities in detail.

Legal services. Legal advice is necessary for every fund at its inception, and further legal advice should be available when needed. In addition, a periodic review of trust documents should be made at least every three years to ensure that the changing circumstances of the fund and the evolution of the law have not made the documents obsolete.

For discussion of the legal factors that affect them, funds can be classified into three categories: public funds, ERISA funds, and other trusts.

Public funds are established by specific legislation (usually at the state level). This legislation sets forth the purpose of the trust, the organization of the trust, the responsible parties, and the benefits to be paid. The legislation may also establish risk policy guidelines by mandating the maximum percentage in equities.

ERISA is the dominant legislation for corporate and jointly trusteed retirement funds. Plan documents must be designed to conform to the strictures of this law, one of the most basic of which is that every plan must have written documents. Beyond the establishment of the plan there are numerous requirements for legal advice in complying with the 280 pages of ERISA. As case law develops, these requirements will continue to grow.

Other trusts, which consist largely of endowments, are governed by the laws of the states in which they were established.

Certified audits. Funds covered by ERISA and public funds must be audited by public accountants. Such an audit typically covers a reconciliation of the beginning and ending book (cost) values of a fund, with all contributions and purchases and sales that have been made during the period under examination. The audit also spot-checks for receipt of dividends and interest.

Actuarial services. For defined benefit pension funds the sponsoring organization makes a "reasonable" contribution in order to provide adequate funding to meet pensioners' needs. Determining the amount of the contribution requires analyzing the age, sex, salary levels, and probability of termination/disability/death/early retirement of employees; inflation; and the return on investments that is available in the marketplace. (See Winklevoss in Bibliography.)

OPERATING A FUND

Setting policies and guidelines. After the purposes of the sponsor's organization and the ways in which the fund can support those purposes have been reviewed by the sponsor, the next step is to decide who should set policies and guidelines for the fund. The answer to this question is, without doubt, that the board of directors or the board of trustees should establish policies. Since the fund is important to the sponsor for both financial and legal reasons, the highest authority in the sponsoring organization should have the final say about the fund's policies. The source of information upon which the directors or the trustees will act is a function of the size of the organization, the importance of the fund to the success of the organization, and the availability of experienced personnel within the organization. The larger the sponsor, the greater will be the effort made by staff members as opposed to that made by officers or directors. The greater the importance of the fund to the sponsor, the greater should be the involvement of the highest levels of the organization. Finally, the greater the availability of competent personnel within the organization, the greater will be its ability to supply services internally as opposed to going outside for them.

Writing a statement of purpose. Even for a fund not covered by ERISA it is vital to have a written statement of purpose describing what the fund is intended to do, how the fund relates to the objectives of the organization, and how the fund's goals are to be carried out. The statement of purpose should be as specific as possible, and it should be reviewed at least annually to ensure that it is still relevant and complete. The statement of purpose should be distributed to all board members and to all people and organizations that provide services to the fund. The statement of purpose can also serve as the basis for communications with employees about the reasons for the existence of the fund and the procedures for carrying out its functions.

Establishing a risk/return investment policy. This important subject is the basis for Chapter 3, and consequently it will not be discussed here.

Assigning responsibility for operating the fund. In addition to assigning the responsibility for setting policies and guidelines, a person or a group should be assigned the responsibility for operating the fund on a daily basis. Within the four organization types the choices are:

1. Corporation
   a. Board of directors
   b. Subcommittee of the board of directors
   c. President
   d. Vice president of finance or a subordinate
   e. Vice president of administration or a subordinate
   f. Vice president of personnel or a subordinate
   g. Vice president of pension investing
   h. Outside consultant
2. Jointly trusteed funds
   a. Board of trustees
   b. Subcommittee of the board
   c. Administrator
   d. Outside consultant
3. Public funds
   a. Chief executive (governor, mayor, etc.)
   b. Administrator
   c. Finance officer
   d. Pension board
   e. Outside consultant
4. Charitable organizations
   a. Board of Trustees
   b. Subcommittee of the board
   c. President
   d. Vice president of finance or a subordinate
   e. Vice president of administration or a subordinate
   f. Vice president of personnel or a subordinate
   g. Vice president of pension investing
   h. Outside consultant

The investment aspects of a fund are sufficiently complex and unrelated to the activities of most organizations that it is desirable to have someone within the organization charged with continued, long-term responsibility. Long-term responsibility is emphasized to express concern over the situation in which a stint of overseeing fund investment managers is part of a career path for financial managers. Although such experience is useful both to the organization and to the financial manager, it is highly unlikely that the organization's goals will be very well supported by the fund if the person responsible for it is transferred to a new position just as he is finally beginning to understand the old one. Since it usually takes several market cycles to become familiar with the investment process, it is unlikely that an organization will derive much benefit from a fund administrator who occupies his position for only two or three years.

A second reason for assigning responsibility for the investment aspects of a fund on a long-term basis is that boards of directors or boards of trustees are usually ineffective at *carrying out* the policies they have adopted. Thus it is desirable to give an individual the authority and responsibility for implementing and monitoring such policies with regard to the fund. Further, since the composition of many boards changes rather rapidly, it is desirable to provide a measure of stability to the post. Thus it appears preferable to assign continuing responsibility for the fund to a person who can accept this responsibility over a long period of time. It is then entirely appropriate to rotate subordinate personnel who can use the time spent working on the fund to broaden their experience within the organization.

Choosing assets types and investment managers.   In order to implement the investment policy, security types and investment managers must be chosen. These important subjects are discussed in Chapters 4 and 5.

Other services.   Also required are custodial, recordkeeping, monitoring, legal, and accounting services. In addition, pension funds require actuarial services. Custodial services are described in detail in Chapter 13; monitoring services are treated in Chapters 6–10; and actuarial services are discussed in the Bibliography. As to legal and accounting activities, since sponsors do not appear to have problems in these areas, they will not be analyzed here.

3

Choosing
an investment policy

A unique characteristic of risk is that it exists only in the future but can be measured only in the past.

The choice of an investment policy (a risk policy) for the fund is one of the most important and perplexing problems faced by fund sponsors and fund managers. In very few cases is there a conscious decision, based on rational analysis, as to what the policy should be. Consequently this area will be discussed at considerable length, always in the context of the perspective described below:

1. The purpose of the fund is to support the objectives of the organization sponsoring the fund.
2. The investment policy or risk/return posture of the fund should be such as to maximize the probability that the fund will achieve its goal of supporting the organization.

19

This chapter will discuss a framework for answering the question "How much risk can the fund take?" by looking at the definitions of risk and diversification and then asking what sources of risk confront the fund, what the historic and theoretical risk/return relationships are, how much risk a particular fund can endure, what specific risk policy decisions must be made, and how those decisions should be made.

WHAT IS RISK?

The most widely accepted *definition* of risk is variability of rate of return. The more uncertainty there is about the rate of return on an instrument over some future period, the greater is the risk. Suppose that a sponsor wishes to measure return on a portfolio each quarter and that after a number of quarters it wants to measure the risk that the portfolio has taken. It can first look at 90-day Treasury bills, which have no risk in a 90-day period. That is to say, if it buys a three-month Treasury bill it can tell now exactly what its rate of return will be over the next three months. If it buys a 5-year Treasury note, the return over the quarter is less certain, since interest rates may move up or down, with a corresponding impact on the security's value. A 20-year Treasury bond has even more uncertainty than the 5-year note because the effect of changes in interest rates will be greater for a 20-year instrument than for a 5-year instrument (see Chapter 4). A 20-year *corporate* bond has greater uncertainty than a 20-year *government* bond because the corporate bond may suffer from changes in its quality (i.e., the ability of the issuer to pay interest and principal on time) as well as changes in the general level of interest rates. Common stocks have even greater risk because they do not have a fixed maturity, and consequently their prices are affected by the full force of changes in economic conditions and specific company factors. Thus the uncertainty of rate of return is a useful measurement of risk.

The amount of risk that a fund has taken can be quantified by calculating the rate of return of the fund or its sectors, finding an average rate of return for the whole time period, and measuring the variability of return around the average. The exact methods for doing this include mean absolute deviation, standard deviation, and variance. These techniques are described in the mathematic's refresher (see Appendix B).[1]

The most annoying limitation of this measurement is that it can only be made retrospectively. That is, until the rate of return is known, the variability of that return cannot be measured. One alternative is to assume that the future will be like the past and to use past variabilities as a measure of future variabilities. There is certainly merit to this approach, though surprises await the investor who relies too heavily upon it. Another alternative is to start with a base of past variabilities and then to estimate the changes caused by new factors. For instance, a company which had a certain historic variability might have more variability in the future if the company's capitalization were changed such that the debt to equity ratio were greatly increased. A second limitation of the variability approach is that traditionally most investors have not viewed unexpectedly high rates of return as risk. That is, if a stock is expected to rise 10 percent and it actually rises 15 percent many investors have trouble with the notion of considering the extra 5 percent as risk. However, under the definition of risk as uncertainty of future value this extra profit is risk. A third criticism of the variability notion is that significant risks within a company may cancel each other out, presenting the appearance that very little risk was taken, when in fact the opposite was true. An admittedly exaggerated example might be a situation in which the president of a mining company absconded with $10 million in assets at the same time that a new mine worth $10 million to the company was discovered.

Despite the limitations of variability as a measure of risk, it is hard to find a better measure. Most other approaches to risk are intuitive, and hence unmeasurable, or they involve measurements which aim at the problem but really do not address it directly. For instance, the quality of management and its impact on stock price are important, but they cannot be measured. The equity/bond ratio is an example of a measurement which aims at the problem but does not address it. If a sponsor does not know the risk level of stocks and bonds, knowing how

---

[1] As an alternative to measuring variability against the average, it can be measured relative to a market index, as is the case in a beta model (see Chapter 8).

much of its assets are in stocks as opposed to bonds does not give it a very precise measurement of risk.

Consequently the variability approach has gained considerable acceptance among sponsors, academics, monitoring organizations, and investors.

DIVERSIFICATION

Probably the most important development in investments in the last 25 years is the exploration of the idea that certain types of risk can be eliminated through diversification. An important corollary to this idea is the principle that return can be expected to increase only as an investor increases his *undiversifiable* risk, not as he increases his diversifiable risk. It is desirable that these ideas be examined in greater detail.

Diversification is the spreading of assets among a variety of securities or among securities in a variety of markets with the goal of reducing risk in a portfolio without reducing expected return. A simple example may serve to demonstrate this principle. Let us assume that there is one buyer of services, namely a government wanting to purchase arms, and two arms suppliers, both of which are exactly the same in all respects. Let us further assume that the government has decided to purchase arms from only one company and that the successful company has been permitted to receive a return such that its value in the marketplace will triple. Since the company which does not get the contract will have no customers, it will go out of business and its stock will go to zero. Exhibit 3–1 shows the results to the shareholders of each arms supplier's stock if initially each stock was selling for $100 per share.

Thus an investor has an expected gain from buying either stock of 50 percent, consisting of a 50 percent chance of making $200 and a 50 percent chance of losing $100. However, although the *expected* gain is 50 percent, the *actual* outcome would be a gain of $200 *or* a loss of the entire $100 investment, depending on which stock was bought. A smart investor would recognize the opportunity for diversification. He would spread his money between the two stocks, recognizing that in doing so he is minimizing his potential loss. If he purchased both stocks he would guarantee that one of them would be wiped out com-

EXHIBIT 3-1
Example of the arms suppliers

| | Price per share | | Gain/(loss) |
Company	Initial	Final	to investors
Winner.....................	100	300	200
Loser......................	100	0	(100)

The *expected* results, which are obtained by considering not only the gains and losses of each outcome but also the probability of each outcome, are:

Company	Initial price per share	Probability of winning	Gain from selecting it	Expected gain
Winner.............	100	.5	200	100
Loser..............	100	.5	(100)	−50

$50 expected return on $100 investment = 50%

pletely and that the other would triple in value. Since the odds of either company receiving the award are equal, he would buy equal amounts of each stock. He would then have a $100 gain on a $200 investment, or a return of 50 percent, with no risk. The result would be that the investor diversified away risk without reducing his expected rate of return.

The existence of the principle of diversification is the first point of this section. The second point is that not all types of risk can be diversified away. For instance, a stock market investor cannot diversify away stock market risk. He can own stocks which are less risky or more risky, but as long as he owns stocks he will have stock market risk. He can deal with this risk in three ways. First, he can diversify by investing in more than one market. That is, he can invest in bonds as well as stocks, or in foreign stocks as well as domestic stocks, and thus spread his risk through diversification *among* markets. Second, he can establish a limitation on the amount of risk *per dollar invested* in any market. That is, he can buy risky stocks or conservative stocks with his stock market money, and he can buy risky bonds or conservative bonds with his bond market money. Finally, he can diversify *within* each market and within the chosen risk level in order to eliminate all nonmarket risk, as in the example of the arms suppliers. It is important to understand the difference between the second and third ways to reduce risk since the former involves a proportional reduction in return whereas the latter implies no reduction in return for a reduction of risk. This distinction will be described below. Techniques for measuring these risk factors will be discussed here and demonstrated in Chapters 8 and 9.

By definition, each marketplace consists of many securities, each of which is affected by at least two sources of risk. The first source is market risk, and the second is nonmarket, or specific, risk. (These risks are also sometimes referred to as nondiversifiable and diversifiable risks, for reasons which will soon become apparent.) In other words, looking at a stock market such as that in the United States, we recognize that the rate of return for a given stock can be impacted by factors within the company, such as management, earnings, and new products, and by market factors, such as the general level of the economy, interest rates, and inflation. Further, in any given period unexpectedly favorable or unexpectedly unfavorable things can happen to either the market or the individual stock. The basic point to be considered is that there is no way for the investor in stocks to escape the unexpected effects of the economy, but that he can minimize unexpected effects on individual stocks by buying many different stocks. Each time he adds another stock to the portfolio he hopes to take advantage of the arms supplier effect, wherein the return that the investor expects to make is maintained but the risk that he will not make it is reduced.

A convenient method for describing the diversification level of an equity portfolio is to measure its correlation with the market (see Chapter 8). This is done by making a regression analysis of the rate of return of the portfolio relative to the rate of return of the appropriate stock market index. A portfolio which is 100 percent diversified would consist of all the stocks in the marketplace and would be weighted in the same proportion as are the stocks in the marketplace. That is, a security which represents 1 percent of the value of the entire stock market would be represented by a 1 percent holding in the portfolio, and so on for each security. With a portfolio constructed in this manner, 100 percent of the fluctuation in the portfolio could be traced to fluctuation in the market and the portfolio would be said to be 100 percent diversified, or to have an R^2 of 100. At the other extreme, if the portfolio contained only one stock, the market risk would be a much smaller percentage of the total risk and the specific risk would be a much greater percentage. For a typical stock we might find that about 30 percent of the risk in the stock is market related and that 70 percent is specific. In other words, 70 percent of the fluctuations in the stock are attributable to company-related matters, whereas only 30 percent are attributable to the market. It is clear that in this case the investor whose only holding is that stock has a significant exposure to the unexpectedly favorable or unfavorable factors which might affect the stock. If the investor is very confident that he has information regarding the stock which the marketplace does not have, then he may wish to put himself in a position of owning only that stock and being 70 percent dependent on his information or judgment.

Most investors, and particularly institutions, find this approach to be unsuitably risky. These investors would be willing to sacrifice the exceptional return which might come from having one excellent stock for the knowledge that they would avoid the possibility of having a disaster from one very unsuccessful stock. They might then add a second stock to the portfolio, and find out that this increases the percentage of market risk from 30 percent to, say, 50 percent. By continuing to increase the number of stocks in the portfolio, and by weighting them in the same proportion as they appear in the marketplace, the investor will find that his R^2 quickly rises to the 85–95 percent level. If the investor feels that the market is essentially efficient, or that the potential gains from being "right" are not worth the risk of being "wrong," he may establish a diversification policy which aims to have 100 percent of the risk in the portfolio as market risk. In this case he is willing to sacrifice any opportunity for making extra risk-adjusted return for the comfort of knowing that he will never have negative risk-adjusted return. (Further, he also increases his expected return by reducing his transaction costs to practically zero.)

A distinction must be made between two important but different meanings of the "amount" of market risk in a portfolio.

The total risk in a portfolio, as we have just discussed, can be composed of varying percentages of market risk and specific risk. This is a diversification issue. But we can also look *just* at the percentage of the portfolio which represents market risk and view that portion as risky or conservative.

We have thus discussed the subject of diversification, the significance of portfolio diversification and nondiversification, and the difference between the level of market risk and the percentage of the portfolio's total risk which is market risk. We can now address the remaining issue concerning diversification, namely that the traditional idea that higher risk leads to higher return refers to market risk and not specific risk. This certainly makes sense in the example of the arms suppliers. In that case the market consists of only two stocks, each of which is identical to the other. It makes no sense for an investor who buys either of the companies, and thus increases his specific risk relative to that of an investor who buys both, to achieve a higher return than the investor who buys both. In other words, if the investor could diversify away his risk, he does not deserve to be paid for assuming that risk. If anything, it seems as though there should be a penalty for his failure to act in his own best interests, and in fact there is, in the sense that he has increased his risk without a commensurate increase in the expected return.

There are many cases in which investors *do* deserve to have a higher rate of return because they are assuming risks which cannot be diversified away. An investor owning long-term bonds will find his total rate of return more variable than that of an investor owning short-term cash equivalents. No matter which bonds are owned and in what proportions, the investor will find that over any reasonable period the bond portfolio will be more variable in returns than the cash equivalents portfolio. There being no way to avoid or diversify away this risk without also reducing the expected return, the marketplace adjusts the rate of return on the riskier securities such that, in the long run, they provide a higher return than do less risky assets. Another example would be a portfolio invested 60 percent in an index fund and 40 percent in Treasury bills. This portfolio is inherently riskier than a portfolio invested 50 percent in an index fund and 50 percent in Treasury bills. Because stocks are more variable than Treasury bills, the investor in the more aggressive portfolio is virtually certain to have a higher level of risk. For this he can expect, in the long run, a higher rate of return.

Having considered how to measure risk and having looked at diversification, we can now turn to an analysis of the sources of risk in portfolios.

THE SOURCES OF RISK

Assuming that investments are limited to those available on the planet Earth, the broadest source of risk is *world market risk*. Such risk is impossible to avoid. If some calamity befalls the Earth, there is no possible way to avoid the risk or to hedge against it. This is an important demonstration of the principle of diversification, or more correctly, the lack of diversification.

Because there is no hedge against world market risk, we can ignore it and move on to the next broadest category of risk, *international market risk*. The risks to an investor of investing in the markets of another country are political, currency, business, and liquidity (or interest rate) risks. The political risk is that the foreign government will either confiscate property, as in the case of the nationalization of U.S. industry by Cuba and Chile, or pass laws unfavorable to the investor, such as laws which prevent him from removing his capital or income from the country. The currency, or foreign exchange, risk is that the value of the foreign country's currency will decline, thus wiping out part of the value of the investor's capital. Foreign exchange risk to an outsider is the equivalent of inflation risk to an investor within a country. The third risk, business risk, refers to the fact that the general level of business within a country may decline precipitously, thus causing the value of investments to decline also. The fourth risk, liquidity risk, refers to a potential diminution in the value of capital caused by rising interest rates resulting from a lack of liquidity in the economy.

The *national market risk* to a fund investing *in its own country* consists of similar types of risk: political, depression, and liquidity. *Political* risk from the point of view of an investor *inside* a country can derive from confiscatory taxation or antiproductive regulation, and, regrettably, we do not need to look abroad to find examples of these problems. Although the definition of a confiscatory level of taxation is a matter of opinion, it seems reasonable to suggest that when the government takes a larger share than the producer of revenue, the level has reached confiscatory proportions. An example in this country is the double taxation of dividends. Assuming a corporate tax rate of 48 percent, the government takes more than 50 percent of income from any recipient of dividends who pays more than 4 percent in taxes ($1 in dividends × 48 percent = $0.48; $1.00 − $0.48 = $0.52; $0.52 × 4 percent = about $0.02; $0.02 + $0.48 = $0.50, or a 50 percent tax). Another example is the taxation of nonearned income, which can be taxed at rates of up to 70 percent for individuals. Examples of antiproductive regulations are so abundant as to require several pages just for listing. Among them are price controls on oil and gas, rent controls, pollution controls, interest rate ceilings, and rate fixing in various regulated industries. This is not to deny that there is value in some of these regulations but only to point out that these exercises of government power reduce the return to investors, and hence are a risk which must be recognized.

The risk of *depression* is widely understood. Few, if any, countries in the world are pursuing policies which will lead to depression in the customary way. That is, there is so much emphasis on stimulating economies that a depression induced by lack of demand is unlikely to occur. Given this stimulus, it is far likelier that investors will suffer loss from an inflation-induced lack of *liquidity*. That is, money will be created so rapidly that inflation will reach high rates. When this occurs, paradoxically, a shortage of liquidity also occurs, since money is needed to finance very expensive inventories, plant and equipment, residences, and so on. This increases interest rates and leads to a decline in security values because of the increase in returns available from alternative investments. Thus, if Treasury bill rates go from 6 percent to 8 percent, bonds and stocks become less attractive in a risk/return sense, and consequently yields on stocks and bonds must rise and their prices decline for the market to return to equilibrium. Inflation can also lead to a depression that results from lack of government stimulus. Interestingly, in countries with progressive tax rates, such as the United States, a high rate of inflation forces up income, and therefore people move into higher tax brackets even though their functions are the same in relation to the overall economy. Government receipts automatically rise and move the budget into balance or surplus. This decreases government stimulus and can lead to depression.

Portfolio risk consists of how assets are *diversified* and distributed among risk categories (as well as how the risk categories correlate with one another) and also of *marketability risk*, the risk that the investor will have to suffer a decline from the perceived market value of the fund because of the necessity for liquidating all or part of the fund at a bad time.

Two types of risk relate to factors affecting individual securities as opposed to factors affecting the general economy or a portfolio. These are security risk and company risk. *Security risk* refers to the attitude that the investment community takes toward a particular security, such as when growth stocks are in or out of favor, and also to the marketability risk of being unable to sell the security at or near the price of the last transaction. *Company risk* refers to traditional financial and business risks.

Financial risk should be distinguished from business risk since these types of risk can occur for opposite reasons. *Business risk* refers to the lack of viability of a product or of the company's position in the market for that product. In other words, if a company's main product is unviable, as was the case for buggy whips when the automobile became popular, the company is likely to fail. On the other hand, a product may itself be quite viable, as are computer products for IBM, but a company may find its market position insufficient to justify continuing to produce it. *Financial risk* for a company refers to the condition in which the company has insufficient cash to pay its bills. Interestingly, this condition can occur because of too few sales or too many, since a large backlog of sales means large amounts of money tied up in inventory and accounts receivable. Financial risk can also come about because general market conditions make money unavailable at a particular time for a company of a given credit risk.

THE RELATIONSHIP BETWEEN RISK AND RETURN

The question of the appropriate investment policy is frequently stated as the question of how much risk the fund can endure. Implicit in this question is the view, first, that the more risk a fund endures, the higher is the return that can be expected, and second, that a fund should seek the highest return by increasing risk to the maximum acceptable point. If return *decreased* as risk increased, the risk policy question would make no sense, as all funds would seek to have the lowest risk and the highest return. Nonetheless, before we blindly follow the "high risk equals high return" approach we should explore the risk/return relationship in more detail. Therefore, four questions will be addressed in this section of the chapter:

1. Does return go up as risk goes up?
2. If so, over what period can we be reasonably certain that this will occur?
3. What is the relationship between risk and return (that is, as risk doubles, does return go up by 10 percent, 50 percent, 100 percent, etc.)?
4. How stable are risk and return for each asset type, both absolutely and relatively among assets?

Looking at the Exhibit 3–2 results for the five ten-year periods from 1926 to 1975, we see information which can be used to address these questions. In answer to questions 1 and 2, it does appear that as risk rises, so does return. Within each period, risk rises as we move along the spectrum from short-term governments to stocks. However, return does not fall neatly into line with the rise in risk. This is especially noteworthy (and discouraging) for the most recent of the five periods, 1966–75, when return declined in a straight-line fashion as risk increased. Even for other periods, there are cases in which return decreased as risk increased. For instance, for the earliest period, 1926–35, return decreased from 4.6 percent to 4.3 percent moving from long-term governments to intermediate-term governments. There were similar occurrences during the 1946–55 and the 1956–65 periods. We might thus conclude that

EXHIBIT 3–2
Return and risk for four asset types

	Common stocks		Long-term governments		Intermediate-term governments		Short-term governments	
	Average return	Standard deviation	Average return	Standard deviation	Average return	Standard deviation	Average return	Standard deviation
Date								
1926–35	9.0%	31.4%	4.3%	5.4%	4.6%	5.0%	2.8%	1.4%
1936–45	11.0	21.9	4.6	3.0	3.0	2.2	0.5	0.4
1946–55	15.4	16.0	1.2	3.2	1.7	1.7	1.4	0.6
1956–65	11.7	15.6	2.2	5.7	3.2	4.0	3.3	0.8
1966–75	4.1	19.6	4.5	8.1	5.0	4.0	6.8	1.6

Source: Merrill Lynch Institutional Computer Services Department.

return tends to rise with risk but that this relationship need not hold even for periods as long as ten years.

Exhibit 3–2 provides little help in answering question 3 as to the specific relationship between risk and return, at least using average returns and standard deviations as the measurement. This is especially true in the last ten-year period, when risk and return moved oppositely.

Exhibit 3–2 shows that riskier assets tend to have higher returns than do lower risk assets and that although this ordering is fairly stable, the absolute levels of return and risk vary considerably. For instance, stocks had ten-year average annual returns varying from 4.1 percent to 15.4 percent and long-term governments had returns of 1.2 percent to 4.6 percent. Risk varied from 15.6 to 31.4 for stocks and from 3.0 to 5.7 for long-term governments.

As to question 4 we have some useful information. Neither risk nor return is stable for any asset type, but the relationship between risk and asset type holds true in every case. That is, for each period stocks are riskier than long-term bonds, which are, in turn, riskier than intermediate-term bonds, which are riskier than short-term securities.

This study is rather discouraging for those sponsors and investment managers that wish to be precise in controlling their portfolios. Results in the real world appear to be too unstable to permit any degree of precision in portfolio control. However, it is useful to see the results and to recognize how variable they might be. Sponsors should take this into consideration when establishing their risk/return policies.

HOW MUCH RISK CAN A FUND ENDURE?

In order to answer this question we must know the estimated risk/return spectrum available in the marketplace (as shown in Exhibit 3–3) and the "utility" or risk/return preferences of the fund and of the people responsible for it.

EXHIBIT 3–3

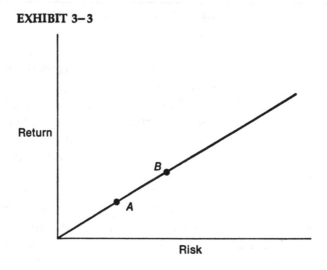

Assume that Exhibit 3–3 shows the risk/return spectrum available as of a point in time for "efficient" portfolios (meaning that for any given level of risk there is no portfolio with a higher return and that for any given level of return there is no portfolio with lower risk). Even for efficient portfolios it is not possible to say whether an investor should be at point A, point B, or any other point on the line. This is because each investor has a slightly different view toward how much risk he can take. There is no clear-cut method for measuring the utility of an investor. However, the issues can be discussed and rational, if imprecise, policies can be developed. There are two fundamental considerations in analyzing the fund's utility. These are:

1. How important is the success of the fund to the success of the organization?
2. What are the financial characteristics of the sponsor?[2]

A third consideration has been created by the particular provision of ERISA which enables the Pension Benefit Guaranty Corporation to attach 30 percent of a corporation's assets. This has the effect of reversing the risk policy wherein a corporation whose fund was in very bad shape would have normally taken very little risk but now might take the opposite tack—namely, "Let's shoot the works"—because it is already suffering maximum exposure to the 30 percent attachment.

Since these factors differ in importance for each of the four major fund types, the factors will be discussed in relation to the type of fund.

Corporate retirement plans

Since the passage of ERISA, every retirement plan has become important to the corporation, and benefit obligations must be met regardless of the financial characteristics of the sponsor. Nonetheless, it is useful to review how the factors discussed above impact the way in which a corporate fund's investment policy should be structured.

Importance of the fund. The first consideration in determining the importance of the fund to the organization is to determine what percentage of its employees are covered by the plan and what the characteristics of those employees are (e.g., do they have special skills which would be very difficult to duplicate in the marketplace, as do airline pilots). Obviously, the higher the percentage of employees covered by the plan or the more important the types of employees covered, the more important the plan is to the success of the organization.

A second consideration in determining the fund's importance to the organization is the place of pension benefits in the

---

[2] For endowment funds these two questions are interrelated since if the sponsor is weak financially, the fund grows in importance, and vice versa.

hierarchy of total compensation. If, as is the case with some public utilities, a good pension is given more weight in relation to current salary than would be the case in, say, the advertising industry, then the success of the fund is relatively more important to those public utilities.

It is suggested here that the more important the plan is to the organization's success, the less is the risk that can be tolerated. The greater the consequences of the fund's losing its value, the less is the risk that the fund should take.

Financial characteristics of the sponsor. The greater the financial strength of the corporation relative to the size of the fund, the greater is the fund's ability to bear risk. The most important measurements of the corporation's financial ability to bear risk within the fund are:

1. *Pretax income relative to the pension fund contribution.* The higher the percentage of the pretax income which flows to pension fund contributions, the more conservative the fund should be, since a risky posture might lead to large losses in the fund that would have to be made up with higher contributions, with a significant impact on the sponsor.

2. *The stability of pretax income.* The more stable the earnings of a company, the greater is its ability to bear risk. A highly cyclical company, on the other hand, may find that it must increase pension fund contributions when earnings are low, again with a significant impact on the sponsor.

3. *Pretax income relative to unfunded vested liability.* The greater the liability relative to income, the more conservative the approach should be, since, again, unfavorable investment results would cause a large percentage of earnings to be diverted to elimination of the liability.

4. *Corporate assets relative to unfunded vested liability.* If the liability were eliminated through the liquidation of assets rather than paid off over time through income, the impact on the company can be measured by comparing the assets of the company to the liability of the fund. This possibility has become more significant since ERISA allows the Pension Benefit Guaranty Corporation to assume 30 percent of corporate net worth in the event of inability to meet pension obligations. If a company's assets are low relative to the fund liability, a conservative posture is implied.

Exhibit 3–4 presents information on these financial characteristics for a large number of corporations, so that each sponsor can determine its relative risk-bearing characteristics.

EXHIBIT 3–4
Financial characteristics of selected large public corporations as related to pension fund contributions and liability (1979)

A. Pension fund contributions as a percentage of pretax net income		B. Stability of earnings (standard error of five-year earnings growth)	
Percentile	*Percent*	*Percentile*	*Stability*
1	0.8	1	1.4
10	4.2	10	4.4
20	5.9	20	6.9
30	7.4	30	9.3
40	8.9	40	13.0
50	11.0	50	15.9
60	13.7	60	21.1
70	18.0	70	28.4
80	23.8	80	37.4
90	36.8	90	58.6
99	−17.6	99	260.0

C. Ratio of pretax income to unfunded vested liability		D. Ratio of assets to unfunded vested liability	
Percentile	*Ratio*	*Percentile*	*Ratio*
1	*	1	*
10	*	10	*
20	*	20	*
30	*	30	*
40	24.8	40	210
50	7.9	50	83
60	4.7	60	48
70	2.9	70	31
80	1.8	80	20
90	0.7	90	12
99	−8.0	99	3

* No unfunded vested liability.
Source: Merrill Lynch Institutional Computer Services Department.

Jointly trusteed funds

Importance of the fund. This depends on the proportion of total compensation which the fund represents. For instance, a fund which provides retirement equal to 10 percent of a given employee's normal income could be viewed as less important than a fund which provides a pension of 40 percent of the same employee's normal income. Presumably, the greater the importance of the pension benefit, the less the risk that can be tolerated, for if a risky policy is pursued unsuccessfully, the risk is increased that the fund will not be able to pay benefits. If employees have been led to believe that their pensions will be substantial, and have planned accordingly, this could have significant negative effects on them. Of course, the establishment of the Pension Benefit Guaranty Corporation has done much to reduce this risk.

Financial characteristics of the sponsor. Since the union itself is not providing benefits, we must look to the employer organizations which provide funding for the plan to assess the ability of the sponsor to take risk in the fund. This can be done in the manner described previously for corporations. However, since the employer organizations typically provide a specific contribution rather than guaranteeing a specific benefit, these organizations are concerned only with meeting their contributions and need not worry about the extra risk involved with guaranteeing a specific level of benefits, as is the case with corporate funds. Consequently, the financial characteristics of the employer organizations are less important in jointly trusteed funds than they are in corporate funds.

Public funds

Importance of the fund. Although the fund is likely to be an important benefit to employees, the importance of various public retirement plans to their respective members seems to be fairly standard. In most cases the plans are very important to the members, and this importance is especially great in the many contributory plans (the employee who is contributing to a fund is not likely to have much other savings).

Financial characteristics of the sponsor. In recent years this issue has taken on an importance that it has not had since the days of the Great Depression. In the postwar period most people would have considered it almost unthinkable that a public fund might not be able to pay its pension benefits, but recent events have made this possibility more likely, though it is still quite remote. Factors that have led to this greater likelihood of default by public funds are the increased percentage of the work force employed by government (and thus the fewer remaining employees to support the public funds through their tax dollars), increased benefits to government employees, increased borrowing by public governments at all levels, and taxpayer revolts which could sharply reduce government tax revenues. The financial characteristics which determine a particular government's ability to meet its pension obligations are:

> The percentage of the government's total revenues that is consumed by pension contributions.
> The trend in this percentage.
> The government's revenues relative to its unfunded vested liability.
> The impact of inflation on the government's revenues.

Endowment funds

For endowment funds the two measures of the ability of a fund to bear risk—that is, the importance of the fund and the financial characteristics of the sponsoring organization—are closely allied, since the charitable institution's work activities are directly supported by the endowment fund. Consequently, these two areas can be considered together for this category of fund. In measuring the importance of an endowment fund to the sponsoring organization, the questions to be asked are:

1. What percentage of the organization's income comes from the endowment fund's income?
2. Conversely, what percentage of the fund's income is required to meet this demand from the organization?
3. How large are the fund's assets relative to the organization's assets?
4. How large are the fund's assets relative to the organization's anticipated capital expenditures?
5. What impact would be felt by the organization if the fund's income increased or decreased by 10 percent? 20 percent? 50 percent? 100 percent?

6. What impact would be felt by the organization if the fund's assets increased or decreased by 10 percent? 20 percent? 50 percent? 100 percent?

The Investment Committee of the National Association of College and University Business Officers collects information on the investment policies and results of the association's members. According to questionnaires submitted by 91 institutions, it appears that on average approximately 100 percent of the institutions' current income was spent. However, only 22 institutions spent exactly their entire income, with the other institutions spending either more or less than their entire income. The questionnaires also indicated that roughly 57 percent of the institutions' assets were invested in equities. This information, though rather sparse, does provide some perspective on how endowment funds are structured and on the income requirements therefrom.[3]

THE UTILITY OF THE PEOPLE RESPONSIBLE FOR THE FUND

In viewing the issue of utility, or choosing an appropriate place on the risk/return spectrum, we typically think in terms of the investor, in this case the sponsoring organization. However, practical experience and knowledge of human nature dictate that we also consider the utility of the people responsible for the fund. A simple example clearly demonstrates why this should be done. Assume that you are the pension manager for a company which has an extraordinarily high return on sales and on equity; is not labor intensive, and hence allocates only a small percentage of its income to the pension fund; and has been informed by the company actuary, Crystal, Ball & Co., that the fund will have a net positive cash flow for at least the next century and that the fund currently has assets in excess of its vested liabilities. You are preparing an extensive memorandum indicating that the company has an enormous ability to bear risk in the fund and consequently should pursue an ag-

---

[3] J. Peter Williamson, "How Well Are College Endowment Funds Managed?" *Journal of Portfolio Management*, Summer 1979.

gressive policy in order to achieve a very high rate of return in the long run, thus making it possible to either reduce contributions or increase benefits. Your superior, the company president, not known for mincing words, informs you that he wants no possible embarrassment from pension fund investment and that "you will be removed from your position if the fund achieves a negative rate of return for any successive two-year period." Clearly, in these circumstances your perception of the fund's ability to bear risk will be changed considerably by the utility of the president and by your own utility, which may be dominated by your desire to retain your job.

Given a recognition of this phenomenon, it is interesting to consider the factors that affect the utility of the various parties to the pension fund:

Member of Board of Directors: Since I'm nearing retirement age, any benefit to the company achieved from having an aggressive policy will be achieved long after I am gone. Therefore, I will tend toward a conservative policy to eliminate any problems that might disrupt my last years with the company.

Pension Administrator: In terms of progressing within this company, the chances of helping my career by taking big risks in the fund seem to be much less than the chances of hurting my career by being unsuccessful in a high-risk policy. This leads me to be conservative. However, if I do an especially good job here, other, larger companies might hire me to oversee their funds. Perhaps I should be more aggressive.

Investment Manager: If I am not at all imaginative in running this fund, the chances are that I will keep the business and get my share of the estimated 8 percent per year in investment return and another 8 percent per year in new contributions, which means that the assets under my management will grow at a hefty 16 percent per year. However, if I take more risks, I may be able to build a name for myself and my organization and attract more new clients.

Actuary: If I am conservative in my assumptions, the company will probably not have to increase its contributions over and above my estimates, and plan participants will be highly likely to receive their benefits. On the other hand, the company may wish to reduce its current contributions in order to increase its net income, which can be done if I choose less conservative assumptions. Perhaps my firm will be replaced if I am not aggressive enough.

Company Shareholder: I don't want the company to run afoul of ERISA or have to make excessive contributions due to poor investment results. However, the greater the return we can get on fund assets, the lower the contributions will be and hence the higher my stock price and dividends.

Although the consideration of these utility factors is potentially embarrassing ("After all, it is the sponsor and the fund for which we are presumably concerned"), nonetheless failure to consider them can be disastrous for the fund since a supposedly long-term policy may be abandoned at just the wrong time. For instance, suppose that a professional analysis suggests that a fund can bear a high level of risk and therefore should be invested largely in equities and that the sponsor goes along with this recommendation even though the conservative tendencies of its officers make them very uncomfortable about the plan. If the stock market were to decline precipitously, the board of trustees might liquidate the equity portfolio near the bottom of the market and opt for short-term fixed income investments just when it should be doing the opposite. Conversely, a conservative fund might sell its bonds at the top of the market to move into equities that supported a board of trustees's bias toward more aggressive securities.

GENERAL PHILOSOPHY

The preceding discussion of utility was intended to be fairly objective. That is, the discussion implicitly assumed that two organizations with the same characteristics would choose very similar risk policies. However, it is possible to take another step forward in the analysis of utility and to consider that investors may come to different conclusions as to the appropriate policies even when the facts are identical. Perhaps a suitable analogy is that of the two people viewing the same glass of water, one of whom suggests that it is half full while the other insists that it is half empty. The comparable investment philosophies can be described as follows:

Philosophy 1: Maximum return for a given level of risk. The responsible parties should analyze the fund's ability to bear risk and attempt to find investments which will achieve the highest level of return consistent with this risk level.

Philosophy 2: Minimum risk for a given level of return. The responsible parties should estimate the required return that the fund needs in order to meet its obligations and then find those securities which have the lowest risk consistent with this rate of return.

A sponsor actuated by philosophy 1 might analyze the historic returns and risks of various asset types, further analyze its cash flow needs, and decide the highest level of risk which the fund can endure without disrupting the sponsor's earnings. Once this level of risk has been identified, securities are chosen which will have high rates of return consistent with this risk policy. Philosophy 2 is obviously more conservative. Rather than viewing risk as the dominant force, it looks at the minimum return which is adequate for the fund's needs and on that basis attempts to find appropriate securities. Both of these philosophies are defensible. The decision as to which course to follow may reflect the general philosophy of the organization, a specific philosophy applied to the fund, or the utility of the participants.

SPECIFIC POLICY DECISIONS OF FUND SPONSORS

Now that we have reviewed risk, diversification, and utility, we can turn to the specific policy decisions that fund sponsors must make. These are:

Which ones?

What proportions?

What risk level?

What diversification level?

How much discretion to give the investment manager in changing each of the above?

These questions can be asked regarding two major areas which sponsors and investment managers must address: countries and asset types. A sponsor must consider which countries to invest in, what proportions to invest in each country, how aggressive or conservative the assets in each country should be, and how well diversified those assets should be (that is, to what extent the approach will emphasize security selection as opposed to just mirroring the market). Similarly, these questions can be raised regarding asset types: which asset types (stocks, bonds, etc.), what percentage in each asset category, how aggressive each category should be (i.e., should the fund own risky stocks or conservative stocks, etc.), and how diversified each asset type should be. Finally, the sponsor must decide to what extent the investment manager will be allowed or encouraged to change these decisions. For instance, it is possible to suggest that 60 percent of assets on average should be in equities but that the investment manager can vary this percentage between 0 percent and 100 percent, depending on his market outlook. On the other hand, it would also be possible to say that the 60/40 asset mix should be maintained for each quarter. Each of the above choices will be examined in an attempt to present its implications for the fund.

The rationale for foreign investment

Before discussing the decisions regarding the countries in which to invest, it is well to consider the rationale for investing in foreign assets. Although very few U.S. pension funds invest in foreign assets, in most other countries this practice is common. Five arguments can be made in favor of foreign diversification.

First, from a pure investment standpoint, there are opportunities abroad which are not available in the United States. For instance, diamonds, gold, certain metals, and, increasingly, oil and gas are either nonexistent in the United States or are more abundant overseas. Also, much as it hurts to admit it, not all of the brains are located in the United States and certain foreign companies have achieved successes which are worthy of consideration by large institutional U.S. investors. Second, the long-term economic outlook for the United States is less attractive than it was 20 years ago. This can be seen most obviously by considering the diminishing supply of energy and other natural resources. Although it is difficult to find comparable statistics, some observers suggest that the United States has a lower level of capital investment than do other countries, particularly Japan. This would indicate that production efficiency and job creation trends in the United States are unfavorable compared to those of other countries.

Third, foreign investments could be made for the purpose of avoiding severe economic or political disaster in the sponsor's own country. Fourth, and an area worthy of considerable exploration, investments in assets denominated in foreign currencies provide a hedge against inflation. Given a high level of inflation in the sponsor's country, traditional stock and bond investments may suffer severe losses of purchasing power. To the extent that foreign countries have lower inflation rates, their currencies will tend to be much stronger than that of the sponsor's country. Therefore, the foreign investment will provide a return from currency reevaluation as well as from normal investment returns. Obviously, this process could work to the detriment of the sponsor as well as to its benefit. The fifth argument in favor of foreign diversification is that it permits a given level of return to be earned with less risk. This can be seen from the example in Exhibit 3–5. In this case it is assumed that investments can be made in two countries, in both of which an identical rate of return can be earned (10 percent) and an identical variability of return exists (±5 percent). On the surface it would seem to make absolutely no difference to the investor in which country he places his funds, since both countries have the same return and risk. The key question to be answered is, "Are the markets of the two countries highly correlated, or do they move independently?" If the two markets are perfectly and positively correlated (i.e., they move exactly together), it makes no difference in which country the investor places his assets. In this case the returns in both countries would be the same in each period. The ideal situation, however, would be one in which the two markets had positive expected returns but were negatively correlated (i.e., they tended to move in opposite directions). In this case, when one market is declining, the other would be rising, and the fund could achieve average (+10 percent) results by investing half of its assets in each of the two countries. Average results would also be achieved when the two markets reversed their roles. Consequently, the return would be very stable around the average return expected, and it would be very high relative to risk. Examples of this phenomenon are shown in Exhibit 3–5 under

EXHIBIT 3–5

Condition 1: Perfect positive correlation (identical results)

	Year 1	Year 2	Year 3	Cumulative (not compounded)
Country A.........	10%	5%	15%	30%
Country B	10	5	15	30
Investor	10	5	15	30

Investor return = 10% each year with risk of ± 5%

Condition 2: Perfect negative correlation (opposite results)

	Year 1	Year 2	Year 3	Cumulative (not compounded)
Country A.........	10%	5%	15%	30%
Country B	10	15	5	30
Investor	10	10	10	30

Investor return = 10% each year with risk of ± 0%

the assumption that each market returns 5 percent, 10 percent, or 15 percent in each year (i.e., an average return of 10 percent ± 5 percent) and that 50 percent of the available funds are placed in each market at the beginning of the period.

There are two common arguments against foreign diversification. The first is that U.S. pension funds are investing on behalf of workers in the United States and that since pension funds are a major source of the capital which is required to stimulate the growth of jobs, this money should be kept here. The second argument is that foreign investments have foreign exchange risk as well as investment risk and that since the liabilities of most of the pension funds in this country are denominated (for future pensioners) in dollars, the assets should also be denominated in dollars. Although both of these arguments have merit, it is likely that in future years large U.S. funds, particularly those of international corporations, will invest in securities denominated in foreign currencies.

As to the appropriate amount to invest in foreign assets, there is no set of rules which can be followed. However, it is instructive to compare the values of assets outside the United States with those of assets inside the United States in order to gain an idea of the general proportions of the various securities markets. This information is provided in Exhibit 3–6.

Specific decisions concerning countries

Deciding which countries to invest in can be based on a number of factors. The *size* of the securities market is one basis. Obviously, the greater the size of the market, the more investment opportunity there is within the country. Also, according to capital market theory, an investor should apportion his assets according to market evaluation. Another possibility is to consider the *historic growth rate* of each country's economy or stock market in order to anticipate those countries which will have superior growth rates in the future. An investor who is concerned with the low level of capital reinvestment in the United States relative to that of other countries may wish to choose countries based on the *reinvestment rate*. It is also possible to use a "bottom up" as opposed to a "top down" approach. In other words, the investor may wish to participate in some *particular industry or company* and to develop an international position in this manner. Finally, the *previous experience* of the sponsor or the investment manager may provide a basis for choosing countries. For example, a corporation which has a subsidiary in West Germany may find it easier to invest in that country than in others.

Decisions on what proportions to invest in different countries can be made on the same bases as decisions on which countries to invest in. That is, the decisions can be based on size, the growth rate, the reinvestment rate, a choice of particular industries or companies, or the comfort level derived from previous experience.

Given the lack of historical data on the risk levels of individual securities, it will be difficult for the sponsor to develop precise guidelines on the risk level of securities to be owned in foreign countries. Most sponsors will therefore choose an approach utilizing a "market" risk level or will hire managers who use traditional methods of securities selection.

EXHIBIT 3–6
Market capitalization and turnover

	1978					1977				
	Total market capitalization		Annual turnover			Total market capitalization		Annual turnover		
	$ billions	Percentage of total	$ billions	Percentage of total turnover	In percentage of each market	$ billions	Percentage of total	$ billions	Percentage of total turnover	In percentage of each market
United States	815.2	54.8%	199.9	47.8%	24.5%	800.7	60.9%	154.8	54.7%	19.3%
Canada	60.6	4.1	10.9	2.6	18.0	52.9	4.0	6.9	2.4	13.0
Europe										
United Kingdom	110.1	7.4	18.6	4.4	16.9	86.4	6.6	17.6	6.2	20.4
West Germany	73.3	4.9	17.3	4.1	23.6	57.3	4.4	12.0	4.2	20.9
France	37.6	2.5	10.6	2.5	28.1	25.7	2.0	4.5	1.6	17.5
Spain	14.6	1.0	1.5	0.4	10.3	17.9	1.4	1.5	0.5	8.5
Netherlands	21.0	1.4	4.5	1.1	21.4	18.1	1.4	3.6	1.3	19.8
Italy	9.1	0.6	2.3	0.6	25.7	7.4	0.6	1.0	0.4	14.2
Sweden	9.3	0.6	0.4	0.1	4.3	9.1	0.7	0.4	0.1	4.4
Belgium-Luxembourg	11.4	0.8	1.2	0.3	10.9	9.5	0.7	1.1	0.4	11.5
Japan	278.7	18.7	142.4	34.1	51.1	189.7	14.4	77.4	27.3	40.8
Hong Kong	14.8	1.0	5.8	1.4	39.4	11.5	0.9	1.3	0.5	11.4
Singapore	9.2	0.6	1.5	0.4	16.3	6.3	0.5	0.5	0.2	7.5
Australia	23.1	1.6	0.9	0.2	3.9	21.8	1.7	0.7	0.2	3.2
"World"	$1,488.0	100.0%	$417.8	100.0%	28.1%	$1,314.3	100.0%	$283.3	100.0%	21.6%

Notes:
1. The annual figures for turnover values in U.S. dollars are calculated by converting monthly values at month-end exchange rates.
2. The turnover data refer to common stocks only. These data include listed foreign shares, except in West Germany and the Netherlands.
Source: Capital International, Geneva.

The choice of the diversification level is really the choice of the extent to which the sponsor is willing to go along with the market as opposed to relying on the success of the manager's securities selection. Relying heavily on the manager's ability in this area makes it possible for the fund to have especially good results while introducing the risk that it will have especially bad results. In practice, sponsors are likely to end up with one of two positions. Either the fund will be structured quantitatively, and hence the diversification level will tend to be rather high, or the sponsor will rely on an overseas investment manager to structure the fund, in which case this manager will almost certainly opt for an active approach and a lesser diversification level.

In addition to knowing the basic investment policies of the fund, the investment manager must know to what extent he has discretion to vary the policies set forth by the sponsor.

Specific decisions concerning asset types

The five policy decisions—which ones, what proportions, what risk level, what diversification level, and how much discretion to give the manager to change these policies—must be decided for the various security types. As to "which ones," Chapter 4 contains a detailed discussion of the characteristics of a broad list of security types. Exhibit 3–2 shows approximate risk/return relationships for some of these types. Thus it is possible to get a general idea of the relative risk of each asset type. It should be noted that the actual level of risk may vary considerably from period to period, though it is highly likely that the ordering of asset risks will remain the same. It is inconceivable, for instance, that stocks would be less risky than short-term securities for more than a day or two at a time. The returns that have been associated with some types of assets are shown in Exhibit 3–2.

The second question, what proportion in each asset, is intertwined with the question of what risk level to choose since obviously a given level of risk could be achieved by having, say, 60 percent in conservative stocks and 40 percent in aggressive bonds, or 50 percent in aggressive stocks and 50 percent in conservative bonds. There is no precise basis for making this decision. Two techniques are frequently used, and two additional approaches will be proposed here. The most common method is an intuitive judgment based on the perceived comfort level of the individuals concerned. A second, related approach is to do what others are doing. Exhibit 3–7 shows asset allocation for a broad sample of portfolios.

For sponsors whose funds have cash needs which can be measured with precision, it is possible to establish a portfolio which will generate cash when it is needed. This can be done with either equity or fixed income securities, but it is easier to do with fixed income securities since both their principal and their income can be predicted. In a process called *immunization* the matching of cash flows is carried out mathematically. By matching the "duration" of the assets with the duration of the liability, the portfolio can be protected from changes in interest rates. If interest rates rise, the increase in interest on reinvested income is sufficient to offset the loss of principal. If interest rates decline, a capital gain on principal offsets the decline in reinvested income.

Another method is to use computer *simulations* of future outcomes that might result from various investment strategies. These simulations are usually based on the historic rates of return of stocks and bonds, as well as the historic risk levels of these assets. From this information and from certain assumptions about the growth in the fund's assets that may be expected from external sources, it is possible to broadly anticipate the future.

A simulation is a mathematical representation of the result which would occur based on certain conditions. A "Monte Carlo" simulation is used to estimate expected results based on probable outcomes. For instance, we know that the probability of achieving heads on the flip of a coin is .5 but that since each flip can be either heads or tails, it is possible to have ten heads in a row. If a computer were used to randomly "flip" the coin for 1,000 series of ten flips each, we could see how many times out of 1,000 we would get ten straight heads. This technique can be applied to portfolios by assuming certain estimates about the rates of return on stocks and bonds and the variabilities of those rates. For instance, the historical data supplied by Ibbotson and Sinquefield or Fisher and Lorie (see

EXHIBIT 3–7
Asset allocation of professionally managed retirement and endowment funds

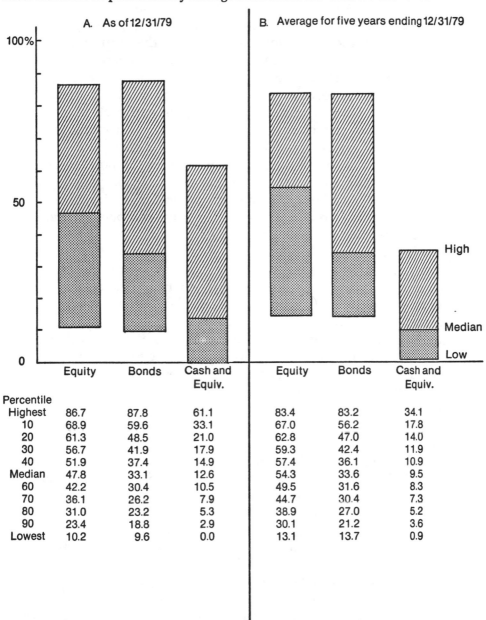

Percentile	A. As of 12/31/79			B. Average for five years ending 12/31/79		
	Equity	Bonds	Cash and Equiv.	Equity	Bonds	Cash and Equiv.
Highest	86.7	87.8	61.1	83.4	83.2	34.1
10	68.9	59.6	33.1	67.0	56.2	17.8
20	61.3	48.5	21.0	62.8	47.0	14.0
30	56.7	41.9	17.9	59.3	42.4	11.9
40	51.9	37.4	14.9	57.4	36.1	10.9
Median	47.8	33.1	12.6	54.3	33.6	9.5
60	42.2	30.4	10.5	49.5	31.6	8.3
70	36.1	26.2	7.9	44.7	30.4	7.3
80	31.0	23.2	5.3	38.9	27.0	5.2
90	23.4	18.8	2.9	30.1	21.2	3.6
Lowest	10.2	9.6	0.0	13.1	13.7	0.9

Source: Merrill Lynch. Institutional Computer Services Department.

Bibliography) can be used as a basis for estimating the probability of the expected results. A sponsor can then simulate the chances of meeting certain financial goals of the fund for different asset mixes. Although this can be very useful, it is essential to recognize the limitations imposed by the importance of choosing the correct assumptions, the impact of changing inflation rates, and the need to consider liabilities as well as assets.

Two other approaches can be taken in establishing an asset allocation policy. The use of a *comparative* approach involves reviewing the characteristics of the company, comparing them to the characteristics of other companies, and then choosing a policy which is appropriate in comparison to the policies pursued by the other companies. For instance, if a company has a greater ability to bear risk than do other companies, then it would establish a policy which is aggressive compared to those pursued by the other companies.

Using what might be called a *historic return/preference* approach, the investor projects the fund's cash requirements, assesses the utility or the willingness to bear risk of the key members of the fund sponsor, reviews the fund's general philosophy to see whether the fund wishes to emphasize return maximization or risk minimization, reviews historic stock and bond market returns, and establishes a policy consistent with the fund's preferences and historic market relationships.

Ideally, a corporation might use both approaches and then work to integrate the two into a single policy. Then approval would be received from the board of directors, the policy would be communicated to the investment managers, and periodic reviews would be made to see whether the managers were following the policy and whether the policy was adequately serving the needs of the sponsor.

The comparative method. XYZ is a manufacturing firm serving a number of highly competitive industries. It was established about 50 years ago, is growing about in line with the gross national product, and is labor intensive. When comparing its financial characteristics, as described on pages 34 and 35, to those of other corporations, it discovered that:

1. A high percentage of its pretax income was flowing to pension fund contributions. Thus, if the fund pursued an aggressive policy and the results were poor, the corporation

would be significantly impacted by the increased contributions that would be required to make up the deficiency in funding. This indicated that a conservative risk posture was appropriate.

2. The corporation's pretax income was not stable. If a serious recession hit the economy, the corporation's profits might be in a cyclical trough at the same time that the stock market declined seriously. Thus, if an aggressive policy were pursued, the corporation might have to increase its contribution when its earnings were low. This suggested that a conservative policy was appropriate.

3. The corporation's pretax income was high compared to the unfunded vested liability. The pension plan was well funded. Thus, profits would be less seriously impacted if a funding deficiency arose than would have been the case if a large liability existed. This indicated that an aggressive policy was possible. Although the analysis presented here seems to conflict with that presented in number 1 above, this combination of circumstances is not impossible. Corporations have widely varying characteristics, and each plan must be assessed in terms of a number of characteristics and a judgment made as to its overall risk-bearing ability.

4. The corporation's assets were low relative to the size of the unfunded vested liability. This indicated a relatively low ability to bear risk. For instance, if the company had to liquidate its assets to pay pension benefits, the company's basic operations might be severely impacted.

Based on this information, the corporation decided that it was somewhat below average in its ability to bear risk. It then reviewed the activities of other sponsors (Exhibit 3–7) and found that the median corporate pension fund had 47.80 percent of its assets in common stocks and that the 60th percentile had 42.21 percent. It decided that it wanted to be halfway between the median and the 60th percentile and thus chose 45 percent in equities. Approval for this policy was sought and received from the board of directors, and the policy was communicated to the investment managers in writing.

This procedure could be extended to include other relevant characteristics. For instance, it would be possible to compare the age level of the company's employees with that of other companies' employees. A company with a relatively old work force should invest conservatively since its fund may lack sufficent time to endure short-term stock market aberrations while waiting for long-term superior rates of return.

The comparative approaches are helpful and have a fiduciary appeal. That is, if the fund administrators are doing the same thing as everyone else, with some adaptation to their own circumstances, it is hard to fault them too much. On the other hand, it is possible that each organization's circumstances are different and that, to quote an old Wall Street saying, "The majority is always in the wrong." Thus a more analytical approach has appeal as well.

The historic return/preference method. 1. Using the historic return/preference method, the company made a five-year projection of the cash requirements for the fund and concluded that a 7 percent per year compound return (40 percent cumulative) was required to meet the fund's future needs. Based on the Fisher and Lorie results (Exhibit 3–8), the sponsor noted that in equities this objective was not achieved 40 percent of the time.[4] This percentage was regarded as excessive, so it was considered inappropriate to invest the fund 100 percent in equities. It was deemed acceptable for the fund to miss this objective 20 percent of the time. Therefore, the fund was invested 62.4 percent in bonds earning 9 percent per year and maturing in five years (53.9 percent cumulative for five years) and 37.6 percent in stocks returning 17 percent cumulative (stocks earned less than 17 percent in only 20 percent of the five year periods), for an appreciation of 40 percent to $140 = (153.9 × .624 + 117 × .376). In this case the fund would achieve or exceed its objective 80 percent of the time.

2. Suppose that the corporation decides that the most it can afford to add to its planned contribution to the fund is $1 million per year, or $5 million over a five-year time horizon. Suppose further that the fund has $25 million, so that the $5 million deficiency represents a 20 percent loss. The fund can then make an estimate of the highest percentage in equities which would permit attainment of the goal of having at most a 20 percent loss over the five-year period. To phrase the issue another way,

---

[4] That is, 40 percent of the time an investment of $100 grew to less than $140 in five-year periods. See Exhibit 3–8B Five-year periods

EXHIBIT 3–8
Historical stock market results (the amounts to which $100 would have accumulated during selected periods) 1926–1976

A. The five best periods and the five worst periods

Three-year periods		Five-year periods		Ten-year periods	
Year Ended	Result	Year Ended	Result	Year Ended	Result
Best		Best		Best	
1935	232	1936	278	1958	580
1945	214	1954	272	1959	538
1956	204	1958	264	1956	484
1928	203	1955	261	1951	475
1936	196	1956	235	1952	468
Average	209.8	Average	262.0	Average	509.0

Three-year periods		Five-year periods		Ten-year periods	
Year	Result	Year	Result	Year	Result
Worst		Worst		Worst	
1931	35	1932	46	1938	85
1932	37	1933	52	1937	95
1974	72	1934	61	1939	99
1933	80	1931	66	1974	120
1975	84	1941	71	1940	126
Average	61.6	Average	59.2	Average	105.0

B. Decile distributions

Percentile	Three-year periods	Five-year periods	Ten-year periods
Best	232	278	580
10	196	235	472
20	171	209	421
25	161	196	395
30	159	185	352
40	140	168	266
50	134	160	247
60	126	140	212
70	120	126	199
75	114	122	192
80	105	117	162
90	85	71	123
Worst.............................	35	46	85

Source: Lawrence Fisher and James H. Lorie, *A Half-Century of Returns on Stocks and Bonds: Rates of Returns on Investments in Common Stocks and U.S. Treasury Securities, 1926–1976* (Chicago: University of Chicago Graduate School of Business, 1977). Exhibit XXXII.

What percentage invested in stocks, with the remainder in Treasury bills, would have a high probability of exceeding 80 percent of the current value. It is possible to use a number of alternative definitions of "high probability"—the average five-year term, the bottom 20 percent, the bottom 10 percent, and so on. In this case we will use the average of the five worst five-year periods measured in the years 1926–76. As shown in Exhibit 3–8, this is 59.2 percent. That is, an investor who started with $1 in each of the five worst five-year periods would have ended up with an average of 59.2 percent of his investment. We can thus apply the formula shown below to find the applicable percentage in equities:

Amount in stocks × Dollars left in stocks
for each dollar invested
+ Amount in bills × Dollars earned in bills
= Desired goal.

Assume bills earn 5% per year or 27.6 for five years.
If the amount in stocks = x and the amount in bills

$$
\begin{aligned}
&= 1 - x, \\
(x)(0.592) + (1 - x)(1.276) &= 0.8 \\
0.592x + 1.276 - 1.276x &= 0.8 \\
-0.684x &= -0.476 \\
0.684x &= 0.476 \\
x &= \frac{0.476}{0.684} \\
x &= 0.696 \\
1 - x &= 0.304
\end{aligned}
$$

Thus, we conclude from the historic return/preference method that, based on the assumptions that Treasury bills will yield 5 percent and that stocks will do no worse than the average of the worst five five-year periods in the years 1926–76 (a loss of 40.8 percent to 59.2 percent of the original investment), a portfolio of 69.6 percent equities and 30.4 percent Treasury bills will be worth at least 80 percent of its current value five years from now.

3. The sponsor can view historical returns and risk levels (particularly the latter) and see the extremes of the results which may occur. For instance, looking at the historical rates of

return for the years 1926–76 (Exhibit 3–8B), the worst three-year period in the U.S. stock market left investors with about 35 percent of the assets that they possessed at the beginning of the period. The sponsor can look at its fund's position and make a judgment of the psychological and financial impact that this would have on the sponsor. Suppose, for example, that the sponsor felt that the most it could withstand in a three-year period without severe repercussions from board members or without endangering its operating success would be a 30 percent drop in assets. This would indicate, using the above formula, that the sponsor should not have more than 56.7 percent in equities, assuming that the balance is in riskless assets earning 5 percent per year. Of course, this further assumes that the stocks owned by the sponsor are as risky as the overall market. If the sponsor owned more risky or less risky stocks, the percentage in equities would be adjusted accordingly.

There are limitations to the historic return/preference approach, however. Assume that the sponsor views results in terms of the worst case or some form of "adjusted" worst case. For instance, the worst five-year period in the stock market during the years 1926–76 saw an investor losing 54 percent of his assets. The average loss of the worst five five-year periods is 40.8 percent, indicating that 59.2 percent remain. Assume that Treasury bills earn 5 percent per year, so that over a five-year period they would return $27.60 for each $100 invested. An investor could ask what percentage in equities will allow him to meet his objective of a 40 percent gain in fund assets over five years assuming that stock market results are no worse than the average of the five worst five-year periods in the years 1926–76. We would like to apply the formula from the previous example, but this is not possible, since the Treasury bill rate is less than the actuarial rate and we are expecting a loss on stocks. Consequently, no combination of stocks and bonds will achieve the actuarial rate of 7 percent per year.

Any methods which are based on historical information are subject to the criticism "But things are different now." It seems to many observers that the last 50 years had almost every conceivable set of good and bad conditions, so that future results are highly unlikely to fall outside the extremes of those years. The strongest argument to suggest that things are now different is an analysis of inflation rates. In recent years the inflation rate has risen severalfold, as have interest rates. Whereas in the past Treasury bills averaged a return of about 2½ percent and stocks a return of 9 percent, it now appears that Treasury bills are closer to 7 to 10 percent, so stocks should be much higher. Those finding this analysis appealing can base their simulations on "real" (inflation adjusted) returns rather than actual returns.

In addition to prescribing the basic policy toward risk described by the percent in equities, the sponsor must also consider the impact on portfolio risk of the risk level of the individual asset categories such as equities. Logically, the risk level of equities would be established as an investment policy. However, this usually is excessively restrictive to the investment manager. Thus the sponsor typically must allow the manager to choose the equity risk policy with the sponsor adjusting the percent in equities to achieve the desired overall policy.

The preceding analysis assumes that the portfolio owned was completely diversified, i.e., that no attempt was made at stock selection. Obviously, to the extent that the portfolio is not diversified, there is further risk. Through unsuccessful stock selection the investment manager who has followed the sponsor's directions as to percentage in equities and as to the risk level of the equities owned may still achieve a lower return than expected. Thus, in an actively managed portfolio it is necessary to consider further variations in the rate of return from securities selection and their impact on the portfolio.

In addition to setting policies regarding the asset types to be owned, the proportions in these asset types, the risk level, and the diversification level, the sponsor must establish policy regarding the extent to which the investment manager will be permitted to vary those policies. A fund may average 50 percent in equities by going between 0 percent and 100 percent or by going between 49 percent and 51 percent. A similar situation exists with regard to the risk levels of the securities owned. Finally, changing the diversification level can have an important impact on the fund's results. Sponsors with many investment managers may find it appropriate to reduce the managers' flexibility in changing policy decisions for two reasons. First, sponsors with many managers usually hire each manager for a specific purpose; if a manager changes that purpose, this partly defeats the objective for which the manager was hired. Second, as the managers change policies, their actions may offset one another. As one manager is increasing the fund's percentage in equities, another manager may be decreasing it, the only result to the fund being that its transaction costs have increased. Thus, the policy toward changing objectives should receive direct consideration from the sponsor.

THE USE OF CONSULTANTS

Establishing an investment or risk/return policy is one of the most difficult responsibilities faced by sponsors. In establishing such policies, it may be desirable to use computer simulations to help understand the impact of various allocations of stocks and bonds. For both of these reasons it may be desirable to utilize consultants in establishing and periodically reviewing these policies. To make these projections even more useful it is necessary to integrate an analysis of both liabilities and assets. In other words, projections of future needs for funds must be coordinated with the current availability of assets. The consultant should be helpful in this regard. Further, the consultant may have available sophisticated analytical tools for making projections, as well as historical information on securities markets for use in simulations. This information, if properly used, can be valuable in the decision-making process. Obviously, however, all projections are necessarily tentative and they are highly dependent on the input on which they were based. Thus they must be used with judgment and they should be reviewed formally at least every third year.

4

Choosing
asset categories

"Do what you will, the capital is at hazard."[1]

Once the sponsor has explored the question of the appropriate
investment or risk policy for the fund, it must turn to the issue
of what types of securities have the appropriate characteristics
for the investment policy chosen. For purposes of this analysis
it is helpful to divide asset types into two broad categories,
marketable and less marketable, and then within each category
to list asset types in order of risk, starting with the least risky.
Within each broad category a natural division occurs between
fixed income investments and equity investments.

---

[1] From *Harvard College* v. *Amory* (1830), the Massachusetts court case which established the "prudent man" rule. In that case the court held that all securities have risk
and that stocks are not de facto inappropriate trust investments. The quotation is from
Harvey E. Bines, *The Law of Investment Management* (Boston: Warren, Gorham, &
Lamont, 1978), p. 1–32.

Fixed income investments represent loans by the holder (in this case the fund) to the issuer, which is usually a corporation or a government. The issuer is required to pay a stated amount of interest and to return the principal at a stipulated time. If it does not, the holders of the fixed income obligation can force the issuer into bankruptcy. Equity investments, on the other hand, represent ownership of the issuer. Equity investments can only be issued by corporations, since ownership in governments is not sold. Holders of equity securities are not entitled to specific income or to a return on their investment; rather, they participate in the success of the corporations through dividends and capital appreciation.

MARKETABLE SECURITIES

Although all assets are obviously marketable to some extent, there are obviously wide differences in the liquidity of various asset types. Since the characteristics of the fund will determine its need for liquidity, and hence marketability, it is useful to describe the liquidity spectrum of asset types.

Fixed income

Cash is the most marketable asset since it has already been turned into the medium of exchange which defines liquidity. In terms of rate of return, cash has a zero percent return and no risk is associated with that return. That is, an investor who holds cash will always have a zero percent rate of return. His only concerns are the stability of the institution in which the cash is deposited and the inflation risk which impacts all monetary assets.

Cash equivalents. This category of assets includes all short-term fixed income securities which can be quickly converted into cash. These include U.S. Treasury bills, federal funds, certificates of deposit, and commercial paper.

U.S. Treasury bills. The instrument with the greatest safety of principal is the short-term U.S. Treasury bill, since it is guaranteed by the U.S. government, which has a virtually unlimited ability to create funds to pay its debts. Treasury bills are offered in units of $10,000 face amount and are auctioned by the Treasury every week.

The maturities of Treasury bills range from 91 days to 364 days. Treasury bills, like many other types of cash equivalents, are sold at a "discount." This means that the return to the holder comes, not from interest payments, but from the difference between what he paid and the face value at maturity. This rate is not the same as the true rate of return or the bond equivalent rate of return (consult Appendix 4–A for a clarification of these distinctions).

Federal funds. These are one-day loans made between banks. Each bank is required to have a certain percentage of its deposits backed up by cash or by its own deposits at one of the Federal Reserve banks. Since some banks have deficiencies and others excesses, loans are made between banks for short periods of time.

Certificates of deposit. These are, in effect, the savings accounts of corporations and other large investors. Banks needing funds for lending purposes will pay interest at specified rates on deposits of $100,000 or more. Subject to interest rate ceilings established by the Federal Reserve, the banks can make any arrangement they want as to the size, the interest rates paid, and the maturities.

Commercial paper. Commercial paper represents the corporate counterpart of certificates of deposit. Whereas banks attract funds by paying interest on certificates of deposit, corporations, particularly those which finance purchases by *their* customers, issue commercial paper. Most issuers of commercial paper sell it through dealers, though a few very large corporations are able to issue it directly.

Notes. Whereas the typical maturity on a cash equivalent is one year or less, notes are generally considered to be fixed income obligations with a maturity of between one and ten years at the time of issuance. Unlike cash equivalents, notes usually bear a coupon, and consequently they are really just short-term bonds.

U.S. Treasury notes. The highest quality notes are those issued by the U.S. Treasury, because these notes are free from default risk.

U.S. government agency notes. These notes represent an instrument of very high quality, since even though they are not directly guaranteed by the U.S. government, there is a strong presumption that the federal government will not allow its agencies to go into bankruptcy.

Corporate notes. The quality of corporate notes depends on the creditworthiness of the issuer. Creditworthiness is a function of profitability, the stability of earnings, and the degree to which earnings have been committed.

Bonds. Bonds are frequently divided into three categories: those secured by specific assets, such as mortgage bonds; "unsecured" bonds, which are secured by the general credit of the issuer and are more properly known as debentures; and convertible bonds, which are discussed under equity instruments. A further distinction can be drawn between bonds which are taxed and municipal, or tax-free, bonds.

Mortgage bonds. In order to increase the quality rating of a bond, and thus enable the issuer to pay a lower interest rate, some bonds are secured by specific assets of a corporation. Such mortgage bonds are most commonly found in the public utility field, secured by such assets as pipelines. Although certain types of assets can be removed from the parent corporation in case of default, most people feel that if, for instance, a pipeline is of no use to the corporation transporting natural gas, it will certainly be of no use to the investor. Consequently, the risk for mortgage bonds is not a great deal lower than the risk for straight debentures.

Debentures. These bonds are sometimes called unsecured, but they are more appropriately recognized as general obligations of the issuer, and they represent a claim on all assets which are not specifically mortgaged. They are junior to tax liens and to mortgage bonds (but only with respect to the pledged assets).

Subordinated bonds. These bonds are issued with the specific agreement that other creditors, such as banks, have higher priority in obtaining the company's assets in case of default. For surrendering part of their security, investors, of course, demand a higher rate of return on such bonds.

Municipal, or tax-free, bonds. Bonds issued by the various states, municipalities, and certain political subdivisions thereof are exempt from taxation by the federal government and by the state in which they are issued. These bonds bear relatively low coupons because investors in high tax brackets find that they have a higher aftertax return by buying, for instance, a 4 percent tax-free bond than by buying an 8 percent taxable bond. This, of course, would be true for any investor in a tax bracket greater than 50 percent. Clearly, a pension or endowment fund which pays no taxes on current income would be twice as well off if it owned the taxable bond than if it owned the municipal bond.

Guaranteed investment contracts. In recent years some sponsors have responded to a desire for high income and stability of return by purchasing from insurance companies contracts guaranteeing a fixed rate of return for a specified period, usually five years. Each of these contracts is offered separately to the purchaser, so a considerable variety of alternatives is available. Although these contracts are offered by insurance companies, they do not represent insurance. That is, there is no pool of participants who are pooling assets for protection against some uncertainty. Rather, these instruments are like debentures. The insurance company borrows money under stated conditions and provides no security other than the general credit of the issuer.

Equity securities

There are four types of equity securities: preferred stocks, pure common stocks, securities having both the privilege to buy common stock and some right to income, and those with privileges to buy (or sell) common stock without any right to income.

Preferred stock. This category of investment can be called either fixed income or equity. In terms of priority in liquidation, preferred shareholders come after debenture holders and before common stock owners. From the point of view of the investor, preferred stock is more like a fixed income investment than like an equity investment, since, assuming that the corporation is not in default, regular dividend payments are received. Further, the holder of nonconvertible preferred stock has no right to extra rewards should the corporation be particularly successful. Preferred stock is not usually a good investment for portfolios which do not pay taxes on their income, because corporations bid up the price of preferred stocks (and thus reduce the yields of such stocks) in order to take advantage of the Internal Revenue Code provision which allows corporations to deduct from their taxable income 85 percent of the income that they receive through dividends from other corporations. (Since corporations pay dividends out of *after*tax earnings, it would be highly unfair for the corporation holding preferred shares in another corporation to pay taxes on income from preferreds.) Because of this tax advantage, corporations bid up preferred stock prices to a point at which the yields are generally too low to be attractive to tax-exempt portfolios. Thus, virtually all tax-exempt institutions find it desirable to avoid preferred stocks.

Convertible debentures. The least risky type of equity investment is the one which carries with it a fixed obligation to pay income and a promise to return the original investment (in dollars) at some time in the future. This type of investment is the convertible debenture or bond. Convertible bonds carry an interest rate and a maturity date, as do other bonds, but they also have a conversion right which allows the holder to exchange them for a certain number of shares of stock during a certain period of time. In return for this privilege, which can be quite valuable if the underlying stock rises dramatically, the holder of convertible debentures sacrifices one or more of three things. First, the interest rate is usually lower than that of other debt instruments of the company. Second, the debentures are usually subordinated to other debt, so that in the event of bankruptcy other creditors have a superior claim. Third, a conversion premium is usually built into the conversion rate. For instance, a $1,000 bond might be convertible into only $900 worth of stock if the conversion took place on the date that the bond was issued. The interest rate level and the amount of the premium are determined at the time of the offering, based on the supply of and demand for the issue.

Convertible preferred stock. Convertible preferreds, like convertible bonds, carry both a fixed return and the right to participate in the success of the corporation. Unlike convertible bonds, convertible preferreds represent an equity interest in the corporation, and therefore they are junior to all bonds. Further, the right to receive dividends on convertible preferreds is not contractual, and if a corporation's board of directors feels that it is not wise to pay such dividends it can choose to withhold them. (In this case the corporation cannot pay dividends on its common stock.) For the reasons given above, convertible preferreds, like straight preferreds, are typically not purchased by tax-exempt institutions.

Common stock. This asset category represents the basic unit of ownership of the corporation. The holders of common stock are the owners of the corporation. They have rights to dividends only to the extent that such dividends have been earned by the corporation and declared by the board of directors. No fixed return accrues to the common shareholder, and in the event that the corporation is liquidated, his right to the corporation's assets has the lowest priority. On the other hand, there is theoretically no limit to the benefit which the common shareholder can derive if the corporation is successful.

Warrants, options, and "rights." These types of securities represent neither loans to the corporation nor ownership in it, but rather the privilege of buying a certain number of shares at a fixed price for a given period of time. The three types have a great deal of similarity with one another, with only nuances relating to the circumstances under which they were issued or their life span determining the designation applied to them. Warrants are typically sold in connection with offerings of debentures, and they become "detachable" from the debentures at some point after issuance. The combination of debenture and warrant provides an instrument very similar to a convertible bond. Options are issued by investors seeking to gain income or to reduce the risk of their portfolios. (Chapter 5 has a section detailing how option investing can impact portfolios.) "Rights" are issued in connection with "rights offerings." Corporations desiring to raise additional equity capital sometimes allow existing shareholders the right to purchase additional shares. For instance, a corporation whose stock is selling for 20 and which desires to add 4 percent to its equity capital base may allow each shareholder to purchase one share at 18 for each 25 shares owned. In this case the rights would sell for approximately eight cents each, as the holder of 25 such rights would be able to buy one share at a $2 discount (25 × $0.08 = $2). Warrants frequently do not expire for a number of years; options typically expire in three to nine months; and rights expire about two weeks after their issuance.

LESS MARKETABLE SECURITIES

The categories of less marketable securities can include any of the security types discussed under marketable securities plus most real estate and natural resource investments.

Fixed income

Privately placed notes and bonds. Marketable notes and bonds are offered to the public through a formal prospectus indicating that the securities have been registered with the Securities and Exchange Commission in Washington. The registration process attempts to ensure that investors are informed of all the relevant facts before they risk their money. Not surprisingly, the registration process is costly and time consuming. This process can be avoided if the securities to be sold are offered, not to the public in general, but to a limited number of sophisticated investors.

In order to avoid the registration process corporations are willing to pay a higher interest rate on the bonds they sell. On the other hand, certain investors with long time horizons and large portfolios are willing to sacrifice the ability to sell their holdings in the marketplace in order to receive a higher yield on their investments. Consequently, the privately placed security has achieved a niche in the investment portfolio of many insurance companies. In recent years banks and pension funds have also increased their activity in this type of investment. Typically, private placements carry an interest rate ¼ to ½ percent (25 to 50 basis points) above that available on public issues. They also usually provide for the repayment of substantial portions of the issue before maturity.

Mortgages. These fixed income securities are, in a sense, privately placed mortgage bonds. That is, a borrower induces a lender to provide funds under certain terms and conditions, one of which is that a specific piece of real estate is pledged as collateral for the loan. Unlike mortgage bonds, however, normal real estate mortgages do not have the full faith and credit of the issuer behind them, but generally only allow the lender to take possession of the collateral in case of default.

Equity investments

Letter stock. This type of equity, which was issued in the speculative market of the late 1960s, represents a method of securing equity capital without going through the SEC registration process. The purchaser of the stock signs an agreement, or "letter," indicating that he has purchased it for investment and not for resale. A legend to this effect is placed on the stock certificates in order to alert the transfer agent not to effect a transfer from the holder to a second holder without being assured that it is proper to do so. Letter stock developed a tainted reputation, through no fault of its own, when some mutual fund investment managers purchased letter stock at a discount from the price of the publicly traded shares and then immediately considered the letter stock to be at full market value in calculating the mutual fund's net asset value. This led to immediate increases in the net asset value of the funds they managed, and hence to artificial performance results.

Equity real estate. The ownership of land or of improvements thereon is another potential investment for tax-exempt portfolios. Such investments can be made directly or through commingled funds. Some caution must be exercised in the direct ownership of income-producing real estate to avoid the "unrelated business income" provisions of the Internal Revenue Code. These provisions suggest that it is appropriate for a tax-exempt fund to invest money and pay no taxes on its income, but that it is not appropriate for such a fund to operate a business in competition with taxable organizations.

Natural resources. It is possible for funds to invest in natural resources such as oil and gas, and given the existing inflationary trends, it is somewhat surprising that more such investing has not been done. Perhaps this is so because many such investments are structured as tax shelters, which are of no interest to tax-exempt funds, and perhaps it is so because no one else is doing it.

Royalties. Although investment in royalties is uncommon, some funds have invested in rights to receive royalties on certain patents or trademarks.

APPENDIX 4-A
Rate of return calculations for fixed income securities

A. Return on bond carrying coupon paid once per year
    Price: 100. Coupon: 6%. Maturity: One year.
    Return: 6/100 = 6%.

B. Return on instrument with 6% discount (no coupon).
    Price: 94. Coupon: None. Maturity: One year.
    Return: (100 − 94)/94 = 6.38% (100 − 94)/94 = 6.35%

C. Return on bond paying semiannual coupon (the normal case)
    Price: 100. Coupon: 6%. Maturity: One year.
    Return: Value of first coupon + Value of second coupon + six months' interest on first coupon = 3% + 3% + 3% (0.03) = 6.09 (assuming 6% reinvestment rate).

D. Bond equivalent return of 6% discount instrument
    Price: 94. Coupon: None. Maturity: One year.
    Return: 5.83% (i.e. ½ of 5.83 = 2.915; 2.915 + 2.915 + 2.915(.02195) = 5.83%

A and B show returns assuming annual compounding. C and D show returns on a bond-equivalent basis, that is, with semiannual compounding. Note that the bond yield (C) understates the true annual return.

E. Terminal wealth: The amount that an investor has at the end of a specific period. Terminal wealth depends on the intial amount, the timing and the amount of income, and the rate achieved on reinvested income (assumes no interim contributions and withdrawals).

F. Return (also called realized compound yield): The compound annual return on the beginning value which will provide the investor with a specific terminal wealth (assuming no interim contributions and withdrawals).

For calculations of return when portfolios have contributions and withdrawals, see Chapter 6.

APPENDIX 4-B

Approximate market value of major public securities types, December 31, 1977 ($ billions)

Short-term private investments		
Commercial paper		65.1
Banker's acceptances		25.5
Certificates of deposit ($100,000 or more)		165.8
U.S. government		
Direct obligations		459.9*
Bills	161.1	
Notes	251.8	
Bonds	47.0	
Federal and federally sponsored credit agencies		109.9
State and local governments		260.0
Mortgages		1,023.5
Corporate bonds		298.1
Corporate stock		1,080.9†
Listed	837.6	
New York Stock Exchange	796.6	
American Stock Exchange	37.6	
Other exchanges	3.4	
Over-the-counter	243.3	

* Excludes $255.3 billion of nonmarketable debt.

† Includes $73.9 billion in investment companies, of which $68.4 billion is over-the-counter, and $119.4 billion in intercorporate holdings. Excludes $187.0 billion in closely held stock.

Source: Securities and Exchange Commission Statistical Bulletin; Statistical Abstract of the U.S. 1978.

5

Choosing
investment managers

Managing money is an easy business. There are only two rules.
Rule 1: Don't lose money.
Rule 2: Don't forget rule 1.

"There are very few old geniuses."

Old Wall Street saying

After deciding on investment policies and asset categories, the
fund sponsor must turn to the question of who will make the
actual investment decisions—that is, who will be the investment manager. A number of decisions must be made, including whether the fund should be managed internally or externally; how much discretion the investment manager should
have; whether the assets should be invested directly in securities or indirectly through pooled or commingled funds;
whether the style employed should be active or passive, and if
active, then what active style should be employed; and how
many managers are needed. Each of these decisions may be

interrelated with other decisions discussed in this or other chapters. This complicates the process of answering the many questions that the sponsor faces, but by analyzing each of these matters separately, a framework of decision is provided for the sponsor. In addition, the Appendix includes a questionnaire assist sponsors in screening prospective investment managers.

INTERNAL VERSUS EXTERNAL
INVESTMENT MANAGEMENT

This area has been touched on in the Chapter 2 discussion of assigning responsibility for operating the fund, but additional comments are desirable. Although some people suggest that a monkey throwing darts can achieve as high a return as the most knowledgeable investment manager, there appears to be no trend whatsoever toward the use of this method of investment. Rather, the trend is quite the opposite, with sponsors desiring more and more sophistication from their investment managers. Because of this trend, most organizations are unlikely to feel that they have the level of capability needed to manage large investment porfolios of varying asset types. Clearly, such expertise can be hired or developed by very large sponsors, and in fact a number of large sponsors are doing this. In considering whether to use internal staff or external managers, sponsors should address the following questions:

1. What are the advantages of internal versus external investment management?
2. What expertise does investment management require?
3. Does this expertise exist within the organization?
4. If not, do budgetary considerations permit hiring people with the necessary qualifications?
5. Can senior officials of the organization properly supervise the activities of an investment manager?
6. Is the organization willing to expend the time and effort that are required to manage investment funds?
7. Is the organization willing to accept the risk associated with this function?

The advantages of internal versus external investment management. The principal advantages of internal management are that it gives the sponsor far more control over investment policies and over the individual securities held, that the people making investment decisions will be more familiar with the sponsor's needs, and that the sponsor can develop a better insight into the problems faced by outside investment managers. The advantages of external management are that the outside manager typically has far more resources, that he may have special capabilities such as in dealing with private placements or mortgage investments, that he may be able to demand lower commission costs from brokers and dealers, and that for bond investing he may be able to get better prices by combining smaller blocks of bonds into more marketable larger blocks. Although the outside manager has less time to spend on a particular fund than would an insider, he develops insight and perspective from viewing many sponsors with different needs. If the truth were known, it would probably be found that the real reason behind most moves from external to internal investment management is performance, or more precisely, the feeling that "we can do as well as those guys."

The expertise required for investment management. The investment manager working within the organization will need knowledge of the two major decision areas, namely how to allocate assets *among* sectors and which securities to buy *within* sectors. That is, he will need to decide what allocations to make among stocks, bonds, liquid assets, and other investments, and he will also need to decide which stocks to buy, which bonds to buy, and so on. The importance of the allocation question, and hence the significance of the manager's expertise in this area, rests to a large extent on the sponsor's position with respect to setting an overall risk policy. If the sponsor establishes firm guidelines as to the percentage of the portfolio which should go into each asset sector, then the manager's activities can be concentrated in security selection. Conversely, if the sponsor has only general guidelines, then the investment manager must choose as well as implement the fund's investment policy. The type of expertise required to make intelligent allocations among investment vehicles is knowledge of economics, particularly monetary economics, and experience with stock and bond market levels over at least two market cycles. (Of course, familiarity with the sponsor and its fund is vital.)

The knowledge required to invest in equities includes much of the experience indicated above plus a strong knowledge of individual industries and companies. Investment in fixed income securities requires a strong knowledge of monetary economics as well as experience with a large number of bonds and bond issuers. If the manager is to invest in real estate he must have a thorough knowledge of the evaluation process for investing in mortgages and real estate equities as well as a network of contacts which will provide a source of investments. Such a network is necessary for both real estate and private placements, which are characterized by less liquid markets than are public investments.

An important factor which the investment manager must concern himself with is lead/lag relationships, which can frustrate even knowledgeable investors. The market discounting function usually causes information to be reflected in securities prices before most investors recognize that this has happened. Consequently, in reflecting on any piece of information, the investor must always remind himself that "this may be true, but if it is already recognized by the market, then it may be too late to act on it."

Does investment management expertise exist within the organization? The vast majority of foundations, public organizations, and labor unions will not have sufficient in-house expertise to manage portfolios unless people have been hired expressly for this purpose. Corporations, on the other hand, will tend to have more of the required experience because of their frequent need for investing excess cash in securities and also because of their sale of securities to finance their own activities. A corporation's investment expertise will depend partly on the extent to which its activities involve buying and selling securities and partly on the extent to which it makes investment decisions itself, as opposed to relying on outside investment organizations. A further consideration is the extent to which the corporation is diversified. Highly diversified companies are in a sense a portfolio which senior officials must manage. If management is accustomed to evaluating merger and acquisition candidates, it may find planning a securities portfolio to be within the realm of the company's abilities.

Are the costs of hiring in-house investment managers justifiable? The budgetary considerations are quite straightforward, involving only the cost of using an internal investment staff versus the cost of using outside managers. The cost of outside investment management is typically based on the size of the account and on whether the relationship involves management only or management plus custody and record keeping. Let us assume that the sponsor intends to undertake only investment management activities and will leave custody to a bank. The cost of outside management is usually about one half of 1 percent for accounts in the $1 million to $5 million area, with a reduction in the fee to as low as $1/10$ percent for amounts up to $100 million. Investment advisers usually charge more than banks, and banks which are performing custody work usually charge a fairly modest incremental fee for providing management in addition to custody. This charge may be only one or two tenths of 1 percent. Thus, the difference in cost between internal and external investment management will be largely dependent on whether the alternative to in-house investment management is the bank providing custody or some other organization. On a $10 million portfolio the investment management fee might be $25,000–$50,000 per year, and for a $50 million fund with three managers the fee might be $100,000–$200,000 per year.

Although an in-house staff of any size, from one person part time to a cast of hundreds, is conceivable, it would appear that an effective organization should have at least one person concentrating on each major asset category and an overall investor/manager who would be responsible for asset allocation, liaison with the rest of the sponsor organization, and administration of the investment management group. That is, an in-house group which is managing stocks and bonds should have three professionals, and in addition it should have clerical and administrative support from two clerical people. Reasonable estimates for salary might be $75,000 for the department head, $50,000 for an experienced investment manager for one asset sector, $40,000 for a somewhat less experienced person for the other asset sector, $15,000 for a senior clerical person, and $12,000 for a junior person. The salary budget of $193,000 per year should be doubled to $400,000 to provide a total budget which would include subscription services, office space, travel, communications, and other typical expenses. However, brokerage commissions, custodial fees, and accounting and auditing expenses are not included. On the basis of these estimates and considering only cost, a fund below $50 million in size would probably not justify the expense of internal investment management (½ percent of $50 million = $250,000) and a fund of over $100 million might justify it. The above analysis assumes that the entire portfolio is managed internally. In the more common case the sponsor decides to manage part of the portfolio internally and to leave the balance to outside managers. If a sponsor decides to manage one third of its assets internally, the fund would have to be about three times as large, or over $300 million, to justify internal management on a cost basis. Since some sponsors view having an internal staff as an important advantage in understanding the activities of outside managers, they may be willing to have higher operating expenses in order to gain the added insight provided by internal management. Since the costs of both external management and internal management vary greatly, each sponsor should calculate its actual outside costs and compare them to its estimated internal costs in order to find the break-even point.

Can the organization supervise an investment manager? The supervisory requirements placed on senior officials are much the same whether the fund is managed internally or externally. In either case the control systems discussed in subsequent chapters will be adequate for these purposes. It should also be noted that in either case controlling an investment process is different from controlling other areas of the sponsor's activities and consequently does not fall within the direct experience of most senior management personnel.

Is the organization willing to manage funds? This question must be asked by the sponsor, but it cannot really be answered by an outsider. There will certainly be much "discussion" within the organization before a board of directors or a board of trustees will agree to internal management. This decision will relate to the perceived risks and benefits of internal versus external management, including the risk of embarrassment.

Is the organization willing to accept the risk of fund management?   In reality there is probably very little difference in risk to the *organization* between internal and external management. That is, if the manager does well and the fund prospers, the organization will benefit, regardless of who was responsible for the success. Similarly, if the manager is unsuccessful, the organization will suffer commensurately. The risk to the individuals within the organization is a different matter. Many officials will feel that a mistake made by an outside investment manager is the investment manager's fault, whereas bad results obtained by an internally managed fund might reflect on the personnel who decided to use internal management, a practice contrary to that of most sponsors. Moreover, most sponsors would find it easier to remove an account from an outside manager who is operating unsuccessfully than to disband an equally unsuccessful internal staff. ERISA tends to support the notion that it is less risky for the sponsor to have an outside manager by saying that under certain conditions a sponsor can escape liability for the acts or omissions of its investment manager by choosing outside managers.[1]

In summary, the advantages of internal management to the sponsor are greater control of the policies pursued and the securities purchased, greater familiarity of the investment manager with the goals and characteristics of the organization, and greater ability of the investment manager to devote time to the sponsor's portfolio. The disadvantages are a lack of the perspective gained by viewing many different customers and their portfolios and, presumably, a much lower level of resources available to the investment manager. The cost of internal management is normally greater than that of external management for small funds (about $100 million or less) and less than that of external management for large funds.

Sponsors wishing to begin internal management might consider the following approach. Rather than moving a large piece

---

[1] These conditions are that the outside investment manager must be "qualified" (meaning that it is a bank, an insurance company, or a registered investment adviser, as defined), that the manager must acknowledge in writing that he is a fiduciary, that the sponsor must have been prudent in hiring the manager, and that the sponsor must have been prudent in continuing the use of the manager (see ERISA, Sec. 405).

of a diversified portfolio in-house immediately, a sponsor may divert the annual contributions or the annual contributions plus income on investments to the in-house pool. Further, the sponsor might start with a reasonably passive bond portfolio as the first step toward investing. In this way relatively small amounts of money will be invested in the less risky assets, and consequently the sponsor can begin an internal operation without taking undue risk.

THE INVESTMENT MANAGER'S DEGREE OF DISCRETION

It is possible for the sponsor to have an investment manager but to give him only part of the responsibility for investing. The degree of discretion is a function of the organization's willingness to become involved in the investment process and of the extent to which it has defined its investment policies (see Chapter 3). The degree of discretion ranges from allowing the managers to have the most control to allowing them to have the least control:

1. The manager makes all decisions.
2. The sponsor provides either general guidelines as to percentage in equities, such as "Do not exceed 60 percent in equities," or specific guidelines, such as "The equity/fixed income ratio will be maintained as close to 60/40 as possible."
3. The sponsor provides either general or specific guidelines as to the risk level (beta) of the equity portfolio.
4. The sponsor provides either general or specific guidelines as to the quality of stocks or bonds.
5. The sponsor reviews all recommendations prior to their execution.

Historically, the two most common approaches have been 1 and 5, though the less extreme positions are now more prevalent. In most cases the manager makes all decisions, though it may be justifiably argued that even though there are no specific guidelines as to percentage in equities, the investment manager and the sponsor have an implied agreement that extremes such as 90/10 or 10/90 are unacceptable and that a more moderate posture is preferred.

Because of ERISA and because of poor equity results in most

of the 1970s, fund sponsors are increasingly specifying explicitly what they wish their investment managers to do. It has become much more common to have not only the percentage in equities established, usually at least with a maximum, but also to prescribe bond quality and even stock quality.[2]

The policy of granting no discretion to the investment manager has three basic advantages. First, the sponsor retains complete control over what investments are held. Second, there is a greater opportunity for the sponsor to learn to understand the manager and for the manager to get to know the sponsor. And third, the manager is required to think out and articulate his reasons for making a suggestion, rather than potentially "shooting from the hip." Of course, the policy of reviewing all recommendations prior to their execution partly defeats the purpose of having an investment manager. Obviously, it makes no sense to have an investment manager if the sponsor or the committee of trustees rejects a large percentage of the investment manager's suggestions. Also, many investment managers indicate that the time lost in obtaining approval for recommendations causes the fund to lose part of the benefit of the recommendations. Some managers have even gone so far as to provide documentation that discretionary accounts tend to have better results than do nondiscretionary accounts. If the manager is a large organization this may be true since the nondiscretionary account will be among the last to buy and sell all the time. Some skeptics, on the other hand, would contend that this is all rationalization on the part of the manager who wants to avoid the extra paperwork and effort required by nondiscretionary accounts.

A less dramatic example of limiting the manager's discretion occurs when the sponsor requires that all purchase recommendations be reviewed in advance but gives the manager authority to act on sale recommendations without prior approval. The logic here is that it is advisable to act promptly to prevent a loss but it is not necessary to act hastily to achieve a potential gain.

As a practical matter the policy of reviewing all transactions prior to their execution imposes a discipline on the manager to think of the long term rather than the short term, since the

---

[2] Paradoxically, some sponsors contend that because of ERISA they do not *dare* to specify a policy lest it be wrong and they be blamed.

manager will know that by the time a transaction is approved and the order executed any short-term trading benefits will be lost. The success of the nondiscretionary approach will be largely contingent on the degree to which the manager's recommendations are accepted. If they are accepted as a matter of course, the manager will feel confident in his role and can act freely to apply his best judgment on behalf of the fund. If the manager is frequently overruled, he will be frustrated. In that event it is unlikely that a successful relationship between the manager and the sponsor will be achieved. Every investment manager who has nondiscretionary accounts can provide instances in which a perfectly valid recommendation was turned down because a trustee had a brother-in-law who lost money in a similar stock.

As a final point, a method of operation that is guaranteed to lead to a poor relationship between the sponsor and the investment manager is one in which an investment committee reviewing all recommendations not only turns down the manager's proposals but also makes proposals of its own. This not only reduces the value of the manager, it turns him into a research assistant who is expected to be a "jack-of-all-stocks." If in fact the trustees do not wish to accept the manager's choice of a given purchase, they should ask the manager to make an alternative suggestion rather than provide choices of their own. If the trustees find themselves rejecting an uncomfortably large percentage of the investment manager's recommendations, it might be feasible to have the manager make two purchase recommendations rather than one in order to give the trustees an opportunity to pick one and thus reduce the embarrassment to both parties. If too many recommendations are rejected, the sponsor should consider using a new adviser or managing the fund internally.

DIRECT VERSUS INDIRECT INVESTMENT FUND OWNERSHIP

Sponsors that are willing to relinquish discretionary control over purchase and sale decisions on individual stocks will find it possible to own securities either directly or through participations in commingled (pooled) funds. Both banks and mutual fund management organizations provide pooled funds in which sponsors can invest. Typically, tax-exempt funds have not invested in mutual funds because of the high operating costs of mutual funds and because of their image as being for individual investors, so the commingled portfolios provided by banks are the prime subject of discussion here. The advantages of a pooled fund are ease of administration, high diversification, and low cost. The disadvantages are the sponsor's inability to adapt the investments of the commingled fund to its own objectives and the sponsor's inability to control the risk posture of the commingled fund.

Advantages of commingled funds

Ease of administration. From an administrative point of view the holder of a commingled fund owns only one security. He need not be concerned with collecting dividends and maintaining custodial records. Since commingled funds almost never issue certificates, he need not worry about custodial problems or the physical transfer of securities. His interest is represented by electronic bookkeeping entries only.

Diversification. Since a pooled fund combines the assets of many contributors, it can achieve a high degree of diversification by purchasing a large number of securities. Theoretically a small portfolio could achieve a similar level of diversification, but small portfolios do not typically invest in large numbers of securities. Both sound investment practice and ERISA require that portfolios be diversified. The implications of high and low levels of diversification are described in Chapter 3.

Cost. Just as it is easier for the fund to own participations in a commingled portfolio, so it is easier for the investment manager to combine the assets of many sponsors into one fund. He need not provide separate management for the sponsor, nor need he provide individual custodial and extensive record-keeping facilities. Consequently, he is able to charge lower fees to the fund sponsors.

Disadvantages of commingled funds

Unadaptable to sponsor needs. Since a pooled fund represents the assets of many sponsors it is obviously impossible to adapt the portfolio to the needs of each sponsor. Consequently, the sponsor must choose a pooled fund which most appropriately fits its needs and then accept the decisions of the investment manager as to what securities the pooled fund will hold. This limitation can be partly avoided by investing in commingled funds with different objectives.

Sponsor unable to control risk. A sponsor that wishes to achieve a specified risk level must constantly monitor the risk policies of the commingled fund in which it invests. For instance, if a sponsor wishes to be 50 percent in equities and 50 percent in bonds, it may invest in two commingled funds, one equity oriented and the other fixed income oriented. If the manager of the equity-oriented fund decides that the market is going down, he may cut back the fund's position in equities to 50 percent. The sponsor might then find that it had not invested 50/50 but that it owned 50 percent bonds, 25 percent equities, and 25 percent cash equivalents. Of course, the manager of the equity-oriented fund may be right in his opinion on the market, but the real point is that he may have been chosen only for his ability to choose equities, whereas he is in fact changing the fund's investment policy by attempts to time the market.

The single-sponsor commingled fund

When a corporation has many subsidiaries, and particularly when those subsidiaries are acquisitions, the corporation will tend to have a great number of pension plans. This can create havoc with the investment process since even the smallest pension plans deserve the best efforts of investment managers. In addition, these plans may have very different characteristics or the employees covered by them may be in different age groups or salary classifications. It thus becomes impossible to establish an overall investment policy which is appropriate for all of the plans. To cope with such situations some large sponsors have established their own commingled funds. In the simplest form there would be two such funds, one for equities and the other for bond investments. A plan whose needs might allow high short-run variability in the hope of high long-run return might have 90 percent of its money in the equity fund and 10 percent of its money in the fixed income fund. Another plan within the same corporation might have different goals which could be met by having 10 percent in equities and 90 percent in bonds. Carried to an extreme, this approach could provide for a private placement fund, a mortgage fund, and so on. It is also possible to have more than one manager within each asset category, such as a growth stock manager and an income stock manager. The only disadvantage of the separate commingled fund structure is that it is difficult to have a manager who times the market by moving from stocks to bonds.

ACTIVE VERSUS PASSIVE INVESTMENT MANAGEMENT STYLES

Although this subhead appears to deal with a very recent subject, passive strategies have been used in fixed income investing for many decades. Traditionally bonds have been managed under a buy-and-hold philosophy, which is certainly passive from the manager's point of view. It should be recognized, however, that the bond portfolio itself is not passive under this structure, but is constantly changing. This is because, for instance, a bond portfolio with a 20-year maturity now will have a 19-year maturity one year from now. The ways in which the portfolio changes will vary, depending on the amount and the allocation of new money received, on how interest income is deployed, and on how many bonds are being redeemed.

The passive management of equity portfolios is a rather new phenomenon. Numerous studies have indicated that when many purchase and sale decisions are made, investment managers as a whole do not add sufficiently to portfolio results, on a risk-adjusted basis, to justify either the fees they charge or the transaction costs they incur. Thus, some investors have opted for passive equity portfolios which attempt to mirror the market or some market index. The issue of "indexing" is an emotional one, with strong opinions being voiced on either side. Suffice it to say that passive strategies are available and that fund sponsors would do well to consider them, just as they consider all the other alternatives which may affect their funds. Even if a sponsor has a strong aversion to passive management, it should at a minimum be prepared to respond to this issue in periods when the fund underperforms the market.

HOW MANY INVESTMENT MANAGERS?

If a passive strategy is adopted, it probably makes sense to choose no more than one manager for each asset category (stocks, bonds, etc.). If active management is preferred, or if only part of the portfolio is to be managed passively, a decision must be made as to the number of managers. The alternatives for this decision can be outlined as follows:

1. Should all of the funds be managed by one manager?
2. If more than one manager is chosen, should the managers be generalists investing in both stocks and bonds, or should they be specialists by asset category?
3. Should more than one manager be chosen for an asset category, and if so, on what basis?

Using more than one manager has these advantages: diversification, the increased resources available to the sponsor in the way of investment or other ideas, and the potential ability to achieve the best efforts of a number of specialists. On the other hand, there are certain problems associated with having more than one manager. These problems include the higher cost (since almost all managers charge on a declining fee scale basis), the greater administrative burden on the fund sponsor, and, most important, the increased burden on the sponsor, which must then decide how to allocate money among managers. This burden is greatest when the managers are asset category specialists, since then the decision as to asset allocation falls entirely on the sponsor. That is, if one manager controls equities and the other controls bonds, the sponsor makes the asset allocation decision by establishing the amount that each manager has to invest. Even worse, the sponsor may be reluctant to change the allocation policy because it is cumbersome or embarrassing to move assets from one manager to another. Thus, having a single manager eases the sponsor's administrative burdens, reduces its costs, and enables it to rely more heavily on the manager in making decisions as to the appropriate asset allocations. On the other hand, using multiple managers increases diversification, permits the sponsor to choose specialists, and increases the sponsor's involvement in asset allocation.

Within a given asset category, such as equities, it is possible to have more than one manager. The typical reason for doing so would be to increase diversification (that is, to decrease the chances that the fund will be harmed if a manager has particularly bad investment results) and to balance styles (a concept related to diversification). In the former case, the sponsor may decide that it is desirable to have a growth philosophy in the portfolio but that more than one manager of growth stocks will be chosen in order to diversify the results. Conversely, it may be considered desirable to have a portfolio which reflects the market as a whole in terms of proportions of growth stocks, income stocks, value stocks, and so on, and the sponsor may try to achieve high risk-adjusted rates of return by choosing the best growth manager, the best income manager, and so on.

ACTIVE INVESTMENT MANAGEMENT STYLES

For the purposes of this analysis, active management styles have been defined in terms of economic approaches, equity styles, bond management styles, market timing, and modern portfolio theory. It must be recognized that these distinctions are somewhat arbitrary and that it is possible for an investment manager to use more than one style over several periods or even within the same period.

Economic approaches

Investment managers, broadly speaking, use one of two economic approaches: top down or bottom up. The top-down approach involves viewing the economy as a whole and attempting to identify the areas of the economy which have either the most favorable or the least favorable prospects, and weighting portfolios accordingly. The bottom-up approach involves purchasing those securities which have the highest potential return (or, hopefully, the highest risk-adjusted return) and constructing a portfolio from these stocks.

Equity styles

Five different equity styles have been identified: the income, growth, value, quality, and size styles. A related area, the use of options, is discussed later in this chapter.

The income style involves purchasing stocks in order to maximize current income. Investors utilizing this style will be highly concerned with yield (the annual dividend divided by the price), the stability of dividends, and the growth of dividends. The stability of dividends is primarily a function of the stability of sales and earnings and of the company's cash position. Growth in dividends is a function of growth in sales and earnings and of the relative need to plow back earnings into the business as opposed to distributing them to shareholders

The growth style involves buying companies with rapidly growing sales and earnings which are enhancing their value by reinvesting their profits into the company. The growth philosophy can be contrasted to the income orientation by saying that the income investor wants to receive his return currently, whereas the growth stock investor is willing to achieve his return, with compound interest, in the future. A growth company is one which has been plowing back earnings and is presumably witnessing a high rate of growth in sales, earnings, and either dividends or the ability to pay dividends.

The value style, sometimes referred to as the Graham and Dodd method, is one in which the investor tries to buy assets at a discount to market price. Typical measures of asset value are book value or owner's equity (assets minus liabilities), net working capital (current assets minus current liabilities), quick assets (cash on hand plus accounts receivable minus current liabilities), and net assets (current assets minus all liabilities).

The quality style presumably emphasizes an investment in securities of the highest quality not in those of lower quality. Measuring the quality of stocks is obviously subjective, and quality ratings are not used as frequently for stock investments as they are for bond investments. Nonetheless, at least one organization (Standard & Poor's) publishes quality ratings for a large number of common stocks and most professional investors have strong intuitive notions as to the quality of various stocks.

Some investors have a preference for larger companies, and others have a preference for smaller companies. Investors preferring larger companies typically point to the greater diversification and stability that are frequently found in the larger, older companies, and they also point to the usual higher liquidity of larger companies in the marketplace. That is, it is easier to buy and sell shares in larger companies because more of their shares are outstanding and because more investors are interested in them. Investors who prefer smaller companies typically point to the fact that many institutions prefer companies with large capitalizations and that more opportunities for high return are therefore likely to be available among smaller, less popular companies.

It is possible to consider risk as a reflection of style. However, risk considerations are made here in terms of the quality, value, size, and income characteristics of the companies owned. It is not very likely that any investor has a style emphasizing high risk; it is much more likely that investors in high-risk portfolios are subjecting themselves to high risk because they feel that in this way very high risk-adjusted returns are achievable. An investment style which emphasizes low risk will be evident in other style measurements.

Bond management styles

The approaches to bond management are partly but not completely analogous to the styles in managing equities. Almost all bond investing is for income, and no growth is possible with bonds in the sense that their final maturity value is fixed at the time of purchase. However, undervalued bonds may be sought; quality is, of course, important in bond purchases; and some investors prefer the issues of larger or smaller organizations for reasons similar to those employed by equity managers. Four management activities can be performed by bond managers, and it is helpful to understand these methods in order to understand bond management styles. The four activities are swaps based on interest rate anticipation or market timing, swaps between sectors of the market, swaps based on the valuation analysis of individual bonds, and market inefficiency swaps.

Rate anticipation swaps. If rates are expected to decline, bonds with longer term maturities will have higher rates of return than will bonds with shorter term maturities, and vice versa (see Exhibit 5–1).

EXHIBIT 5–1

When yields decline, longer term bonds rise more sharply than do shorter term bonds.

	Coupon	Maturity	Level of interest rates 8 percent: Price	7 percent: Price	Percentage change in price
Bond A	8%	One year	100	101	1%
Bond B	8	Two years	100	102	2

If interest rates decline from 8 percent to 7 percent, each bond is worth roughly 1 percent per year more than the prevailing rate. To equalize this change, the one-year bond rises about 1 percent and the two-year bond rises about 2 percent (ignoring call provisions and compounding).

Sector swaps. Investment managers may identify changes in the historical spread relationship between sectors of the bond market. For instance, an investor may recognize that historically U.S. government bonds have traded at x basis points below those of triple A issuers. If the current relationship is such that the spread is below x basis points, the investor may wish to buy the government bond. This is because, regardless of the level of interest rates, if the spread widens, the investor would have been better off in the government (lower yielding) bonds. If the spread widens because the government yield declines, the investor will have a capital gain on the government bond. If the spread widens because the triple A bond rises in yield, the triple A bond will suffer a capital loss, which will give it a lower return than that of the government bond. Similar swaps can be made between short-term and long-term bonds; among industrial, utility, and financial bonds; and between bonds with high and low coupons (see Exhibit 5–2).

EXHIBIT 5–2

Swapping between bond sectors occurs when sector yield spreads are "excessively" narrow. Assume that the yield spread between governments and corporates has historically ranged between −0.05 and −1.00 percentage points (5 and 100 "basis points").

Current market

Government yield	Corporate yield	Spread
8.00%	8.10%	−0.10%

Investor decides to swap from corporates to governments because he feels that the spread will widen, in which case he will be better off in governments.

If the spread widens by the government yield declining, the government bond will rise in price.

If the spread widens by the corporate yield rising, the corporate bond will decline in price.

Swaps based on bond valuation analysis. The third method of active bond management is to view the companies which issue bonds as to their creditworthiness, with the thought of selling bonds which are declining in creditworthiness and of purchasing bonds which are rising (see Exhibit 5–3.) Viewed another way, this method emphasizes the default risk of the issuer. Factors to be considered in looking at default risk relate primarily to funds available, both cash on hand and cash being generated by the business, relative to the bond charges, including interest and the payment of principal.

Market inefficiency swaps. A fourth activity for increasing the return on a bond portfolio is to look for situations in which bonds of similar characteristics sell at dissimilar yields due to

EXHIBIT 5–3

Bonds with improving credit will outperform other bonds.

Current market yields of
AA-rated bonds

Strong	*Average*	*Weak*
8.40	8.50	8.60

Bond X, trading at an 8.60 yield to maturity, has a new product which is selling well and improving the company's cash position, with the result that investors view the bond as an "average" AA rather than a "weak" AA. The yield declines to 8.50, and the bond rises in price.

imbalances in the marketplace. Such situations can occur when bond dealers develop excessive long or short positions and wish to lighten their holdings in order to reduce their risk, or when sinking fund purchases are made in order to meet agreements to reduce the amount of bonds outstanding over a prescribed time, or when issuers of new bonds offer higher rates to attract buyers. In these circumstances, market inefficiency swaps may be made for a small gain in yield, perhaps even three to five basis points.

Market timing

An active style which appears to be used by most managers at some point, but by very few managers with great emphasis, is market timing. By market timing is meant changing the allocation of assets from stocks to bonds to cash equivalents in order to avoid losses in the worst performing category and to emphasize investment in the category which is producing the highest returns. Market timing can be viewed as either defensive, that is, to preserve capital, or offensive, to maximize return. It so happens that because of the characteristics of compound interest, which are explored in Chapter 6, a manager who is successful in maintaining portfolio value need only achieve average returns in favorable periods in order to have extraordinary overall results (see Exhibit 5–4). Thus the potential for high returns is available, though achieving them is another matter.

Four methods of market timing have been identified: traditional economic, monetary economic, technical, and valuation. The traditional economic approach involves looking at employment, production, government spending, and so on, and deciding when the economy will be expanding and contracting its physical production. The intent is to be invested when the economy is expanding and to reduce investments when the economy is contracting.

The monetary economic approach is similar, except that instead of viewing the physical growth of the economy the investor analyzes the economy's monetary growth. In simplest

EXHIBIT 5–4
Results obtained from investing $100 in stocks, bonds, and Treasury bills and from perfect and perverse (always wrong) timing, 1973–1978

Successfully timing the market can produce enormous benefits for a fund.

Investment	Ending value	Compound annual rate
S&P 500	$123.8	4.4%
Merrill Lynch Master Bond Index	131.9	5.7
90-day U.S. Treasury bills	136.8	6.5
Perfect timing*	209.0	15.9
Perverse timing*	55.7	−11.0

* For perfect timing, at the beginning of each quarter the portfolio is 100 percent invested in the index which will have the highest return for the quarter. For perverse timing, investment is in the index which will have the lowest return.
Source: Merrill Lynch Institutional Computer Services Department.

terms, this school of thought suggests that consumers (including business and government) use money to purchase needed goods and services and that the excess available after such purchases goes into securities. When the available supply of money is growing faster than the demand for goods and services, the excess (initially) moves into securities. The purchase of securities leads to higher prices, lower yields, and the enhancement of asset values. If monetary growth is below the physical growth of the economy, then interest rates rise and lower security prices result. There are two ways in which this process can be frustrated. The first way is a decline in the velocity of money. That is, the excess money, instead of being spent or invested in securities, lies fallow in consumers' pockets or bank accounts. The second and far more significant way occurs when the excess money is absorbed not by rises in security prices but by rises in the prices of goods and services—*inflation*.

The technical method of market timing involves viewing historical patterns of prices and estimating when market sectors are undervalued or overvalued based on those patterns. Viewed another way, the technical approach looks at the supply and demand factors for stocks and bonds over and above the fundamental causes of changes in supply and demand.

The valuation method of market timing may use either an absolute or a relative approach. An absolute valuation approach might suggest that when common stock yields rise or price earnings ratios decline to certain points, stocks are attractive. A relative valuation approach might suggest that when the differential between the yield on stocks and the yield on bonds reaches a certain level, then stocks are attractive relative to bonds.

Modern portfolio theory

Modern portfolio theory (MPT) is a process for quantifying risk and return in investment portfolios. Traditional investment practice (TIP) utilizes quantitative or intuitive judgements to set investment policies, choose individual securities, and structure portfolios. For TIP, the best portfolio is the one which contains the best securities and the emphasis is on return. MPT portfolio management, on the other hand, is quantitative rather than intuitive, and it emphasizes the portfolio rather than the securities held.

MPT began when Harry Markowitz (see Bibliography) discerned that portfolios can behave quite differently from the securities of which they are composed and that rational investors should be primarily concerned with their portfolios rather than with the securities owned. Markowitz noted that the impact of a security on a portfolio is dependent on three things:

1. The security's return.
2. The security's risk or uncertainty of return.
3. The movement (covariance) of the security in relation to the movement of every other security in the portfolio.

A strange-sounding but correct implication of this theory is that adding a risky security to a portfolio will frequently make the portfolio less risky. An even stranger implication is that adding a risky security to a portfolio may reduce the portfolio's risk even more than would adding a conservative security. The determining factor is how each of the proposed additions to the portfolio correlates with each other stock. If the stock being added is highly correlated with the other stocks in the portfolio, it does little to reduce the risk of the portfolio. On the other hand, if the stock being added is highly uncorrelated with the other stocks in the portfolio, it reduces the risk of the portfolio. That is, if the new stock tends to move down when the portfolio moves up and tends to move up when the portfolio moves down, it will reduce the portfolio's risk. This phenomenon, the diversification effect, was described in Exhibit 3–1 in the example of the arms suppliers and in Exhibit 3–5 in regard to the benefits of foreign diversification.

Three types of equity models will be described: the Markowitz or covariance model, the Sharpe or single-index model, and the multi-index model. Under the Markowitz model the investor attempts to estimate the rate of return of each security being considered, its risk, and its covariance or comovement which each other security. With this information an investor can assemble a group of portfolios, each of which has the highest level of return for its level of risk or the lowest level of risk for a given level of return. He can then choose from these so-called efficient portfolios the one which best balances his desire for return with his tolerance for risk. This method is the theoretically most correct way to invest, but it is also largely unworkable.

Although it is possible for investors to make reasonable estimates of the expected return of securities and perhaps to make reasonable estimates of risk, it is unlikely that an investor could determine how each security being considered would move in relation to each other security in the future. This problem might be dealt with by using historical relationships (though these are not particularly reliable) or by grouping stocks into broader categories, such as by industries or market sectors, and making estimates for the categories. The steel industry could thus be compared to the drug industry. This certainly appears more feasible than calculating how each drug stock will correlate with each steel stock, though the usefulness of this model is tied heavily to the accuracy of the estimates.

The Sharpe or single-index beta model greatly simplifies this problem, though with some loss of accuracy. This approach suggests that each security can be viewed in relation to the market rather than to each other security, thus greatly reducing the number of correlation studies which must be made. An investor then chooses a level of risk (beta) in relation to the market and attempts to find the portfolio which best meets the client's needs. Presumably this means some combination of highest return and least probability of deviating from the return anticipated, based on the portfolio's risk level. In other words, the investor might say that he would like to beat the market on a risk-adjusted basis by 1 percent per year, assuming that he is not likely to do worse than the market by one half of 1 percent per year. Any number of combinations of these parameters can be viewed by the investor, and a choice can be made, based on his perception of his requirements.

The multi-index model is similar to the single-index model in viewing each security in relation to the market rather than to each other security. The difference between the single-index model and the multi-index model is that the former has only one market index whereas the latter has more than one. This might mean that in addition to a securities market index the investor would have a second index which measures interest rates, industry effect, or some other economic variable.

MPT can be used to achieve optimization. The investor can attempt to structure a portfolio to achieve certain goals while reducing the (nonmarket) risk that the goals will not be achieved. Most commonly, the investor specifies the beta or yield of a portfolio and runs a program which will scan a list of stocks and allocate money such that the yield or beta will be attained but that in other respects the portfolio will move with the market.

The use of modern portfolio theory in bond management is relatively new. Since bonds are very mathematical in nature, with returns precisely measurable under given conditions, it is somewhat surprising that fixed income securities were not the first area of interest for quantitatively oriented analysts. Perhaps this was due to the lack of a theoretical framework for analyzing bonds. In any event, it is possible for fixed income investors to make assumptions about changes in market conditions or in individual bond prices and to calculate the impact of those changes on their portfolios. It is also possible to view a range of possible outcomes and to gauge the impact of each on the portfolio. This technique might be applied to evaluate the impact of a rise in interest rates from the current level of, say, 8 percent to 9 percent. Or a measurement might be made of the importance of a reduction in the spread between high-quality bonds and low-quality bonds. Since the investor is concerned with his return per year, he must make assumptions about the time over which the change will occur. For instance, if spreads changed from one level to another over a one-month period, the investor would obviously receive his return much more quickly than if the change occurred over a year. Once the investor has analyzed a number of potential portfolios he can array them against their estimated risk in order to choose the one which is most appropriate for the client.

PASSIVE APPROACHES TO INVESTING

Passive approaches to investing are frequently referred to as index funds or market funds although strictly speaking the market fund is only one type of passive portfolio. Index approaches assume that the market is essentially efficient and that consequently investors are not rewarded for attempts to find undervalued securities, or that the risk of trying to out-perform the market is not worth the risk of underperforming it.

In both active and passive approaches to investing performance is defined on a risk-adjusted basis, and transaction costs and management fees are recognized as having a negative impact on return. All such costs must be considered by investors who pursue active strategies which attempt to find undervalued securities. The investor who utilizes the passive approach in its purest sense would own only two types of securities: the indexed or market portfolio and the riskless asset (Treasury bills). Such an investor would choose the level of risk appropriate for him and then weight his portfolio with the two types of securities. An aggressive passive investor would invest heavily in the stock market, with a small percentage, if any, in Treasury bills. A more conservative passive investor would increase the percentage in bills.

Given the importance that the passive investor attaches to minimizing transaction costs, it is well to consider what is meant by the "market" which the investor is trying to track. Strictly speaking, this market would consist of all assets. As a practical matter, however, most investors think in terms of the stock market as a whole and of a broad-based market index in particular. Probably 95 percent of the market funds in operation are index funds that use the S&P 500 index. Although it is certainly defensible to use a proxy for the market instead of trying to buy all the assets in the marketplace, it is questionable whether it makes sense to attempt to replicate the returns of a market index so closely that the portfolio's holdings will be changed merely because the constructors of the index choose to change the securities of which it is comprised.

Investors who establish index funds must consider a trade-off between the ability of such funds to track the market and the transaction and administrative costs involved in doing so. If transaction costs and administrative fees were nonexistent, the investors would hold portfolios which precisely mirrored the market portfolio. For example, an investor attempting to track the S&P 500 index would own each of the 500 stocks in exactly the same proportions as their proportions in the marketplace. As of the end of December 1979, he would own 5.2 percent IBM (the largest holding) all the way down to 0.001 percent of

Kroehler Manufacturing (the smallest of the 500 stocks). In this case, as soon as the investor received additional cash, either through contributions or dividend income, he would use up the cash balance by buying each of the 500 stocks in the same proportions. However, in the real world there are transaction and administrative costs, so investors frequently decide to own fewer than the entire list of securities, and when they make purchases with small cash inflows they usually buy fewer stocks than even the number on their reduced list. A constant trade-off must be made between the cost and the benefit of making a transaction (the benefit being reduced tracking error).

In addition to simply purchasing an index fund as a style of investing, sponsors can utilize index funds as part of an active/passive strategy. The active/passive strategy involves placing a portion of the fund's assets in an index fund, where diversification is obviously very high, and placing the balance with one or more managers who will invest at a low level of diversification in a short list of securities which are expected to have high risk-adjusted returns. Theoretically the fund could place 80 percent of its assets in an index fund and the remainder with ten active managers, each of whom invested all of the assets under his discretion (2 percent of the total fund) in one stock. This might make sense from the fund's point of view, but it is doubtful whether any investment manager would be willing to succeed or fail based on one judgment.

The case for the active/passive strategy is quite strong if one considers that large portfolios with active managers, when viewed as a whole, tend to look very much like index funds, except that they have higher management and transaction costs. Sponsors have rightfully asked, "Why should I pay all that money for management when I end up with a portfolio no different from the overall market?" The answer to this question depends on the sponsor's perception of where its active managers make their contribution. If the active managers achieve their extra return by making thousands of minute buy and sell decisions, the active/passive approach does not seem appropriate. On the other hand, if the sponsor feels that most managers have great conviction about a few stocks and hold a large number of stocks about which they have only slightly positive feelings, then the active/passive approach makes a great deal of sense. Further muddling the issue is the question of whether even the best of investment managers are able to rate which of their stocks will be the superior performers. It may be that even if the manager's overall intuition about his securities is accurate, his opinion on each one of them is subject to a wide range of error. If this is the case, then the active/passive strategy is inappropriate.

One innovation in the index fund area is the market inventory fund (MIF). This approach is used by some sponsors with large portfolios and multiple managers to eliminate the transaction costs which result from purchases by one manager of the same securities that another manager is selling. It is contended that, although such offsetting transactions are rarely simultaneous, they frequently occur within a few days of each other. Consequently, an index fund is positioned between the managers to warehouse securities from the time that one manager sells them to the time that another manager buys them. When the index fund becomes over- or underbalanced in a particular industry, it makes transactions in the normal marketplace. Since the index fund does not have to buy or sell all of its securities in the marketplace, and since index funds can trade at lower costs than other funds, transaction costs are reduced.

Although it certainly must concern sponsors to incur transaction costs when managers are neutralizing each other's efforts, nonetheless sponsors must carefully examine the MIF. The key is the amount of time that it takes for information contained in the manager's buy or sell decision to be reflected in the price of the security that is being bought or sold. Assume that an investment manager holds a stock currently selling for $50 which the manager feels is worth only $48. He then offers the security to the market inventory fund, which, assuming that it is not overweighted in that industry category, agrees to accept the shares. If the price of the stock then drops from $50 to $48, the active manager has saved two points, whereas the inventory fund has lost two points. Thus, the gain achieved by the manager's decision has been offset by the MIF's purchase, with the saving of transaction costs being a small consolation.

A misconception has arisen which has led some investors to overlook this situation. They believe that an index fund automatically tracks the market so that no matter how loaded up it is with castoffs from other managers it will nonetheless track the market. This is clearly not the case. Index funds, like all portfolios, earn the returns achieved by the underlying stocks in the proportions in which the stocks are held. If the active managers are dumping poor stocks into the MIF, and the MIF is not turning around and selling those stocks in the marketplace, the MIF will underperform the market and neutralize the impact of the active managers.

In practice, MIFs probably do save the sponsor money because on average managers probably do not have information which enables them to make superior risk-adjusted returns, so it is pretty much random whether a security is owned by the active manager, the MIF, or not at all. In this case the fund benefits by saving transaction costs while these random purchases and sales of securities take place.

However, it should be noted that although the inventory fund may be solving a real problem, it has not solved the *real* real problem. That is, a sponsor with managers who are structured in such a way that their activities neutralize each other has a bigger problem than merely the transaction costs. If a sponsor feels that offsetting transactions are a significant expense, it should consider some of the techniques described in Chapter 11, where this problem is addressed directly.

An additional way of using index fund technology is to invest passively in a subset of the market. For instance, an investor can decide to own rapidly growing companies, low-beta conservative stocks, high-yielding stocks, and so on. It has been suggested that tax-exempt institutions should invest in high-yielding securities because these are shunned by taxable investors who prefer capital gains to current income. In the process of expressing this preference, individuals and other taxable investors are said to bid up the price of growth companies and liquidate stocks paying high dividends. This is believed to create higher yields and greater expected returns in the high-yielding companies.

THE USE OF PUT AND CALL OPTIONS

With the new procedures developed by the Chicago Board of Trade in 1972, options became readily marketable. Although only a small number of tax-exempt funds utilize option investing, that number may grow considerably. Thus, it is worthwhile to consider the uses of options and their advantages and disadvantages. Since puts have not come into widespread use, the primary emphasis will be on calls.

A call option is the right to buy 100 shares of stock at a specified price for a specified amount of time. For instance, if AT&T is selling at 60, an investor might purchase for $400 the right to buy 100 shares at 60 for the next six months. This means that (ignoring commissions) if the stock rises above $64 per share, the owner of the option will have a gain. Since his investment is only $400, the gain can be a very large percentage of his equity. Similarly, any loss will probably be a large percentage of his capital. However, the investor might say that by buying the option he can have most of the benefits of the upside potential without risking nearly as much money as he would have if he had bought 100 shares at $60 for $6,000.

Clearly, the short-term nature of the option and the option's high volatility relative to the equity invested makes purchasing calls rather speculative and hence generally inappropriate for tax-exempt portfolios. However, in certain circumstances, it may be perfectly appropriate for tax-exempt investors to *sell* options to other investors and speculators. If a fund owns the 100 shares of AT&T, it can sell the option to the speculator without acting imprudently. In this case the fund receives $400 income and is entitled to the dividends paid on the stocks even during the period when the call is outstanding. If the stock rises dramatically, the fund loses the benefit of the dramatic increase. If the stock falls sharply, the fund will still own the stock, but it will have the $400 as a cushion against the loss. In either case the fund has the opportunity of selling the stock and buying back the option contract if it wishes to remove itself from the transaction. Experience indicates that stocks go up and down but that they do not go either to the moon or to zero, and consequently a steady option-writing program can provide income and reduced volatility to the portfolio. However, it is doubtful that any investment medium can provide above-average risk-adjusted returns over the long run. Exhibit 5–5 demonstrates the impact of a covered option on a portfolio.

The above example indicated the position with 100 shares of stock long versus 100 options sold. It is also possible to sell more or less than 100 options for each 100 shares of stock owned.

Two interesting uses of options have been developed recently. The first involves owning a combination of calls and low-risk Treasury bills or commercial paper. For instance, a fund might invest 10 percent of its assets in calls and 90 percent in Treasury bills. This approach permits reasonable participation in a strong market rise, through the calls, while protecting capital in the event of a large decline through the short-term securities.

The second use involves *selling puts.* Whereas a call is an option to buy stock at a certain price during a certain period of time, a put gives the holder the right to sell his shares at a certain price for a certain time interval. Viewed from the point of view of the option seller, the writer or seller of a call has the liability to deliver shares to the holder of the call during the time interval. Thus, if the stock rises greatly in price, the investor who has written the call has a substantial liability. (If the investor owned the shares, this liability would be offset by the increase in the value of the shares that he owned.) The put seller, on the other hand, has guaranteed to purchase shares from the put holder, and consequently he has the liability of purchasing the shares at the agreed-upon price even though they may be far below that price in the marketplace. This may be a less serious problem than it seems to be if the put seller only sells puts on securities which he is anxious to own. In other words, if a stock is at $50 and the investor feels that this is an attractive purchase price, he should be willing to receive a fee of $3 or $5 per share to guarantee to purchase the stock at $50. If the stock goes to $40 and the put is exercised, the investor still ends up paying $50, as he would have without entering into a put transaction, but at least he received the three- or four-point premium for having agreed to give the put holder the right to sell the shares to the investor at $50. The put seller is disadvantaged if unfavorable news is released regarding the stock. In that case, the stock will decline and the put will rise in price. The seller can cut his loss by buying back the put, just as a stockholder can cut his loss by selling the stock.

EXHIBIT 5-5

Impact of change in stock price on value of "hedged" portfolio (assume ownership of 100 shares of stock and short sale of option to purchase 100 shares)

					Value of portfolio just before option expires	
	Value of stock, option, and portfolio with several months remaining before option expires			Percentage change from base		Portfolio
A	B	C	D	E	F	G	H
			Stock	Option	Portfolio		
Stock price	Price of option to buy 100 shares at 50	Portfolio value				Value	Percentage change from $45 cost
50	5	45	—	—	—	50	11.1
48	3.5	44.5	-4	-30	-1.1	48	6.7
46	2	44	-8	-60	-2.2	46	2.2
40	nil	40	-20	-100	-11.1	40	-11.1
30	nil	30	-40	-100	-33.3	30	-33.3
52	6	46	4	20	2.2	50	11.1
54	7	47	8	40	4.4	50	11.1
60	12	48	20	140	6.7	50	11.1
70	21	49	40	320	8.9	50	11.1

1. If the stock price remains unchanged, declines, or rises slightly, the investor is better off having written the option. This can be seen by comparing columns D and H.

2. If the stock is at or above the stock price at the time the option expires, the investor's gain is the value of the option in excess of its conversion value. In this case the option's conversion value was "0" when its price was 5 and the stock price was 50, so the investor's gain was 5. His total investment was 50 for the stock less 5 for the option proceeds, for a net total of 45.

3. The hedged portfolio is less volatile than the stock alone (compare columns D and F).

4. As the stock price declines, the portfolio volatility rises, since the option value gets smaller and smaller (i.e., the portfolio value is completely dominated by the movement of the stock price) (compare columns D and F).

5. As the stock price rises, the portfolio volatility declines, since the option value rises faster than the stock value (i.e., the impact of the stock price rise is increased by the rise in the option price) (compare columns D and F).

6. The relationship between the stock and option prices depends on the striking price, the stock volatility, and the level of interest rates. If these factors are constant, the option price decreases (as the square root of the time remaining) as the expiration date nears.

GUARANTEED INVESTMENT CONTRACTS

Guaranteed investment contracts are fixed income investments whose rate of return is guaranteed, usually by an insurance company. The terms can vary considerably, but the key considerations are the length of time, the rate guaranteed, whether the stated rate is before or after commissions and administrative expenses, whether the interest compounds annually, how frequently the principal can be removed without interest penalty, and any options that permit the sponsor to extend the contract or the issuing insurance company to withdraw it.

REAL ESTATE INVESTMENTS

Investments in real estate can be made either in mortgages or in direct ownership. Mortgages are reasonably straightforward, though care must be exercised in reviewing the collateral, the ability of the borrower to repay, the marketability of the collateral in case of default, and any special terms. Equity ownership can involve 100 percent participation by the sponsor, partnership with other investors or with the developer, or, increasingly, commingled funds. Because of the illiquidity and lack of fungibility of real estate (each piece of real estate is unique), high risks are involved. On the other hand, because of escalating construction costs real estate has proven to be one of the few successful areas of investment in the past decade.

CHOOSING THE INDIVIDUAL MANAGER WITHIN THE INVESTMENT MANAGEMENT FIRM

Thus far this chapter has dealt with the organizational and structural aspects of choosing investment managers. It is, perhaps, equally necessary to recognize the importance of the personal side of the equation. The sponsor should be almost as careful in choosing the individual within the investment management organization as it is in choosing the organization itself. This decision should be based on three factors: the individual's experience, his work load, and intangible personal qualities.

Hopefully, the individual who actually manages the sponsor's fund will have had experience in managing portfolios during several market cycles. It is only after seeing several periods of dramatic over- and undervaluation of securities, and the passing in and out of favor of a number of investment fads, that most people are capable of exercising good investment judgment. Such judgment is a combination of a healthy skepticism, objectivity, humility sufficient to permit changing one's mind when the facts so dictate, the ability to keep one's eye on long-term goals despite the daily contradictions and confusions of the marketplace, and the ability to act independently and decisively when this is warranted by the conditions.

As to work load, it is important that the sponsor and its portfolio achieve adequate attention. This requires that the portfolio manager not have overly burdensome responsibilities in administration, marketing, or managing other portfolios. In the organizations which manage portfolios most intensively (and charge the highest fees), portfolio managers may have only five to ten clients. In large organizations which have many clients of moderate size, portfolio managers may be responsible for many times this number of accounts. The sponsor should know in detail the work responsibilities of its portfolio manager before entering into an investment management agreement.

The third factor to be considered in choosing an individual investment manager is not easily measurable. This intangible includes the ability of the individual manager to communicate with the sponsor, his personal motivation in learning about the sponsor and attempting to do a good job, and his general willingness to respond to the sponsor's and the fund's needs. This does not mean that the individual should be an errand boy for the sponsor, spending his time seeking information unrelated to the fund. But a certain willingness to put in extra effort on behalf of the client is a most desirable attribute in the individual manager.

ADMINISTRATIVE SUPPORT FOR THE
INVESTMENT MANAGER

Although the investment manager's primary responsibility is to make investment decisions, it is extremely important that the investment manager have adequate accounting and reporting facilities. The required services are discussed in Chapters 2 and 13. In addition, it is helpful if the manager has the ability to create special reports which the sponsor may require from time to time. Finally, inquiry should be made as to the investment manager's ability to control short-term cash investments, particularly if the manager is not also the custodian of the assets, and as to the extent to which the manager's statements are reconciled with those of the custodian to provide a cross-check on accounting errors.

SIZE OF THE MANAGEMENT ORGANIZATION

There is little to indicate that the size of the organization, with respect to either number of employees or assets under management, should be an important consideration in choosing an investment manager. Large organizations clearly have more resources, yet it is questionable whether they can necessarily bring these resources to bear to the benefit of individual clients. Smaller organizations have few resources, yet may be better able to coordinate these resources. They also may have a wider range of investment opportunities since they can purchase securities of smaller companies, and can move in and out of the market more easily. One argument, having little merit, raised against smaller organizations is that the portfolio will be in jeopardy if the key manager dies. Just as "a stock doesn't know who owns it," "a portfolio doesn't know who runs it." In the event of the passing of the key manager the sponsor can hire a replacement. This may be awkward at the time but it is a small risk to the fund and one worth taking to have the right manager.

USING CONSULTANTS TO CHOOSE
INVESTMENT MANAGERS

Since the choice of investment managers is so critical, and since the investment management field is both fragmented and specialized, many sponsors consider it desirable to use outside consulting services to assist in the management selection process. A wide variety of such services is available, ranging from those which provide assessments of purely intangible factors to those which have detailed information on the performance of accounts and the qualifications of personnel. In selecting consultants, care must be exercised to ensure that the particular needs of the sponsor are within consultants' capabilities. It should also be recognized that choosing the manager who will have the best performance is not much easier than choosing the stocks which will rise the most. Thus, the sponsor should be realistic about what it expects to accomplish through the use of the consultant.

APPENDIX

Manager Selection Questionnaire

A. *Company background and general description*
   1. Number and location of offices
   2. Year founded
   3. Employees

	Number	Average number of years of professional experience
Portfolio managers		
Equity only	_____	_____
Bond only	_____	_____
Balanced	_____	_____
Research analysts	_____	_____
Economists	_____	_____
Marketing	_____	_____
Trading	_____	_____
Administration	_____	_____
Other	_____	_____
Total	══════	══════

Number added _____ lost _____ in past two years

Note: Since filling out numerous questionnaires can be burdensome to investment managers, this format has been offered as a standard to the Investment Counsel Association and to the Bank Administration Institute, the primary trade organizations of the two groups managing most separate (non-commingled) portfolios. In this way sponsors can easily screen managers, while managers need only prepare a lengthy response once each year. Both parties can then key in on the most relevant areas requiring further discussion.

4. Company is
   Bank _____
   Insurance company _____
   Registered investment adviser _____
   Other _____
5. Ownership of company
   Employee percentage _____
   Is company affiliated with a bank, insurance company, broker or dealer, mutual fund? (Circle appropriate reply)
   Name the parent company.
   Name any mutual funds managed.
6. Clients

	Number	Total assets	Largest account	Smallest account	In last two years, number of accounts Added	Lost
Employee benefit						
Corporate	___	___	___	___	___	___
Jointly trusteed	___	___	___	___	___	___
Foundation	___	___	___	___	___	___
Personal trust	___	___	___	___	___	___
Individual	___	___	___	___	___	___
Mutual funds	___	___	___	___	___	___
Other	___	___	___	___	___	___
Total	___	___	___	___	___	___

7. Number of accounts per portfolio manager _____
   $_____ assets per manager
8. Company objective for annual growth of assets under management?
   0–5% _____ 5–15% _____ 15–25% _____
   Over 25% _____
   What, if any, maximum asset limit is planned? _____

	Minimum account size accepted	
	With no cash flow	*With at least 10 percent cash flow*
$500,000 or less	_____	_____
$500,000–$1,000,000	_____	_____
$1,000,000–$2,000,000	_____	_____
$2,000,000–$5,000,000	_____	_____
$5,000,000–$10,000,000	_____	_____
Over $10,000,000	_____	_____

9. Has company been profitable in each of last three years? Yes _____ No _____
Please enclose a recent financial statement.
10. Does company have formal plans and budgets?
Yes _____ No _____

B. *Investment philosophy*
   1. Asset types managed

		Approximate percentage of	
	Total assets	*Total discretionary assets*	*Total employee benefit assets*
U.S. securities (active management)	_____	_____	_____
Fixed income	_____	_____	_____
Equities	_____	_____	_____
Privately placed	_____	_____	_____
Bonds	_____	_____	_____
Equities	_____	_____	_____
Options	_____	_____	_____
Real Estate	_____	_____	_____
Mortgages	_____	_____	_____
Equities	_____	_____	_____
Other	_____	_____	_____
Market (index) funds	_____	_____	_____
Equities	_____	_____	_____
Bonds	_____	_____	_____
Venture capital	_____	_____	_____
International	_____	_____	_____
Equities	_____	_____	_____
Bonds	_____	_____	_____
Total	$_____	$_____	$_____

2. Management style

	Balanced fund	Equity-oriented fund	Bond-oriented fund
a. How important is market timing (changing asset allocation or mix) to your management philosophy?			
Very important	———	———	———
Somewhat important	———	———	———
Not important	———	———	———
b. Does your choice of stocks emphasize:*			
Income	———		
Growth	———		
Assets	———		
Quality	———		
Large companies	———		
Small companies	———		
Natural resources	———		
Low P/E	———		
Other (describe)	———		
c. Does your choice of bonds emphasize:*			
Issuer type			
Corporates			
Industrial	———		
Utility	———		
Finance	———		
U.S. Treasuries	———		
U.S. government agencies	———		
Foreign governments	———		
Foreign corporates	———		

* If more than one is checked use 1 for most important, 2 for second most important, etc.

Maturity
   Over 20 years   _____
   10–20 years   _____
   Under 10 years   _____
Quality
   AAA   _____
   AA   _____
   A   _____
   BAA   _____
   Under BAA   _____
Coupon
   Above current   _____
   Current   _____
   Discount   _____
Turnover
   High   _____
   Low   _____

3. Relative importance of investment input

	Balanced fund with full discretion on percentage in equities	Equity-oriented fund	Bond-oriented fund
Asset allocation			
Monetary economic	_____	_____	_____
Interest rate	_____	_____	_____
forecasts	_____	_____	_____
Other economic	_____	_____	_____
Valuation	_____	_____	_____
Technical	_____	_____	_____
Security selection			
Industry factors	_____	_____	_____
Fundamentals	_____	_____	_____
of security	_____	_____	_____
Valuation	_____	_____	_____
Technical	_____	_____	_____
Trading/swapping			
Among sectors	_____	_____	_____
Within sectors	_____	_____	_____
Total input	100%	100%	100%

4. Organization for decision making

	Equities	Bonds
Committee		
Sets policies as to asset allocation	___	___
Establishes approved list of securities	___	___
For equities, sets industry or sector	___	___
For bonds, sets maturity or issuer types	___	___
Team	___	___
Individual manager	___	___
	100%	100%

5. Portfolio control
   Would portfolios with identical objectives tend to have identical security positions?
   Are risk and diversification controlled quantitatively or intuitively?
   How many securities would typically be held in a:
   $10 million stock portfolio? ___
   $10 million bond portfolio? ___
C. *Available investment resources* (sources of information for investing)
   1. Economics
      Monetary economics
      Percentage supplied internally ___
      Percentage supplied by external sources ___
      Names of individuals and/or organizations most heavily utilized:
         (1) ___
         (2) ___
         (3) ___
      Other economics
      Percentage supplied internally ___
      Percentage supplied by external sources ___
      Names of individuals and/or organizations most heavily utilized:
         (1) ___
         (2) ___
         (3) ___

2. Stock market level

    Percentage supplied internally _____

    Percentage supplied by external sources _____

    Names of individuals and/or organizations most heavily utilized:

    (1)

    (2)

    (3)

3. Bond market level

    Percentage supplied internally _____

    Percentage supplied by external sources _____

    Names of individuals and/or organizations most heavily utilized:

    (1)

    (2)

    (3)

4. Industry trends

    Percentage supplied internally _____

    Percentage supplied by external sources _____

    Names of individuals and/or organizations most heavily utilized:

    (1)

    (2)

    (3)

5. Common stock selection

    Percentage supplied internally _____

    Percentage supplied by external sources _____

    Names of individuals and/or organizations most heavily utilized:

    (1)

    (2)

    (3)

6. Bond selection or swaps

    Percentage supplied internally _____

    Percentage supplied by external sources _____

    Names of individuals and/or organizations most heavily utilized:

    (1)

    (2)

    (3)

7. Economic, stock market, or portfolio models
   Percentage supplied internally _____
   Percentage supplied by external sources _____
   Names of individuals and/or organizations most heavily utilized:
   (1)
   (2)
   (3)
8. Other resources (name and describe)

D. *Administration and fees*
   1. Accounting reports provided
      a. Data
         Valuations
            Monthly _____ Quarterly _____
            Trade date or settlement date?
         Cash or transaction statements?
         Performance
            Total portfolio _____ Equity _____ Bonds _____
            Time weighted _____ Dollar weighted _____
            Comparison? versus? _____
            Commentary on reasons for each purchase and sale? Yes _____ No _____
            Commentary on investment outlook?
            Yes _____ No _____
      b. Whose system? _____
      c. Reconciled with bank statement? Yes _____ No _____
   2. Fees on account of size
         1mm $_____
         5mm _____
         10mm _____
         20mm _____
         50mm _____
         100mm _____
   3. Can brokerage be directed?

E. *Performance (if available)*
   1. Time-weighted returns

	1975	1976	1977	1978	1979
Balanced funds					
Number included	____	____	____	____	____
Equity funds					
Number included	____	____	____	____	____
Bond funds					
Number included	____	____	____	____	____

   2. Are funds weighted equally or by value? ____
   3. Are the results typical, above the average, or below the average of those experienced by your clients? ____

This questionnaire prepared by: Name _____ Tel. ____

Information as of (date) ____ .

6

Measuring
investment performance

"If it can't be measured it doesn't exist."

Paraphrase from Lord Kelvin

The science of measuring the performance of investment port
folios has progressed considerably in the last 15 years. The
most significant factor enhancing this development was the
study produced by the Bank Administration Institute in 1968.
This study, called *Measuring the Investment Performance of Pension Funds*, was made by a group of investment professionals
and academics at the instruction of the Bank Administration
Institute, a trade association of banks. Part of the impetus for
the study was, in the view of some observers, the fact that bank
trust departments, which had traditionally managed almost all
investment funds for wealthy individuals and pension funds,
were losing business to investment counseling organizations.
Some of the banks which were losing their assets to these com-

petitors felt that the investment counseling organizations were achieving superior investment performance by increasing the risk of the securities owned. Since risk-adjusted performance measurement was virtually nonexistent at that time, the sponsors of portfolios have been unaware of the increased risk that they were taking in order to achieve higher rates of return. Thus, it was felt desirable to have a prestigious and qualified group prepare an authoritative report on the appropriate method for analyzing investment performance. The BAI study made considerable progress in this regard. It drew four main conclusions:

1. Measurements of performance should be based on asset values measured at market, not at cost.
2. The returns should be "total" returns; that is, they should include both income and changes in market value (realized and unrealized capital appreciation).
3. The returns should be time weighted.
4. The measurements should include risk as well as return.

Market values were required in performance measurement so that at any point in time the fund sponsor could accurately see the value of its portfolio and measure the changes in its value. It was acknowledged that fixed income securities had a maturity date and that holders of such securities could expect to achieve the rate of return indicated at the time of purchase if they held them until maturity. However, it was felt that if the returns of one portfolio were to be comparable with those of another, both portfolios must be measured at their fair market value. In retrospect, it seems obvious that *total rates of return* should have been used, but at the time many organizations were viewing the income from their portfolios in one light and capital appreciation in another. For taxable investors, this makes some sense, though even such investors must consider both capital changes and income. For tax-exempt investors, such as pension funds or endowment funds, the distinction is of very little consequence. Therefore, the appropriateness of using total returns is unassailable.

The reasons for using *time-weighted rates of return* are not nearly as obvious. The time-weighted rate of return is designed to eliminate the effects on the portfolio of the timing and magnitude of external cash flows, whereas the alternative, the internal or dollar-weighted return includes the impact of any such external contributions or withdrawals. The rationale for the distinction and for the use of the time-weighted return is that what is being subjected to a performance analysis is not the *fund's* results but the activities of the *manager*. Since the manager presumably does not have control over the timing of contributions to and withdrawals from the portfolio, it is not appropriate to attribute to him the impact of these cash flows.

The decision to measure *risk* and *return* was simple in theory but difficult in practice. This was because a theoretical framework for measuring risk was lacking and because at that time few investors had the capability for manipulating sufficient data easily enough to develop risk measures even if such a framework existed.

CALCULATING THE RATE OF RETURN

A "rate of return," or, for succinctness, a "return," is the percentage profit or gain achieved for holding an investment or a portfolio *for a particular time*. Price or capital returns are the changes in the value of assets, excluding income. Income returns are the gain or profit from dividends or interest. Total returns are the sum of price or capital returns and income returns. In its simplest form, a return is calculated by subtracting the difference between the beginning and ending value and dividing this amount by the beginning value. The result will be the decimalized return, which, of course, can be converted to a percentage return by multiplying by 100. Alternatively, the return can be calculated by dividing the ending value by the beginning value, subtracting 1 and multiplying by 100 to show the percentage return. Both of these methods are demonstrated below for a security which rose in value from $100 to $105.

$$\text{Return} = \frac{\text{Ending value} - \text{Beginning value}}{\text{Beginning value}} = \frac{105 - 100}{100} = \frac{5}{100}$$

$$= 0.05 \times 100 = 5\%$$

$$\text{Return} = \left(\left(\frac{\text{Ending value}}{\text{Beginning value}}\right) - 1\right) \times 100$$

$$= \left(\frac{105}{100} - 1\right) \times 100 = 1.05 - 1.00 = .05 \times 100 = 5\%$$

Complications enter the process from two sources: the need for accurate valuations and the need to handle cash flows properly. The need for accurate valuations is obvious, since if we improperly measure either the beginning or ending value, we will obviously not have a true rate of return (unless by chance we have made a proportional error in both). The only other difficulty which can arise with valuations stems from the number of valuations required. Obviously, the more frequent the intervals over which return information is required, the more frequently the portfolio must be valued even if there are no cash flows. If there are cash flows, the accuracy of the return calculation will be increased by having more frequent valuations.

This leads us to the second complexity, namely the need to handle cash inflows and outflows to and from the portfolio. At this stage, let us consider only a total portfolio rather than dealing separately with such sectors as equities or fixed income. Clearly, if a contribution has been made to the portfolio, our simple calculation of rate of return breaks down: a portfolio which started with $100 and ended with $120 did not have a 20 percent gain if the sponsor contributed an additional $20 during the period. The fund in this case had a zero percent rate of return, as can be seen from the example below:

$$\text{Gain} = \text{Ending value} - \text{Contributions} - \text{Beginning value}$$
$$= \quad \$120 \quad - \quad \$20 \quad - \quad \$100 = 0$$

Now let us see what would have happened if the fund started with $100, the sponsor added $20, and the fund ended with $130. We know that there is a gain of $10, but the return could have been anywhere between 8.3 percent and 10 percent. If the gain came before the arrival of the $20 contribution, then 10 percent is the correct return; if the gain came after the contribution, then 8.3 percent is correct (see Exhibit 6–1). If the gain came partly in each period, then we must have further information or make some assumption before we can state the return earned. The information that we require depends on whether we are calculating time-weighted or dollar-weighted returns. If a time-weighted return is needed, the required piece of information is the value of the portfolio at the time of the cash flow. If a dollar-weighted return is desired, the necessary information is

EXHIBIT 6–1
Timing of cash flow affects rate of return

Beginning value = 100
Ending value = 130
Cash flow = 20

Case 1: Cash flow came before gain

$$\text{Return} = \frac{\text{Ending value} - \text{Beginning value} - \text{Cash flow}}{\text{Beginning value} + \text{Cash flow}}$$

$$= \frac{130 - 100 - 20}{100 + 20} = \frac{10}{120} = 8.3\%$$

Case 2: Cash flow came after gain

$$\text{Return} = \frac{\text{Ending value} - \text{Beginning value}}{\text{Beginning value}}$$

$$= \frac{110 - 100}{100} = 10\%$$

the exact time at which the cash flow occurred. This will be discussed further below.

TIME-WEIGHTED VERSUS DOLLAR-WEIGHTED RATES OF RETURN

Almost all investment managers and fund sponsors think they understand this subject, but a surprisingly large number do not. This observation is based on experience derived from interviewing prospective job applicants over a number of years in an environment which permitted strenuous cross-examination of the applicants' knowledge. Most of these applicants recognized that the time-weighted rate of return in some fashion excluded the impact of external cash flow and that it was an appropriate measure of the manager's impact on the portfolio. They also recognized that the dollar-weighted return included the effect of cash flows and hence was appropriate for seeing whether a fund had met its rate of return objective. Beyond that, however, most of the applicants were unable to explain the distinctions between the two methods. It is thus advisable to describe these distinctions in detail so that there is no confusion about the two methods.

The time-weighted return (TWR) shows the value of one dollar invested in a portfolio or a portfolio sector for the entire period. The dollar-weighted return (DWR), on the other hand, shows an average return of all the dollars in the portfolio or the portfolio sector for the period. In a sense, the DWR reconciles the beginning dollar amount of the fund plus the cash contributions with the ending value of the fund. The TWR intentionally ignores the fact that money is contributed to or removed from the fund and only looks at the money in the fund during each period.

Consider an investment cycle in which a fund has high returns for one period and negative returns for the next period. If the portfolio has more dollars working when the return is low, the return on the average dollar will be low; in this case the TWR will be higher than the DWR. On the other hand, if more dollars are in the fund when the returns are high, the return on the average dollar will be high; consequently, the DWR will exceed the TWR. In both cases the TWR will be the same. If the fund manager had no control over the number of dollars in the fund, he should be measured on the basis of *his* time-weighted returns, not the *fund's* dollar-weighted returns.

Understanding of the distinction between the two types of returns can be enhanced by noting when the two will be identical, and by seeing an example. The TWR and the DWR will be identical when there are no cash inflows or outflows *or* when the return earned during the period is constant. Since the distinction only arises when there are contributions to or withdrawals from the fund, if there are no such cash flows, the two types of return will be the same. Also, if the return is constant during the entire period, there can obviously be no difference between the two types of return.

The time-weighted return is calculated by measuring the rate of return during a number of subperiods (presumably quarterly or monthly) and "linking" or "chaining" the interim returns (see Appendix B, "Mathematics Refresher"). For example, if the fund earned 6 percent in period 1 and 8 percent in period 2, the time-weighted return is:

$$[(1.06 \times 1.08) - 1] \times 100$$
$$1.1448 - 1 = 0.1448 \times 100 = 14.48\%$$

In order to calculate a time-weighted return, it is necessary to measure or estimate the value of the portfolio at the end of the first year when the cash flow took place. A simple example may serve to demonstrate differences in the two types of returns. Suppose a portfolio begins with $1,000 at the beginning of year one, receives $100 at the end of the year, and has $1,200 at the end of year two. If we know, for instance, that the value of the portfolio was $1,050 just before the cash flow was received, we can easily calculate an accurate time-weighted rate of return, as follows. The return for the first year is $1,050 divided by $1,000 equals 1.05, or 5 percent. The second year's return is calculated by taking $1,200, the ending value, and dividing it by $1,150 (the sum of $1,050 plus $100 equals $1,150). This return is 1.043, or 4.3 percent. The return for the two years is thus 1.043 times 1.05 equals 1.095, or 9.5 percent.

The dollar-weighted return is calculated on an "iterative" or trial-and-error basis. In effect, the dollar-weighted calculation raises the question "What is the rate of return which can be multiplied by the beginning value and the interim cash flows in order to equal the ending value?" Or more precisely, "What rate of return per period equates the initial value and the cash flow received to the ending value?"

In the example above, the iterative procedure, figuratively speaking, asks what rate on $1,000 for two years plus the same rate on $100 for one year equals $1,200. Let's try 10 percent and see what happens. Ten percent of $1,000 for one year is $100, so at the end of year 1 and before the contribution we have $1,100. After the $100 contribution we have $1,200, which earns 10 percent, or $120, for year 2, providing an estimated total ending value at a 10 percent rate equal to $1,320. Since $1,320 is greater than the actual ending value of $1,200, the rate we used must have been too high. If 10 percent is too high, let's try 5 percent. Five percent of $1,000 is $50; 5 percent of $1,050 is $52.50; 5 percent of the $100 contribution is $5; and adding the $100 contribution we get a total of $1,207.50. Again the results exceed the actual ending value, so a lower return must be tried. The procedure keeps doing this until a return is calculated which leads to an ending value sufficiently close to $1,200 to be acceptable. Thus, the dollar-weighted return takes into account both performance and the impact of the timing of cash flows on performance.

The following example demonstrates convincingly the difference between the two types of return. Both funds start with $100 and have the same investment manager, and the manager keeps both funds 100 percent invested in General Motors stock at *all* times. General Motors' price and the contribution to the two funds are as follows:

1. Beginning price: 50; each fund buys two shares.
    Value Fund A: 2 shares @ 50 = 100.
    Value Fund B: 2 shares @ 50 = 100.
2. One year later price rises to 100; Fund A receives $100
    Contribution and buys one share @ 100.
    Value Fund A: 3 shares @ 100 = 300.
    Value Fund B: 2 shares @ 100 = 200.
3. One year later price declines to 50.
    Value Fund A: 3 shares @ 50 = 150; cost = (2 × 50) + (1 × 100) = 200; loss = 50.
    Value Fund B: 2 shares @ 50 = 100; cost = 2 × 50 = 100; gain = 0.

Time-weighted return = 0 in each fund.
Dollar-weighted returns:
  Fund A = −18.1%
  Fund B = 0%

Thus, Fund A showed a loss and had a negative dollar-weighted return. Fund B broke even and had a 0 percent dollar-weighted return. Both funds had a 0 percent time-weighted return. Fund B had no contributions, and thus its dollar-weighted and time-weighted returns were identical. The manager clearly made the same contribution to each fund, since he made exactly the same investments in both funds. The TWR reflects his contribution. The DWR in Fund A reflects both the contribution of the manager (0 percent) and the timing of the contribution, which happened to come when the stock was at a high price.

CALCULATING THE RETURNS ON PORTFOLIO COMPONENTS

Equities

Once the technique for calculating returns is understood it can be applied to all asset categories, with only procedural rather than theoretical questions to be answered. The first such procedural question in measuring returns on equities is what to include in this category. A typical definition of equities would include common stocks, convertible preferred stocks, convertible bonds, warrants to purchase stocks, and options. Other definitions are perfectly acceptable as long as all parties are aware of the classification being used. The need for valuations is the same for all asset categories, and cash flows must also be dealt with. In the case of an individual asset category, such as equities or fixed income securities, the cash flows are the purchases and sales. In other words, a cash flow into equities is an equities purchase and a cash outflow is a sale. Just as the increased value in the total portfolio resulting from contributions is not attributable to return, so a purchase of equities is not attributable to equities return. Assume, for example, a beginning value of 100, an ending value of 120, and a purchase of 20.

$$\text{Gain} = \text{Ending value} - \text{Purchases} - \text{Beginning value}$$
$$= 120 - 20 - 100 = 0$$

Therefore, equities purchases and sales are treated in the same fashion as are total portfolio contributions and withdrawals. An additional factor, namely dividends, must also be considered, since part of the return of an asset category is its income. This subject can cause confusion, since one could properly argue that income should be counted in the total portfolio return if we are measuring "total return." The distinction to be drawn is that cash, the normal form of income payment, is part of the total portfolio but that cash is not part of the equities portfolio. The total portfolio is defined to include all assets, including cash, but the equities portfolio can consist only of equities. Calculation of the return, including income, is demonstrated in this example:

$$\text{Gain} = \text{Price gain} + \text{Income gain}$$

$$\text{Equity return} = \frac{\substack{\text{Ending equity value} - \text{Equity purchases} \\ - \text{Dividends} + \text{Equity sales}}}{\text{Beginning equity value}}$$

Thus, it can be seen that the $5 dividend received on the $100 worth of stock has led to a 5 percent gain, just as would have been the case had the $5 come from capital appreciation. *However*, the return has been calculated as though we were viewing a total portfolio, since the ending value, $105, consists of $100 in equities plus $5 in cash. Thus, the true position of the portfolio at the end of the period is as follows: $100 stock plus $5 cash equals $105 total.

The presentation of the true portfolio position leads to an intuitive difficulty, namely that we all tend to think of the $5 dividend as a positive cash flow to the equities portfolio, whereas in fact the $5 is a positive cash flow to the total portfolio but a *negative* cash flow to the equities portfolio. This can be substantiated in several different ways. First, the $5 increase in cash had to come from somewhere, and since it did not result from an external contribution it must have come from the only other source within the portfolio, namely equities. Since there were no external cash flows, the internal cash balance must net out to zero, which can occur only if the +$5 in cash is offset by a −$5 in equities. Second, we know that the portfolio gained 5 percent during the period and that equities were the source of this 5 percent gain. The only way in which an asset can start out with $100, end up with $100, and have a 5 percent return is if 5 percent of the value of the assets are withdrawn during the period. Finally, since we are drawing no distinction between income and appreciation in our calculation of return we can view the situation in which no dividend was paid but the shares rose 5 percent in value and 5 percent of the holdings were sold. In this case we would obviously treat the sale as a negative cash flow, and logically, therefore, we must treat the dividend in the same way.

Determining how to treat the timing of the dividend received will be addressed below.

The next issue, the handling of stock splits and stock dividends, should be simple now that the principles have been established. Clearly, return is not enhanced by a stock split or a stock dividend, so no special consideration need be given to these events *except* to be certain that the asset price used in the valuation is consistent with the number of shares owned. In other words, if 100 shares of a $50 stock are owned and a two-for-one split takes place, the new position is 200 shares at $25. In both cases the investment is worth $5,000, so there has been no impact on return. This may sound elementary, but it must be remembered that the receipt of the extra 100 shares by the investor invariably occurs well after the stock begins trading at the new price. This is because the company must know who owns its shares at the time of the split in order to distribute the shares properly. Consequently, a time lag exists which can cause errors in a custodial statement if the statement shows the old number of shares and the new price.

Bonds

The return on fixed income (bond) investments is calculated very similarly to the return on equities. That is, it is calculated after adjusting for purchases, sales, and income. The principal distinction lies in accounting for accrued interest. Whereas the value of a common stock investment is merely the market price times the number of shares owned, there are two components to the value of a bond. These are the capital value (or number of bonds owned times price per bond) plus the accrued interest. Since misunderstandings regarding accrued interest can occur, it is well to discuss this area further. The holder of a bond is contractually entitled to receive interest, usually semiannually. Since the bondholder is entitled to this interest, the value of the bond increases every day by that day's accrued interest. If a bondholder sold a bond two thirds of the way through the interest period (four months) he would receive two thirds of the semiannual coupon from the buyer, with the buyer receiving the one third to which he is entitled plus the two thirds which he paid to the seller at the end of the six-month coupon period. Thus, the value of the bond increases every day by the amount of accrued interest until the payment period, when the process starts all over again. Although some distortion in return is possible if there are large purchases or sales in a period within a fixed income portfolio (see discussion of anomaly on p. 136 in the appendix to this chapter), accrued interest should not be a problem in calculating return as long as it is treated consistently. That is to say, if the beginning value of the portfolio includes accrued interest, the ending value must also include accrued interest. It is preferable to include accrued interest in asset valuations wherever possible, though this is usually not practical for investors who wish to measure the rate of return on equities and bonds as well as the total portfolio. This is because many fund accounting statements do not show accrued interest at all, and those which do rarely distinguish among accrued interest on convertible securities (which applies to the equities portfolio), accrued interest on bonds (which is attributable to the fixed income portfolio), and accrued interest on short-term investments (which is included in the cash equivalent portfolio sector).

Cash equivalents

Calculating returns on cash equivalents is no different, in principle, from calculating returns on stocks and bonds. If the cash equivalent is a discount instrument, the market value of the asset includes both accrued interest and capital changes such that a proper rate of return can be calculated from this value. If the instrument carries a coupon, the coupon must be treated just like any other income to a portfolio subsector, namely as a negative cash flow to that subsector and a positive cash flow to the cash holdings of the portfolio. Practical considerations in measuring returns on cash equivalents will be considered below.

Commingled funds

Commingled funds represent a special case in that they are single securities from the point of view of the fund owner. That is, although a commingled fund may own stocks, bonds, cash, or cash equivalents in any proportion, all of the assets within the commingled fund are treated as part of the portfolio's value. Hence the effect of the commingled fund on the return of the overall pension or endowment fund will be considered by merely accounting for changes in the value of the investment in the commingled fund and in the number of shares or units owned.

A caution must be made regarding the treatment of income distributions from commingled funds. A commingled fund can treat income in one of three ways. One alternative is to retain the income within the portfolio, in which case the commingled fund's net asset value is enhanced by the amount of income per share. This causes no problem to the sponsor, since it includes the market value (equals number of shares times net asset value per share) in the value of its fund. A second alternative is for the fund to distribute its income to shareholders in cash. In this case the net asset value of the share declines due to the distribution, and thus the sponsor must treat the cash received as a negative cash flow from the commingled fund and an increase in cash within the sponsor's fund. The third alternative is for the sponsor to choose to have income distributions automatically reinvested in new shares. In this case the net asset value of the fund declines but the number of shares owned by each holder increases proportionately, so that the value of the investment is maintained at the same level before and after the income distribution. Fortunately, since many tax-exempt funds have no need for income, it has become customary for most commingled funds to retain and reinvest income within the commingled fund. A sponsor which wishes to receive a distribution merely sells sufficient shares to achieve the amount of cash required.

Savings accounts

Savings accounts are not often used by large funds, but some smaller funds find them of value for investing small cash positions. Savings accounts should not be a problem if the record-keeping process recognizes that the value of the savings account is enhanced as interest accrues, just as in the case of a bond, which also has interest accruing daily.

APPLYING PERFORMANCE MEASUREMENT
TECHNIQUES TO REAL PORTFOLIOS

We have established that the dollar-weighted return is the average return on all dollars invested, whereas the time-weighted return is the result obtained from calculating the internal rate of return for subperiods between cash flows and "linking" or "chaining" the subperiod returns to find the return for the cumulative period. When we turn to real portfolios we find three practical restraints to accurate calculation of time- and dollar-weighted returns:

1. Information is reported on a calendar period basis, not by cash flow. That is, valuations are presented monthly, quarterly, or annually, not in relation to the timing of cash inflows and outflows.

2. The valuation statements may not be produced as frequently as desired. The accuracy of the return calculation will be reduced if there are large cash flows and, for instance, only quarterly rather than monthly valuations are available.

3. Cash flows may take place at any time, not just at midmonth. There is obviously a different impact on a portfolio from a $100 contribution in the middle of the month than from a $100 contribution at the end of the month. On a practical basis, however, most performance measurement systems do not permit the treatment of cash flows on each of the 250-odd days possible.

It is obviously not feasible to have reporting periods other than by calendar month, as the whole system of analysis in this and other countries is based on annual periods. Furthermore, since we are dealing with a time-related concept, namely rate of return *per period*, it makes sense to have the reporting done on a calendar month or quarter basis. Thus, a problem requiring that some assumptions be made is automatically built into the measurement of portfolio performance, since we will not normally have appropriate valuations on the date of cash flows. For purposes of analysis, let us assume that we are viewing the typical case, monthly cash or transaction statements and on-calendar quarterly valuation statements.

In addition to the "exact" method, which requires valuations at each cash flow, there are three methods for calculating time-weighted returns. These are:

1. The linked internal method.
2. The regression method.
3. The linked apportioned contribution method (a term applied here but not in wide use).

The *linked internal* method involves measuring the internal rate of return for each period between valuations (in this case quarterly) and linking or chaining the results, as demonstrated in Appendix B. This method assumes that the return *within* each quarter is uniform. Even though we know that dollar-weighted returns are not usually good estimates of time-weighted returns, if we break the subperiods up sufficiently and if there are no large cash flows during a period when the market had a large return, this method will yield adequate results.

The *regression* method is the most accurate way of calculating rates of return when valuations are available only quarterly. This method involves estimating the value of the portfolio at interim periods within the quarter, such as monthly, on the assumption that an estimate of the monthly valuation is more useful than the linked internal method's assumption that the rate of return during the quarter was equal each month. An estimate of the interim market value can be made if two things are known: the rate of return on the market during the monthly subinterval and the relationship (beta) of the portfolio's return to the market's return. If we know that the portfolio is, for instance, 10 percent more volatile than the market and that the market rose 10 percent during a month, we can assume that the portfolio's value was more likely to have risen by 11 percent than by either the 10 percent which the market earned or the average of the quarter, as would be assumed by the linked internal method.

An astute reader may recognize both the logic of this approach and the dilemma it poses. We are trying to calculate the portfolio's rate of return, and in order to do this we need to know the relationship between the portfolio's return and the market's return, which obviously requires our knowing what the portfolio's rate of return was! This dilemma can be solved by using the trial-and-error method of trying to find a portfolio beta which will result in an ending value of the portfolio, arrived at by estimation, as close as possible to the actual ending value. The regression method is limited in that it is ordinarily not possible to develop a useful measure of beta without having had at least six to eight quarters of valuations. When 12 to 20 quarters of valuations are available, the regression method gives quite satisfactory results. According to the BAI study, for funds having quarterly valuation statements and monthly cash statements, the expected annual errors in return using the linked internal method and the regression method are 0.48 percent, and 0.17 percent, respectively.[1]

The *apportioned* methods are hybrid approaches to performance calculations. They have a simplicity about them, both conceptually and in carrying out the calculations, which gives them considerable appeal. These methods say, in effect, that the ending value is composed of the beginning value, gains from income and appreciation, and contributions. The contributions cannot be treated as gains, so an adjustment must be made for them. Further, recognition must be made of the amount of time that the contributions were in the portfolio. Therefore, the beginning or ending values will be adjusted by a portion of the contributions. The adjustment can be the exact portion of the period for which the funds were available, thus leading to a return which is "weighted by the time" that funds are available.

APPENDIX: STRANGE BUT TRUE INVESTMENT RESULTS

Experience with the results of hundreds of performance measurement studies indicates that almost any combination of anomalous results is possible. These strange results can cause great frustration to those unfamiliar with how they come about and can cast doubts on valid and useful measurement techniques. These correct but nonintuitive returns can derive from such causes as:

1. Changes in the allocation among equities, fixed income, and cash equivalents.
2. Dollar-weighted versus time-weighted factors.
3. Compound interest.
4. Accrued interest.
5. The use of total returns rather than just income.
6. Conceptual misunderstandings (e.g., all assets not accounted for—thus Equities + Fixed Income = Total portfolio because of cash).

---

[1] *Measuring the Investment Performance of Pension Funds for the Purpose of Inter-Fund Comparison* (Park Ridge, Ill.: Bank Administration Institute, 1968), p 25.

Changes in allocation

One of the strangest things that can occur within a portfolio is for the return of the total portfolio to fall outside the return of the equity and fixed income portions. An extreme form of this event occurs when the equity and fixed income returns are up and the total portfolio return is down. The extreme form is apparent from the following example, which is taken from the results of a jointly trusteed retirement fund.

	Percent return		
Year ended	*Equities*	*Bonds*	*Total portfolio*
12/75.......	19.8	8.1	−2.0

The portfolio had a loss on a time-weighted basis in 1975 even though equities and fixed income securities showed sharp gains in the rising market for stocks and bonds. This seemingly impossible occurrence can take place if three things happen:

1. The rates of return on the asset sectors (equities and fixed income securities) fluctuate greatly (see Exhibit 6–2).

EXHIBIT 6–2
Quarterly portfolio returns: Sector returns vary greatly

Quarter ended	*Equities*	*Bonds*	*Total portfolio*
3/75	15.5	3.5	4.7
6/75	12.4	2.3	3.4
9/75	−16.5	−1.0	−13.5
12/75	10.5	3.1	4.6
Year	19.8	8.1	−2.0

Note that for each quarter the total portfolio returns were in the range between the equity and bond results.

2. The allocation between equities and fixed income securities changes greatly (i.e., the fund policy changes or the investment manager tries to time the market) (see Exhibit 6–3).

EXHIBIT 6-3
Valuations and cash flows: Significant changes in allocation (as percentage of total portfolio)

Quarter ended	Valuations		Purchases (sales) at end of quarter	
	Equities	Bonds	Equities	Bonds
12/74	10	90		
3/75	11	89		
6/75 (before transactions)	12	88		
6/75 (after transactions)	82	18	70	(70)
9/75 (before transactions)	79	21	(59)	59
9/75 (after transactions)	20	80		
12/75	21	79		

EXHIBIT 6-4
Source of total portfolio return

Quarter ended	$\left(\dfrac{Equity}{allocation} \times \dfrac{Equity}{return}\right)$		$+ \left(\dfrac{Bond}{allocation} \times \dfrac{Bond}{return}\right)$		$= \dfrac{Total\ port\text{-}}{folio\ return}$
3/75	0.10	15.5%	0.90	3.5%	4.7%
6/75	0.11	12.4	0.89	2.3	3.4
9/75	0.82	−16.5	0.18	−1.0	−13.5
12/75	0.20	10.5	0.80	3.1	4.6
		19.8		8.1	−2.0

The movement of large amounts of money between sectors at the wrong time led to small allocations to equities in the first, second, and fourth quarters, when equity performance was good, and to a high allocation to equities in the third quarter, when equity results were poor. Consequently, the poor results in the third quarter overshadowed the good results in the other three quarters.

3. Time-weighted rather than dollar-weighted returns are being measured (see Exhibit 6–4).

Dollar-weighted versus time-weighted factors

A second major area of confusion occurs when the portfolio shows a negative time-weighted return but the portfolio has shown a positive gain (or vice versa). In other words, the sum of the initial value plus the net contributions is below the ending market value, thus indicating that a positive investment gain has been achieved. This case demonstrates the fundamental distinction between time- and dollar-weighted rates of return. The case may occur if the portfolio's return was lower when a smaller amount of money was invested in the portfolio and higher when more money was invested in it. If the cumulative effect of the portfolio returns is such that the down cycle does more harm than the up cycle does good, the overall portfolio return will be negative. This apparent anomaly occurred in many portfolios during the period 1973–76. The cumulative effect on $1 invested throughout the poor years 1973 and 1974 was not overcome by the market improvements in 1975 and 1976, yet the portfolio had a great deal more money invested in the latter years due to increased contributions. The result was negative time-weighted returns and positive dollar-weighted returns.

Compound interest

When an investor views his portfolio sometimes he wonders why the results in up and down quarters appear to be equal or perhaps favoring the upside but the portfolio's cumulative return is negative. This results because of the impact of negative returns on an investment portfolio. If a portfolio rises 10 percent one year and declines 10 percent the next, it would appear that the investment has maintained its original value. However, a quick run through the numbers indicates that this is not the case. A $100 investment which achieves a 10 percent return will have $110 at the end of the period, for a gain of $10. A decline of 10 percent leads to a loss of $11 and an ensuing value of $99, or an overall loss for the two periods of $1. The greater the volatility of the portfolio, the more apparent this phenomenon will be. We can see this in Exhibit 6–5, wherein returns are shown for various percentage gains and commensurate percentage losses.

It sometimes appears that the last year's results dominate portfolio returns over the cumulative period. That is, a portfolio which did very well in the last period seems to have done

EXHIBIT 6–5

Result of equal percentage gains and losses			Gain required to recoup losses	
Gain	Loss	Cumulative loss	Loss	Gain required
5%	−5%	−0.25%	−5%	+ 5.26%
10	−10	−1.00	−10	+ 11.1
15	−15	−2.25	−15	+ 17.6
20	−20	−4.00	−20	+ 25
25	−25	−6.25	−25	+ 33.3
30	−30	−9.00	−30	+ 42.9
33 1/3	−33 1/3	−11.11	−33 1/3	+ 50
40	−40	−16.00	−40	+ 66.6
50	−50	−25.00	−50	+ 100
75	−75	−56.3	−75	+ 300
100	−100	−100.00	−100	+ Infinity

well cumulatively, and similarly a portfolio which did badly in the latest year appears to have a poor cumulative result. It can easily be seen that the apparent phenomenon does not really exist. Each year's returns count equally with each other year, so it makes no difference whether the portfolio did well in the first period or the last. This is indicated by the following example:

	Year 1	Year 2	Cumulative
Fund A	−5	+15	0.95 × 1.15 = 1.0925, or 9.3%
Fund B	+15	−5	1.15 × 0.95 = 1.0925, or 9.3%

Accrued interest

With increasing interest in fixed income portfolios, combined with positive cash flow in most pension funds, an anomaly crops up in which returns on bond portfolios which have heavy contributions are lower than those of portfolios invested in the same bonds but with static or negative cash flows. This results not from any complexity of mathematics but rather from limitations in the evaluation process. The source of the problem is the way in which accrued interest is treated in the performance measurement process. When an investor sells a stock he has no right to subsequent dividends that the company pays, regardless of the fact that he may have held the stock for almost the full 90-day period between quarterly dividends. (For purposes of this analysis we exclude consideration of the five-day period prior to the payable date for the dividend, during which the purchaser is entitled to the dividend payment.) That is, a buyer who has not held the stock for more than a few days may still be entitled to the full quarterly dividend. This is because the company does not have a contractual obligation to pay the dividend, and consequently the buyer cannot hold the seller accountable for it. (Of course, the market price action reflects the presence or absence of the dividend to each party.)

The bond issuer, on the other hand, has a contractual obligation to pay interest, usually semiannually, and thus the holder of a bond should receive interest for each day that he holds it. Let us assume that a bond pays interest on January 1 and July 1 and that a purchaser buys the bond four months into this period. The seller is thus entitled to four months of interest and the buyer to two months. If we assume that the bond has a 6 percent coupon, the seller is entitled to 2 percent interest and the buyer to 1 percent, representing their respective portions of the semiannual 3 percent payment. When July 1 arrives, however, the holder of the bond will be the purchaser and he will at that time receive 3 percent interest from the issuer. In order to properly compensate the seller, the buyer must at the time of purchase pay the seller the accrued interest of 2 percent. Thus, if the bond were traded at par, or 100 percent of value, the buyer would pay $102 to the seller, of which $2 would be interest and $100 principal. For purposes of performance measurement it is necessary to treat the 2 percent interest that the buyer paid as interest paid, or negative interest income. This is not a long-run problem, in that each party is properly compensated for his investment, but for the quarter ended June 30 the purchaser's portfolio, assuming a $100 value at March 31 before the bond purchase was made, will show a negative return of 2 percent. For the six-month period through September the return will be correct, since as soon as July 1 arrives the $3 semiannual interest payment will be received, representing repayment of the $2 paid out and the $1 interest due. However, a distortion occurs for the one period, causing an understatement of return for the period. If there are no additional purchases, the problem corrects itself, but for rapidly growing (or declining) bond portfolios the problem persists, with growing portfolios having an understated return and shrinking port-folios an overstated return. The distortion remains with the portfolio if the fixed income portion of the fund continues to grow. If the fund in the above example were to double on June 30, the portfolio would be penalized by 2 percent ($2 ÷ $100), whereas the correction would be only 1 percent ($2 ÷ $200). Thus, the fixed income portion of the fund would be affected in its time-weighted rate of return until such time as there was a substantial liquidation of bonds. Total portfolio return would also be affected, with the extent dependent on the size of the bond portfolio as a percent of the total portfolio.

The solution to this problem is simple in theory but difficult in practice, in that data sufficient to provide perfect results are typically not supplied on custodial statements. Obviously, the ability to produce an accurate performance measurement re-port is limited by the accuracy of the information provided. Since a performance measurement study typically breaks down returns among equities, bonds, and cash equivalents, it is nec-essary to produce figures on accrued interest for cash equiva-lents, straight bonds, and convertibles (which are frequently included in equities). Even if a total portfolio accrued interest figure is available, it is unlikely that the custodian or other source of accounting information will have recorded accrued interest by asset category so as to permit an accurate break-down. Although this problem is of no great significance, it is an annoyance to people who desire to achieve a high level of accuracy. In coming years, as bank custodians become more sophisticated in their record-keeping processes, it is likely that accrued interest will be reported by asset type.

Total returns

An apparent anomaly can occur for investors who are unac-customed to viewing total rates of return, especially in fixed income portfolios. For example, assume that the portfolio has a yield of 7–8 percent and that the total return for the period is dramatically different, perhaps minus 2 percent to plus 15 percent. Dramatically varying total rates of return result, of course, from changes in the capital value of the portfolio rather than changes in interest income. Changes in the level of interest rates can cause large changes in capital value even in portfolios with no default risk. The impact of interest rate changes on a portfolio is largely a function of the portfolio's maturity structure. This can be demonstrated by looking at the rate of return on individual bonds of different maturities as interest rates change (see Exhibit 6–6).

EXHIBIT 6–6
Percentage changes in bond prices, assuming a current coupon 8 percent bond (i.e., all bonds start out at par) and rate changes to those shown

Maturity	New level of interest rates			
	6 percent	7 percent	9 percent	10 percent
1.........	1.8	1.0	−1.0	−1.8
3.........	5.4	2.6	−2.6	−5.0
5.........	8.4	4.1	−3.9	−7.6
10.........	14.7	7.0	−6.5	−12.2
15.........	19.4	9.1	−8.0	−15.3
20.........	23.0	10.6	−9.2	−17.0
25.........	25.6	11.6	−9.8	−18.2
30.........	27.5	12.4	−10.3	−18.9

These are the percentage price changes due to an instantaneous shift from 8 percent to each of these coupon rates. If the shift is not instantaneous, the total return of the investment should be considered. This total return will include the price change and the income received during the period measured, as well as income on that income.

It can be seen from Exhibit 6–6 that bonds with longer maturities are more volatile than bonds with shorter maturities. A simplified example (which does not *precisely* take compounding into account) may assist in understanding this process. Let us assume that the general level of interest rates rises from 8 percent to 9 percent. Let us further assume that we own three bonds in our portfolio, all of which have 8 percent coupons at the beginning point, with one bond having a one-year maturity, the second bond having a two-year maturity, and the third bond having a three-year maturity. We will also assume that the change in interest rates comes instantaneously right after we purchase the portfolio.

Looking at the one-year bond, an investor would see that the general level of interest rates provides for a 9 percent return for one year and that the one-year bond provides only an 8 percent return. For this bond to have a competitive return in the marketplace it must also yield 9 percent. In order for it to yield 9 percent the investor would have to make 1 percent in appreciation in addition to the 8 percent in interest. For the investor to make 1 percent in appreciation over a one-year period, the $100 value of the bond would necessarily have to drop to $99. Thus, this bond would show an instantaneous negative return of 1 percent.

The investor would apply the same analysis to the two-year bond, but in this case he would not be satisfied with a purchase price of $99, since this would yield him 8 percent per year in interest but only one half of 1 percent *per year* in appreciation. In order to achieve the 9 percent return he must have a 1 percent per year return from capital appreciation, or a 2 percent return for the two years. He would thus be willing to buy the 8 percent two-year bond at $98, with the bond showing an instantaneous return of minus 2 percent in comparison to the minus 1 percent return of the one-year bond.

Carrying the analysis to the three-year bond, we immediately recognize that the investor would be willing to pay only $97 for this bond, which would then have an instantaneous return of minus 3 percent. Recognizing that if interest rates declined the longer term bond would have a positive rate of return greater than that of the one-year bond, we can see the impact of changes in interest rates on bonds of different maturities and the fallacy of expecting the income return to closely correlate with the total return when a portfolio is being measured.

We have thus determined that results of almost any kind can be achieved, and that there is usually a good reason for them!

7

Comparing investment performance

"How's your wife?"
"Compared to what?"

Old vaudeville joke

Although virtually all sponsors are interested in comparing the results of their funds with appropriate benchmarks, it is not easy to determine the appropriate benchmarks. In general terms there are three useful standards against which portfolios can be measured:

1. Comparison with an absolute goal.
2. Comparison with market indices.
3. Comparison with other portfolios.

COMPARISON WITH AN ABSOLUTE GOAL

When a choice is presented as to which of the three standards is appropriate, almost all fund sponsors will choose the first.

141

That is, almost all will agree that the most important measure of a fund's success is whether it meets its objectives. In the case of a pension fund the objective is to return at least as much as the actuarial rate. For an endowment fund the objective is to provide sufficient capital or income to meet the needs of the sponsoring organization. Although achieving these goals is certainly important, in practice this method of comparing results is rather unsatisfying. A brief example will demonstrate why.

In both of the periods shown in Exhibit 7–1, the fund referred to is attempting to achieve or exceed its target rate of

EXHIBIT 7–1

Period	Market return	Fund return
1......	+50%	6.1%
2......	−50	5.9

return of 6.0 percent. It is clear that in an absolute sense the fund met its objective in the first period and failed to meet it in the second period. However, virtually all fund sponsors and investment managers would feel that the fund performed well in the second period and poorly in the first. This is because the returns of investment portfolios are dominated by the returns of the market, particularly in the short run. Consequently, practically all funds will fail to meet their stated objectives in a poor year and will exceed them in a good year. Similarly, even the best managers frequently show negative returns in bear markets and even the poorest managers generally show positive returns in strong bull markets. Thus, although meeting the absolute goal of the fund is certainly important, there is a need for additional benchmarks in order to understand the activities of the fund and to assess whether the manager is doing a good or a bad job in light of the market environment in which he is operating.

COMPARISON WITH MARKET INDICES

In order to look beyond the problems associated with the absolute goal, namely the way in which the market environment dominates returns, it is desirable to measure the market environment so as to assess its impact on portfolios. Thus, it is appropriate to measure the impact of the market on the various sectors of the portfolio.

Equity portfolios

The performance of the equity portion of portfolios (common stocks, convertible securities, and warrants or options) may be appropriately measured against any one of a number of stock market indices. Among these indices are the Standard & Poor's 500, Standard & Poor's 400, New York Stock Exchange Index, American Stock Exchange Index, Value Line Index, Indicator Digest Average, Dow Jones Composite Index, and Wilshire 5000 Index. A detailed discussion of their composition and construction is presented in the appendix to this chapter.

Bond portfolios

Fixed income or bond portfolios can be appropriately compared to bond indices, including the Salomon Brothers Index, the Lehman Brothers Kuhn Loeb Indices, the Merrill Lynch Indices, and the Moody's Index. Two points should be made about the ways in which bond portfolios and indices differ from those for equities. First of all, the bond market is not a unified market in quite the same way as the stock market is. This is because the fixed maturity of bonds creates a spectrum of risk and return quite apart from the characteristics of the bond issuer. Whereas AT&T common stock is AT&T common stock, an AT&T bond with two years until maturity is a quite different investment than an AT&T bond with 30 years until maturity. For this reason it is not easy to find a bond index which is truly representative of the market. Second, because of this maturity characteristic and because an investor may have a fixed time horizon, it is possible for an investor to choose bonds which are appropriate for his portfolio but unrepresentative of the bond market as a whole. Consequently, this investor may find that even a bond index which is truly representative of the bond market may not be an appropriate benchmark for comparing performance. Fortunately, indices describing the returns of the various sectors of the bond market are becoming increasingly available. These bond indices are shown in the appendix at the end of this chapter.

Cash equivalents

The return on cash equivalents (short-term investments or money market instruments) can be compared to the returns on U.S. Treasury bills, certificates of deposit, commercial paper, and banker's acceptances. There are no widely published indices of these instruments, though the rate on U.S. Treasury bills is readily available and easy to measure with high precision. Typically, when cash equivalent returns are available (and frequently returns are not calculated for cash equivalents), they are compared to the return on U.S. Treasury bills or to the return on commercial paper. This is done in a somewhat less formal fashion than are the comparisons with stock market and bond market indices.

Not readily marketable assets

There are no indices known to the author which measure the return on private placements or on such assets as real estate equity investments, and oil and gas investments.

Total portfolios

The total fund typically consists of investments in various market sectors, and consequently there is no total portfolio index which is appropriate for all investors. However, it is possible to construct a hypothetical or "custom" index which is useful in measuring a given investor's results. This index can be constructed by looking at the composition of the fund and weighting market indices accordingly. For example, if a portfolio consists of 60 percent stocks and 40 percent bonds at the beginning of a certain quarter, we can use an index for that quarter which consists of 60 percent of the return on an equity index plus 40 percent of the return on a bond index. If the investor switches to 70 percent equities and 30 percent bonds at the end of the quarter, we might consider the "market" return for the total portfolio for the second quarter to be equal to 70 percent of the equity index's return and 30 percent of the bond index's return. The "market" return for the two-quarter period could then be calculated by linking or chaining the market return of the individual periods. Alternatively, the market index could be calculated by using the average percentage in equities and the average percentage in bonds, in this case 65 percent and 35 percent, respectively. The stock and bond index returns for each quarter would then be weighted 65 percent and 35 percent, respectively, and chained.

Both methods are useful and sensible. The method using quarter-by-quarter returns measures selection but not timing. The average method measures both selection and timing, because in each quarter the measurement considers not only the difference between the equity and fixed income returns in the portfolio and those of the indices but also the difference in the proportions of the two. This is shown in Exhibit 7–2.

The custom index has two limitations. First, the index of each fund will be different, reflecting the fund's composition. Consequently, there is no total portfolio index which is appropriate for all portfolios. Second, since there are no widely published indices covering private placements and other less marketable assets, it is obviously not possible to reflect the portfolio's full composition if the fund contains such assets.

Dollar-weighted indices

The preceding discussion of market indices assumed a time-weighted approach, namely that we were looking at one dollar invested throughout the period and not considering any impact from external cash flows. An alternative approach to the use of indices is to assume that return equaled the return on the index but that the portfolio had cash flow equal to those which actually occurred. In this case the question being asked is, "How much money *would* the fund have now relative to the amount that it *actually* has now had it invested in a certain index?" This approach can be used in a variety of ways for the total portfolio and for the sectors of the portfolio. Logical ways in which the concept can be applied are as follows.

The total portfolio. The assumed ending value of the portfolio can be calculated under the assumption that the fund is

EXHIBIT 7-2

Custom index at actual allocation measures selection only:*

	Period 1	Period 2	Average	Cumulative (not compounded)
(1) Percentage in equities	60	70	65	
(2) Percentage in bonds	40	30	35	
(3) Equity index return	10	20		
(4) Bond index return	5	10		
(5) Custom index return	[0.6(10) + 0.4(5)] +	[0.7(20) + .03(10)]		
	$6 + 2 = 8$	$14 + 3 = 17$		+25
(6) Fund return	10	19		+29
(7) Fund return − Custom index return at actual allocation = Return from security selection and choice of risk level of securities	+2	+2	+2	+4

Custom index at average allocation measures selection and timing:*

	Period 1	Period 2	Average	Cumulative
(1)–(4) Same as above				
(5) Custom index return	[0.65(10) + 0.35(5)] +	[0.65(20) + 0.35(10)]		
	$6.5 + 1.75 = 8.25$	$13 + 3.5 = 16.5$		+24.75
(6) Fund return	10	19		29
(7) Fund return − Custom index return at actual allocation = Return from selection, choice of security risk level, *and* timing..........	1.75	2.5	2.125	4.25
(8) Impact of timing = Custom index at actual allocation − Custom index at average allocation = 25.0 − 24.75 = +.25				

*Selection is used here to include not only security selection but also choice of the risk level of the stocks and bonds owned.

100 percent invested in an equity index, 100 percent in a bond index, 100 percent in a cash equivalent index, or any combination of weightings. The same calculation can be made by assuming that the portfolio is invested in the average commingled equity fund, the average commingled fixed income fund, the average separately managed balanced fund, the best fund, the worst fund, and so on. Another application of this approach is to see whether the fund kept up with its assumed or actuarial rate of return or with the consumer price index. A special case of this analysis can be carried out to see whether the fund achieved a profit or a loss from investments. In this case the fund's ending value is compared with its beginning value plus net contributions and the question implicitly asked is, "Did the fund achieve a return above or below 0 percent?"

Equity or fixed income portfolios. The same multitude of possibilities exists for comparing the actual ending value of equity and bond portfolios with assumed ending values under various assumptions as exists for the total portfolio. Logically, one might compare the actual ending value for an equity portfolio with the results which would have been attained had the fund been invested in equity indices, equity commingled funds, or the equity portions of separately managed funds. The same approach can be applied to fixed income funds, only using fixed income indices and funds to provide the alternative rate of return which might have been achieved.

In summary, comparing portfolio returns to those of market indices is a useful function that can be carried out by comparing a sector of the portfolio to the appropriate market index and by comparing the total portfolio return to an index weighted in the same proportions as the portfolio.

COMPARISON WITH OTHER PORTFOLIOS

Although comparing portfolio results to those of market indices has considerable use, there is still something lacking, both conceptually and emotionally, when only market indices are used as comparisons. The *conceptual* problem is that even though the market indices are supposedly representative of the "market," each index is, in fact, a specific portfolio with characteristics which may or may not be representative of what real funds are like. Further, the market indices have no transaction costs associated with them, and real portfolios obviously incur a certain amount of transaction costs. This creates a negative bias for fund results as compared to those of market indices. As an example of the limitation of using market indices as a sole benchmark for comparison, we can see how the Standard & Poor's 500, viewed as a portfolio, would have compared to a sample of managed equity portfolios for the years 1973 to 1977:

S&P 500 ranked versus equity portfolios (rank of 1 is best)

1973–1977	1977	1976	1975	1974	1973
16	44	22	33	35	17

As can be seen, the Standard & Poor's 500 was not a good representation of the "average" managed equity portfolio, which many people believe that a market index should be.

In addition to the conceptual objections to using only market indices for comparisons, there is also an *emotional* objection. Human beings tend to be greatly concerned with how they fare in comparison with other persons in similar circumstances. For both reasons fund sponsors have come to count on comparisons between their fund results and those of other funds. Consequently, a knowledge of this area is important to all fund sponsors.

Equity portfolios

Portfolios containing only equities should be compared to other similarly constructed portfolios. That is, an equities versus equities comparison is by far the most appropriate basis for comparing the results of an equity portfolio with those of other portfolios. Both the fund and the sample should be either tax-exempt or taxable. In almost all cases in which performance measurement services are provided, the portfolios measured are tax-exempt retirement or endowment funds.

Equity-oriented portfolios

A portfolio can be called an equity-oriented portfolio if it is either invested in equities or it is invested in cash reserves that will be invested in equities at an appropriate time. It is important to distinguish between an equity-oriented portfolio, which conceivably could be 100 percent in cash equivalents, and an equity portfolio, which by definition is always 100 percent in equities. The appropriate comparison for equity-oriented portfolios is, of course, other equity-oriented portfolios. That is, portfolios which can be invested in either equities or cash equivalents should be compared to similar funds.

However, it is not easy to find such a sample for separately managed portfolios. This is because most funds own stocks, bonds, or cash equivalents, and in the reporting process they do not distinguish their cash equivalent reserves for equity investing from their cash equivalent reserves for fixed income investing. Thus, adding the portfolio's cash to the equity sector to calculate an "equity-oriented" return would be misleading, in that some or all of the cash equivalents in the account may, in fact, be in reserve for the purchase of fixed income investments.

Fortunately, an alternative solution is at hand in the form of bank-commingled equity-oriented funds. Although these funds are typically called equity funds, they are more appropriately called equity-oriented funds since they contain both equities and cash equivalents. Increasingly, banks are making available the returns of their commingled funds, so this information can be monitored rather easily. Mutual funds are also a source of information on the performance of equity-oriented funds, and precise information on mutual funds is widely available because these funds are required to calculate and publish their values daily. However, since mutual funds typically invest for individuals rather than tax-exempt portfolios, they are a less appropriate basis for comparison than are bank-commingled equity-oriented funds.

Bond portfolios

Bond portfolios, consisting of intermediate-term and long-term bonds (but not cash equivalents) are appropriately measured against similar portfolios. The tax implications of the fund sponsor must be considered, since a portfolio with tax-exempt (municipal) bonds obviously cannot be compared to one with taxable bonds. This is usually not a problem because most funds desiring performance information are tax exempt. Since the funds are tax exempt, they own higher yielding taxable bonds.

Bond-oriented funds

Bond-oriented funds, unlike bond funds, can own both cash equivalents and bonds, whereas pure bond funds can own only bonds. Thus, as with equity-oriented funds, bond-oriented funds should be compared to similar funds. For the same reason, namely the availability of appropriate data, the results of bond-oriented funds can be compared to those of bank-commingled bond-oriented funds. The necessary data are becoming more widely available.

Cash equivalents, private placements, and other assets

For these categories the available comparative information is sparse. The returns on cash equivalents could be compared to the returns of several "money market" funds which invest in taxable securities. The returns on private placements could be compared to the returns of the few insurance company private placement commingled funds, which are becoming more popular, though these funds may also contain cash equivalents. As to "other assets," it is unlikely that there will be appropriate comparative information for many years to come due to our inability to accurately measure the performance of investments in real estate, mortgages, oil and gas wells, and other relatively unmarketable assets.

Total portfolios

Total portfolios consist of the assets from the various sectors of the overall marketplace. Thus, it is appropriate to compare the total returns of a fund with the total returns of many other funds. However, several cautions are in order.

First of all, returns (and hence comparisons) tend to be dominated by the risk posture of the portfolio and by the particular market results which occurred during the period being measured. That is to say, a fund whose policy is to be 80 percent in equities will look very good in a period when the stock market rises and will look quite poor in a period when it declines. This may be fully attributable to the policy chosen by the sponsor rather than a reflection of the investment manager's skill.

Second, a problem arises regarding how to treat investments which are in less readily marketable securities. One alternative is to include these assets in the total portfolio, recognizing that some investors have large investments in these "other assets" and that other investors have none at all. Recognition must also be given to the fact that some of these assets are valued at historical or amortized cost, and others at some estimate of market value. Obviously, the quality of these estimates affects the quality of the total portfolio return and hence the usefulness of the comparison. An alternative treatment is to exclude less readily marketable assets from the "total portfolio" for purposes of comparing results to other portfolios. Although this solves the question of the accurate measurement of returns, it can be misleading in that not all of the portfolio's assets are accounted for. Perhaps the only solution in this case is to choose a method and to be sure that the portfolio is being measured on the same basis as the funds in the comparative universe.

Third, commingled funds are generally not appropriate comparisons for total portfolios. This is because the total portfolio, which is assumed in this case to be a balanced fund, is not structured in the same way as the commingled funds, which are almost always oriented to either equities or bonds. (Obviously, if the total portfolio contains either no equities or no bonds, then the commingled funds are appropriate comparisons. For purposes of this discussion, however, such a portfolio would not be regarded as a total portfolio but as an equity- or bond-oriented fund.) The fallacy of using commingled funds to compare total portfolio results is the same as the fallacy of comparing equity-oriented funds to equity-only funds, namely that the differences in allocation among stocks, bonds, and cash equivalents will have an important bearing on how the fund performed in a particular market environment. In an up market a balanced fund will tend to underperform bank-commingled equity funds and to outperform bank-commingled bond funds. Since stocks will return more than bonds, the funds with the highest percentage in equities will have the greatest returns. In a down market the reverse will be true. Again, the problem is that we are measuring the investment policy rather than the investment performance of the fund.

In summary, the principal concern of those who attempt to compare their portfolio results with the portfolio results obtained by others is to find a sensible comparative universe. The logical way to do this is to compare the fund being measured with funds which are as close as possible to it in construction—equities to equities, bond to bonds, and total portfolios to total portfolios. Funds containing equities plus cash should be compared to similar portfolios, as should funds containing bonds plus cash equivalents. In this way the most reasonable comparisons of straight returns (not risk-adjusted returns) can be made.

COMPARING RISK AND RISK-ADJUSTED RETURNS

Once an appropriate risk measure has been chosen (see Chapters 8 and 9), comparing the performance of portfolios becomes quite straightforward. The percentage in asset categories, such as equities, of one portfolio versus another can be readily compared. Similarly, the beta, or variability, however measured, of one portfolio can be directly compared with that of other portfolios. Of course, this assumes that the fund sponsor has available to it information on the risk measures of other funds.

Comparing risk-adjusted returns, like comparing risk, is straightforward. The only requirements are that the portfolio's measurement of risk-adjusted performance be similar to that of the sample and that the classification of assets also be similar. For instance, meaningful comparisons cannot be made if the portfolio's equity sector is defined to exclude convertible securities, but the comparative sample defines equity to include convertibles.

COMPARING FUNDS WITH SIMILAR OBJECTIVES OR OF SIMILAR TYPES

The idea of comparing one's fund with other funds that have similar objectives is very appealing. Unfortunately, developing a workable definition for "similar objectives" and finding a sufficiently large sample of funds which fit the objectives are two formidable problems. All funds have as their general objective making money without losing money. More eloquent statements suggest as objectives maximizing return without undue risk of loss of principal. These definitions of objectives are of little help since they include all funds rather than just "similar" funds.

In theory it is possible to compare funds based on their level of risk, such as the percentage in equities. In practice it is not possible to find a sample of funds with exactly the same asset allocation as the sponsor's fund, so typically a range of allocations is considered. In other words, a fund with 63 percent in equities would be compared with funds having between 60 percent and 70 percent in equities. However, in a volatile period there can be substantial differences between funds having 60 percent in equities and funds having 70 percent in equities. Also, if the fund being measured has a very high or a very low percentage in stocks, there will probably not be many similar funds in the same category.

An alternative might be to construct an artificial total portfolio sample by taking a sample of balanced funds and assuming that each hypothetical fund in the sample had the equity and fixed income returns of the real fund but the asset allocation policies of the sponsor's fund. Although a bit awkward to calculate, this alternative has some merit. However, most of the benefit of this procedure could be gained merely by comparing the sponsor's equity to the sample of other equity funds, and making a similar analysis for other asset categories.

Criteria other than the percentage in equities could also be used for establishing similarity of objectives. Among such criteria are the actuarial rate of return and the size of cash inflows or outflows.

It obviously makes sense to compare the results of commingled equity funds with those of other commingled equity funds, and similarly for bond funds and other fund types. However, the rationale for this type of comparison is related to the asset type and policy rather than any characteristic of the sponsor. It is also possible to compare profit-sharing funds with other profit-sharing (but not pension) funds, Taft-Hartley pension funds with other Taft-Hartley pension funds (but not corporate pension funds), and similarly for public pension funds and endowment funds. Although this makes intuitive sense, experience indicates that very few differences between funds are attributable to the sponsor's organization type other than that Taft-Hartley funds and public funds tend to have lower percentages in equities than do corporate pension funds. This is probably the only area in which a comparison by fund type provides useful information. Even so, it is still appropriate to compare equity funds with an equity funds sample, bond funds with a bond funds sample, and the timing scores of funds with the timing scores of other funds.

APPENDIX: COMPOSITION AND CHARACTERISTICS OF VARIOUS STOCK AND BOND INDICES

Since portfolios are so frequently compared to market indices, and since sponsors, investment managers, and consultants place considerable weight on such indices, it is worthwhile to understand more about them. It should be noted that:

1. No one index is useful for all purposes.
2. Each index is composed of a certain list of securities that are weighted in a specific way, and if the list contained other securities or a different weighting scheme, the results would be different.
3. Each index has flaws or limitations which sponsors should be aware of.

Creating indices involves deciding what is to be measured, choosing a list of representative securities, choosing methods for weighting the securities, changing the list of securities, treating income, and establishing the frequency and timing of index availability. Characteristics of the major stock indices follow (see also Exhibit 7–3).

Standard & Poor's 500. Goal is to measure the pattern of common stock movements; 500 large companies are included; changes are made in the list of securities by a committee at S&P; weighting is by capitalization; available daily as to capi-

EXHIBIT 7–3
Common stock indices

Index	No. of securities	Weighting	Calculation technique	Base year
Standard & Poor's 500	500	Market value	Same as NYSE	1941–43 = 10
Standard & Poor's 400	400	Market value	Same as NYSE	1941–43 = 10
Dow Jones Industrials	30	Price	Sum of prices divided by number of companies adjusted for historical splits	Started 1927 (an average, not an index)
Dow Jones Utilities	15	Price		
Dow Jones Transportation	20	Price		
Dow Jones Composite	65	Price		
New York Stock Exchange	All companies listed (1,540 as of 6/30/79)	Market value	Market value of all listed shares adjusted, for capitalization changes	December 31, 1965 = 50 (approximate average share price)
American Stock Exchange	All companies listed	Market value	Same as NYSE except that NYSE subtracts the value of dividends from the index on ex-date, whereas ASE does not	August 31, 1973 = 100
Value Line	1,696 as of 2/80	Equal	Geometric mean of daily price relatives	June 30, 1961 = 100
Wilshire 5000	Changes every month 4,935 as of 1/31/80	Market value	Market value	December 31, 1970 = $798.439 billion

EXHIBIT 7–4
Bond indices

Index	*Securities: No. or par value*	*Securities: Type*	*Type index*	*Weighting*	*Calculation*	*Base*	*Average YTM or coupon*	*Years to maturity*	*As of*
Moody's Industrials	10	AAA	Yield	Equal	Arithmetic average	n.a.	8⅜%	25¾	October 1978
	10	AA					8⅝	23¾	
	10	A					8¾	20⅜	
	10	BAA					9	19⅛	
Moody's Public Utilities	10	AAA					8¾	30⅛	
	10	AA					9	26¼	
	10	A					9⅜	26⅜	
	10	BAA					9⅜	27⅝	
Moody's Railroads	6	AA					4⅝	21⅝	
	10	A					6⅜	20	
	7	BAA					6¼	29½	
S&P Corporate	27	AAA					n.a.	n.a.	
		AA							
		BBB							

	Number of issues	Composition	Quality	Type of index	Weighting	Averaging	Base			As of
S&P Utilities	31		BBB					n.a.	n.a.	→
S&P Municipals	15		n.a.					n.a.	n.a.	
S&P Government	12	Equal amounts of long, medium, short						7.84	18.6	→
Merrill Lynch Corporate and Governmental Mast ...	$540.8 billion par value			Total return	Market value	Arithmetic average of price relatives	December 1972 $100	7.4	11.2	August 1979
Government	$315.4 billion par value							7.2	6.0	
Corporate	$225.4 billion	57% high quality 43% medium quality						7.7	18.5	
Salomon Brothers	3,878		AAA or AA		Market value		n.a.			August 1979
Lehman Brothers/ Kuhn Loeb	About 3,500	All publicly traded								
Dow Jones Industrials ...	10		AAA	Price	Equal	Arithmatic average		n.a.	n.a.	August 1979
Dow Jones Utilities	10		AAA							

tal changes and quarterly about one week after quarter end including dividends.

Standard & Poor's 400. Designed to measure movements of industrial stocks; all other characteristics same as S&P 500.

Dow Jones averages. Industrials. Designed to measure movements of industrial companies—includes 30 large industrials; changes made rarely, generally to reflect mergers or acquisitions; weighting according to price of shares; available daily for price changes.

Utilities. Covers utility companies; otherwise same as Dow Jones Industrials.

Transportation. Covers transportation companies; otherwise same as Dow Jones Industrials.

Composite. Amalgamation of Industrials, Utilities, and Transportation indices.

New York Stock Exchange Index. Represents market value of all common stocks on New York Stock Exchange; issues included changed according to listings and delistings from the NYSE; capitalization weighting; available daily as to price.

American Stock Exchange Index. Reflects value of shares on American Stock Exchange; all issues on ASE included; issues changed when listing so requires; capitalization weighted; available daily as to price.

Value Line Index. Goal is to represent typical price movements of 1696 stocks in Value Line Universe; changes in securities made at discretion of Arnold Bernhard & Co.; weighting is equal, calculated as a geometric average (rather than adding up the values and dividing by the number of securities, the index multiplies daily price relatives and takes the nth root of the ensuing value); price relatives are then compounded to compute the index; available daily as to price. Note: A geometric index always underperforms the corresponding arithmetic index.

Wilshire 5000. Represents the market value of all common stocks on the New York Stock Exchange, American Stock Exchange, and over-the-counter markets; changes at discretion of Wilshire Associates; weighted by capitalization; price index and total performance index available; published weekly as to price.

Bond indices. The information included in Exhibit 7–4 is self-evident.

8

Measuring
risk in equity portfolios

"Measurement of performance of pension funds should be in two dimensions: rate of return and risk." [1]

In Chapter 3 risk was discussed in general terms and defined as uncertainty of the rate of return. In this chapter more precise measurements of risk will be explored in detail, and both the traditional approach to risk and the newer quantitative approach will be considered. It is helpful to view the traditional and quantitative approaches as being at different ends of the same spectrum rather than as opposing philosophies. The traditional measurements, such as price/earnings ratio and financial leverage, are *causes* of uncertainty of the rate of return. Standard deviation and beta can then be viewed as measurements of the uncertainty resulting from fundamental risk.

---

[1] *Measuring the Investment Performance of Pension Funds for the Purpose of Inter-Fund Comparison* (Park Ridge, Ill.: Bank Administration Institute, 1968).

TRADITIONAL RISK MEASURES

Traditional or fundamental risk measures can be divided into two categories: company related and stock market related. Company-related factors pertain to the company itself, whereas stock market–related factors indicate the risk arising from the price that the stock market places on the company's characteristics.

Company-related factors

Debt/equity relationship. The more a company has borrowed to finance its capital expenditures or operations, the greater is the company's risk. In order to avoid bankruptcy a company must pay interest and principal to lenders before it can pay dividends to shareholders. Thus, although a highly leveraged position may contribute to a company's growth rate, it also increases the company's risk.

Stability of sales and earnings. An important measure of a company's risk is the stability of its sales and earnings. The greater their stability, the more confidence investors can have that the company will continue to operate successfully. Quality measurements for stocks, as well as bonds, reflect to a large extent the stability of a company.

Profit margins. The greater the difference between revenues and expenses, the less risky a company is, all other things being equal. If costs rise unexpectedly, a company with narrow profit margins may become unprofitable, wheras a company with wide profit margins will just become somewhat less profitable.

Return on equity or return on assets. The extent to which a company can profitably employ capital is an important risk measure.

Value-related factors

Price/earnings ratio. Probably the most common measure used by equity investors to establish the relative value of stocks is the P/E ratio. Obviously, the more an investor must pay for each dollar of earnings, the greater is the risk of the investment.

Yield. The current return provided by a stock is also an important measure of risk. The greater the income provided by a stock, the less need investors will find to sell it during an unfavorable economic period.

Price/book value ratio. In the same way that an investor can view his stock holding in terms of its earnings or yield, he can also look at the underlying assets of the company whose stock he is purchasing and relate them to the price that he is paying. Subtracting liabilities, or money owed, from the asset figure leaves the net worth, owners' equity, or book value of the shares. In a sense, the investor is looking at the liquidation value of the company and comparing that to his purchase price. Since the assets of the company are calculated on a historical cost basis, rather than on the basis of current market values, there are limitations to this approach.

Most basic texts in finance expand considerably on the financial ratios described above.

QUANTITATIVE RISK MEASUREMENT TECHNIQUES

Since the quantitative approaches define risk as uncertainty of return, quantitative measurements attempt to calculate the degree of risk or uncertainty. This can be done by looking at either absolute or relative measures. The absolute measures include standard deviation, variance, and mean absolute deviation. These are all described in detail in Appendix B. The standard deviation, as the most common measure and one of the simplest, will be described below.

Standard deviation as a measure of uncertainty

When looking at a series of numbers describing the characteristics of some phenomenon, analysts usually think first of reducing the measurement to an average. However, in many cases additional information is required in order to analyze the characteristics of the phenomenon being measured. For example, a person walking across a river would not find it sufficient to know only the average depth of the river. He would want to know the maximum depth of the river as well. Assume that the person was told that the river, which is ten miles long, averages one foot in depth, but that the range is between zero inches and ten feet. This would be additional useful information, since the person would then know that at some point the river is ten feet deep. Suppose further that the person did not know precisely where he was going to cross, and that not every point in the river had been measured, because this was too expensive to do. An intermediate step could be carried out by calculating the depth of the river at a number of places and establishing a distribution or pattern of the measurements. That is, it might be that roughly 90 percent of the river is one inch deep and that about 10 percent is ten feet deep. On the other hand, it might be that 99 percent of the river is one foot deep, nine tenths of 1 percent is one inch deep, and one tenth of 1 percent is ten feet deep. This distribution of measurements could provide very significant information to the person attempting to understand the characteristics of the river which had to be crossed. The standard deviation describes this distribution.

Another example is more relevant to the investment world. Suppose that an investment manager owns a portfolio containing 100 stocks. The manager's style is to preserve capital, and consequently he wishes to investigate closely all securities which are in an unfavorable price trend. He wishes to find a simple way of establishing which stocks are trading in an unfavorable pattern. He could review the list of "new lows for the year" each day in order to see whether any of his companies have traded at a lower price than they have during the previous year. However, this would require waiting until a stock went all the way down to its low point before the investigation process was initiated, by which time the fund would have been injured excessively. The investor could also keep track of stocks which have declined by a given number of points or a given percentage from some previous level. However, some stocks are more volatile than others, and just because they swing widely it is not necessarily serious if these stocks decline below their prior levels. The manager thus wants to have a measurement which shows when an individual stock is trading below *its* normal range. This could be done by calculating the average price of the stocks over a period and the extent to which the stock fluctuates around that average. For instance, AT&T may average 60 and fluctuate between 57 and 63. Digital Equipment may average 60 but trade between 50 and 70. Thus, AT&T would come under scrutiny when it declined below 57, and Digital Equipment when it fell to 50.

This technique can be applied to portfolio rates of return in order to measure the volatility or risk of the portfolios. In other words, a common stock portfolio might average a 10 percent return and fluctuate between −12 percent and +32 percent. A bond portfolio might average 8 percent and fluctuate between a 0 percent and a 16 percent total rate of return. Treasury bills might average 6 percent and vary between 4 percent and 8 percent. This distinction can be seen in Exhibit 8–1.

BETA ANALYSIS

Using the standard deviation, the portfolio's variability or volatility is measured in relation to the average return. In the beta analysis the portfolio's volatility is measured in relation to the marketplace. Since betas are widely used and even more widely discussed, it is imperative that fund sponsors understand how the beta analysis is made. This section describes beta measurements in considerable detail.

Beta is a calculation which results from making a "regression" analysis. Regression analysis is a statistical technique for relating two variables (see Mathematics Refresher—Appendix B). In this case the two variables are the rate of return on a stock or portfolio and the rate of return of the market. As can be seen in Exhibits 8–2 through 8–6, the regression analysis, also called the characteristic line analysis, is made by plotting the rate of return for the security or portfolio against the rate of return of the market during the same period. Each of the graphs contains plots of the quarterly rates of return for hypothetical portfolios. The "line of best fit" is drawn in each case to fit as closely as possible the points plotted. For instance, in Exhibit 8–2 point A represents a three-month period in which the market rose 10 percent and the fund rose 5 percent. A similar point is drawn to represent each quarter or month for which data are available. A line is then drawn which best fits these points. Much useful information can be acquired about a portfolio of equities by performing the characteristic line analysis. Of special interest are the amount of *market* risk in the portfolio, the level of *diversification*, and the manager's contribution through *stock selection* (risk-adjusted return). Alternatively, these factors are known as the beta, the R^2, and the alpha. The beta, or market sensitivity, is measured by the slope of the characteristic line. Three portfolios will be considered for comparison purposes. The first of these (Exhibit 8–3) is an

EXHIBIT 8–1
Variability of return of assets with different risk levels

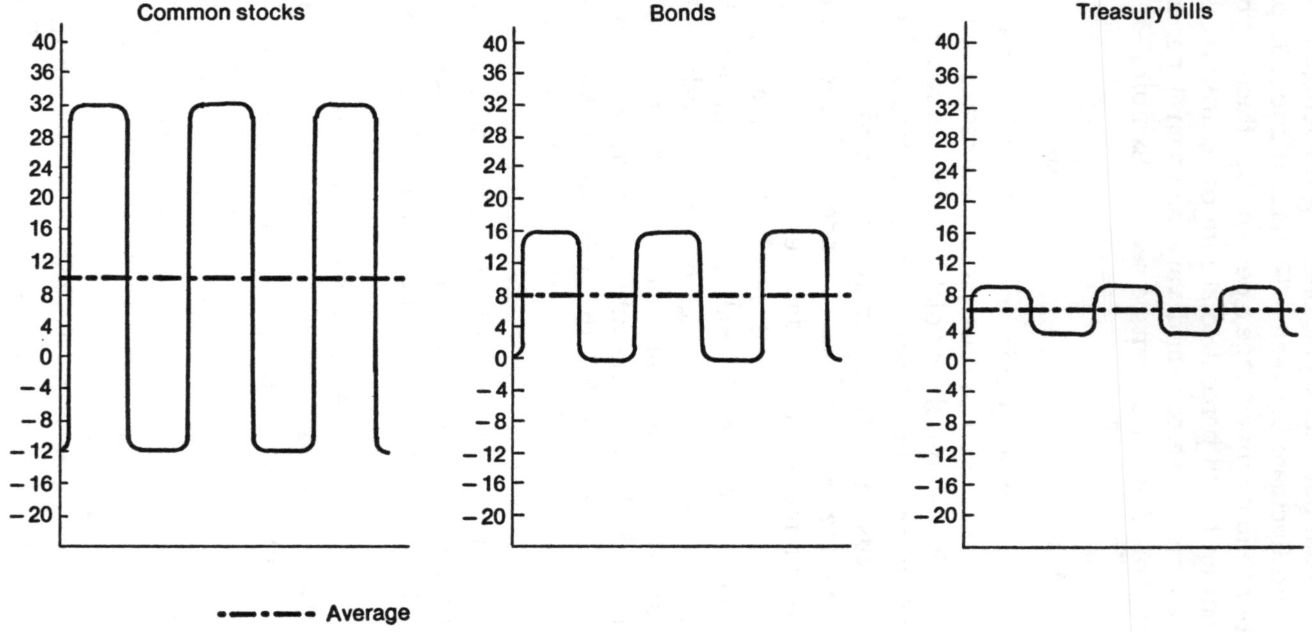
Common stocks
Bonds
Treasury bills
40
36
32
28
24
20
16
12
8
4
0
−4
−8
−12
−16
−20
Average

EXHIBIT 8–2

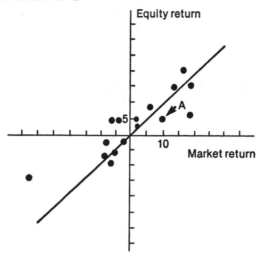

EXHIBIT 8–3

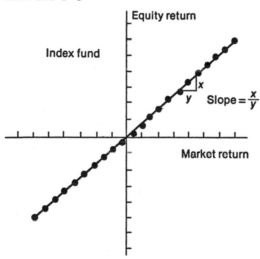

index fund containing the market portfolio, that is, a portfolio containing all the stocks in the market balanced in the proportions in which they appear in the marketplace. The second portfolio (Exhibit 8–4) is an aggressive fund, containing many volatile stocks, such as airlines and emerging growth companies. The third portfolio (Exhibit 8–5) is a conservative fund

EXHIBIT 8–4

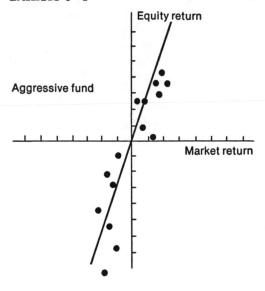

Aggressive fund

EXHIBIT 8–5

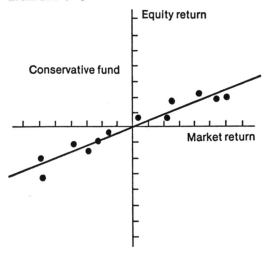

Conservative fund

composed of stocks of utilities, banks, and food service companies. To understand how the characteristic line helps us determine the market sensitivity or risk of the equity portfolio, it is helpful to recall how the characteristic line is constructed. The return of the portfolio and the market is plotted for each quarter. In a quarter in which the market had a return of 10 percent and the fund had a return of 15 percent, a point would be drawn which is closer to the equity portfolio's (vertical) axis than to the market's axis. Similarly, in a period in which the market went down 10 percent and the fund went down 15 percent, a plot would be drawn closer to the axis of the fund. In this case the line would have a steep slope, characterizing a fund which is aggressive (moving up more than the market when the market rises and down more when the market declines). This can be seen in Exhibit 8–4. Conversely, for a portfolio of conservative stocks, the plots would be drawn closer to the axis of the market, indicating that the fund rises less than the market in a rising period and declines less than the market in a declining period. Thus, the slope of the line determines the amount of market risk. This slope is measured by viewing the ratio between the vertical distance and the horizontal distance that the line moves, as is shown on the triangle in Exhibit 8–3. The slope may also be viewed as the percentage change in the portfolio that is expected for a 1 percent change in the market. In the case of the aggressive fund a gain of 1 percent in the market would be accompanied by a gain of more than 1 percent in the fund, thus giving the fund a beta, or market sensitivity, greater than 1. The opposite is true for a conservative portfolio. The index fund, shown in Exhibit 8–3, has a slope of 1. That is, when the market rises 5 percent, the fund rises 5 percent, which is not at all surprising, since the fund is identical to the market. The index fund thus has a beta of 1.0.

In the preceding discussion we tacitly assumed that the portfolio was completely diversified, so that all of the risk in the portfolio was market risk. However, this is usually not the case. In most portfolios there are two types of risk: market risk and specific, or nonmarket, risk. Market risk derives from factors impacting the overall market and economy, such as interest rates, inflation, and unemployment. Specific risk relates to factors affecting the individual companies in the portfolio. Among such factors are the management of the company, the success of the company's new products, and the impact of foreign competition on the company's product line. It is important to distinguish between these two types of risks because market risk is inherent to investors in the stock market, but specific risk can be eliminated through diversification. This is because an investor can own many stocks with the thought that unusual specific factors affecting individual companies will offset each other. For example, one company may have especially bad results during a quarter, but another company may have surprisingly good results during the same period. These two factors offset each other, leaving the investor with a return which on average is what he had expected.

Since there are two types of risk in a portfolio, it is important to measure both of them. We have discussed the significance of beta, or market sensitivity, as a measure of market risk. Beta measures the market risk and helps determine the expected rate of return of a portfolio, given a particular rate of return for the market. However, the beta measurement only applies to the *market* risk in the fund; it tells nothing about the amount of nonmarket, or specific, risk in the portfolio. The usefulness of the beta measurement thus depends on the percentage of the total portfolio risk which is represented by market risk. This can be seen by considering two portfolios, both of which have a beta of 1. The first of these portfolios is the index fund, which contains all the stocks in the market in the same proportions in which they exist in the marketplace. The second portfolio consists of a single stock which happens to have a beta of 1 but has had returns each quarter which are very different from those of the market. It might appear that the beta of 1 is something of a coincidence in this portfolio, since about half the time the fund's return was above what would have been expected and about half the time it was below what would have been expected for a portfolio with a beta of 1. It may be that the fund's return and that of the market were never very similar. The plots for this portfolio are shown in Exhibit 8–6. It can be seen that the plots cover a broad range and do not fall into a neat linear order. This fund can be characterized as having a beta of 1 and a low diversification level. Its condition can be described in two ways: first, we can say that the fund is not very diversified, and consequently its success or failure is highly dependent on the success of the stock owned rather than on the general level of the stock market; second, we might say that we cannot have much confidence that the portfolio's return

EXHIBIT 8–6

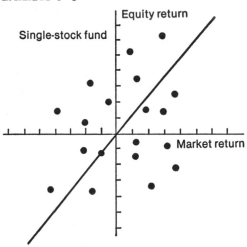

will be close to the return indicated by its beta level. Both statements say the same things but from different points of view. The reader may have recognized that the points in Exhibit 8–3, the index fund, all fall precisely on the characteristic line, whereas the points in Exhibit 8–6, the individual stock, scatter widely about the line. In effect, the diversification measure describes the extent to which the dots fall close to the line. The standard error of beta, also called the standard error of estimate or the standard error of regression, shows the extent to which the dots are dispersed in relation to the line. More frequently, the diversification measure is expressed as the R^2, also known as the coefficient of determination. This measurement, which is linked precisely to the standard error, shows the extent to which the regression line explains the relationship between the equity portfolio and the market. A measurement of zero shows no relationship, and a measurement of 1.00 shows a 100 percent explanation, as would be the case in an index fund.

A third factor which can be determined from the characteristic line is whether a manager was successful on a risk-adjusted basis in adding to the portfolio's return. This can be determined by looking at the intercept of the regression line (also called the alpha). Returning to the index fund in Exhibit 8–3, we note that the characteristic line goes through the origin, or meeting point, of the two axes. This indicates that the fund had a risk-adjusted return of 0.0 or, phrased another way, that the manager neither added nor subtracted return through stock selection. This is obviously what is anticipated with an index fund.

A manager who had success in stock selection on a risk-adjusted basis would find that the characteristic line intercepted above the zero mark, as shown in Exhibit 8–7. We can

EXHIBIT 8–7

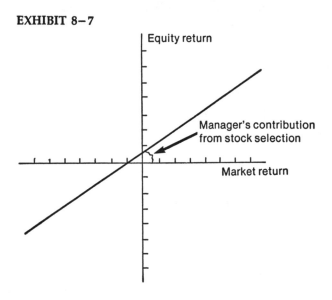

think of this example intuitively by considering a fund manager who invested by starting with an index fund and each quarter sold those securities which were overvalued and placed assets obtained from the sale in securities which were undervalued, but in each case moving the assets in such a way as to maintain the beta of 1. Assume that this activity added 1 percent per quarter to the portfolio's return. In a quarter in which the market rose 10 percent, the fund would rise 11 percent. When the market declined 10 percent, the fund would decline 9 percent, thus still achieving a return 1 percent better than the market. In this case the slope of the line is the same as that of the pure index fund, namely the 45-degree line with a slope of 1.0. However, the line would not go through the origin of the axes, but through the +1 percent mark on the vertical axis. This

1 percent per quarter represents the alpha, or the contribution through stock selection. The gain could have been achieved either by judicious choice of stocks or by increasing or decreasing the beta of the portfolio in anticipation of market movements (a form of timing).

An alternative way of viewing these ideas is shown in Exhibits 8–8, 8–9, and 8–10. Rather than looking at a regression

EXHIBIT 8–8

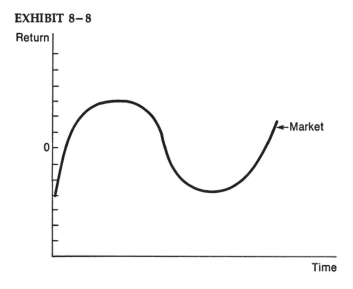

EXHIBIT 8–9

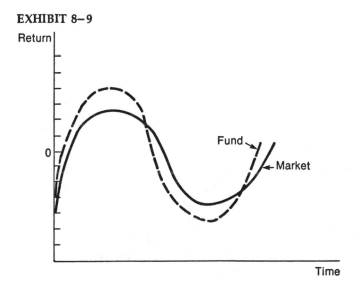

EXHIBIT 8–10

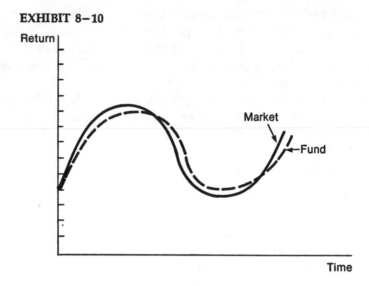

characteristic line, we now look at a more familiar graph show-ing events over time. Exhibit 8–8 shows the stock market (or index fund) through one cycle. Exhibit 8–9 shows a portfolio with a beta of 1.5. The portfolio rises more rapidly than the market in rising periods and declines more rapidly than the market in declining periods. Exhibit 8–10 shows a portfolio with a beta of 0.8; the portfolio moves more conservatively than the market, dampening swings in the market in both directions. In both cases the portfolios have an R^2 of 100, that is, are highly diversified. The idea of diversification can be introduced by recognizing that the portfolio may not have a return exactly equal to that indicated by its beta. Exhibit 8–11 shows a portfolio with a beta of 1.2 and an R^2 of 0.90. In this case the portfolio's expected rate of return is known, but its actual return will vary from the expected return. The width of the shaded area indicates a confidence span around the ex-pected return. In other words, in this case we are saying that two thirds of the time (within one standard deviation) the portfolio's return is likely to be within plus or minus 4 percent of the expected return. For another portfolio (Exhibit 8–12) with a beta of 1.2, but containing only a few stocks and thus having a very low diversification, or R^2, level, this span is much wider. Finally, Exhibit 8–13 shows the portfolio whose manager had 1

EXHIBIT 8–11

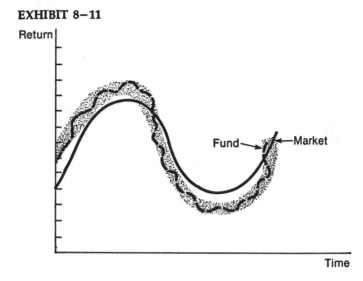

EXHIBIT 8–12

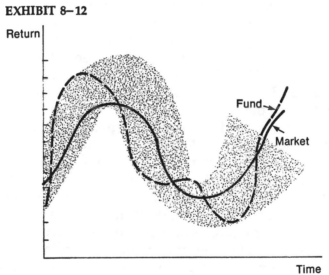

percent per quarter risk-adjusted contribution through stock selection in a portfolio with a beta of 1.0. The actual average return is distinguished from the expected return for this beta level. We can also see the degree of diversification in the port-folio by viewing the shaded area.

The implications of the information provided by the charac-teristic line are extremely important to fund sponsors and in-

EXHIBIT 8–13

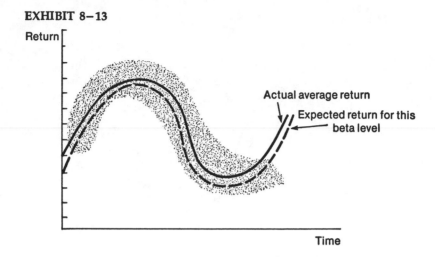

vestment managers. Two policy considerations are represented, and one evaluation of the manager's skill. The two policy considerations are the amount of market risk in a portfolio (beta, or market sensitivity) and the percentage of the total risk in the portfolio which is represented by market risk (diversification, or R^2). The beta, or market risk, question is one of whether or not the sponsor and the manager feel that it is appropriate for the fund to have an aggressive posture. This is largely a function of the characteristics of the sponsor, but it is also impacted by the percentage of the portfolio in equities. For example, a fund might choose to place 50 percent in aggressive equities rather than 60 percent in conservative equities.

The diversification issue is the extent to which the sponsor is willing to make the success of the fund a function of the success of the manager in finding undervalued securities, as opposed to allowing the movements of the marketplace to dominate the fund's return. This is not to say that it is wrong to be undiversified and to depend on the investment manager's success in stock selection. The reason for hiring an investment manager, in most cases, is that the sponsor believes that the investment manager will be able to find undervalued securities, or at least that the sponsor feels it is worth the risk of doing somewhat worse than the market on a risk-adjusted basis in order to try to do better than the market on a risk-adjusted basis. This is the conventional way of investing, and it should not be assumed to be imprudent. The main point is for sponsors to recognize what they are, in fact, doing and to be sure they have some reason for feeling that the manager will be successful in stock selection before they permit a manager to operate with a relatively low diversification posture.

Limitations of the beta measurement

Although the characteristic line beta analysis has considerable usefulness, there are some limitations which should be considered. First of all, the validity of the beta calculation is only as good as the "fit" between the two variables being measured, in this case the rate of return on the portfolio versus the rate of return on the market. The closeness of the fit is measured by the R^2. Generally speaking, if the R^2 is below 50, not much confidence can be placed in the measurement of the beta; if the R^2 is below 80, not much confidence can be placed in the measurement of the alpha, or intercept (selection measurement).

The calculation technique is also limited if there is a significant change in the beta during the period being measured. In other words, if the manager owned highly aggressive stocks at one point in the market and conservative stocks at another point, it is not possible to distinguish between the movements attributable to the market (beta) and those attributable to selection (alpha).

Moreover, the beta measurement is of limited value in looking at an individual stock. This is because the R^2 is usually low, averaging about 0.3. Intuitively, we know that stocks are affected both by the market and by internal factors affecting the company, and we see from the R^2 that about 70 percent of the risk or movement in the stock price is attributable to internal factors and only about 30 percent to movements in the market. Consequently, although the beta measurement is useful for a stock, it is not appropriate to place much weight on the information supplied by the characteristic line analysis. As more and more stocks are added to the portfolio, the specific factors cancel, leaving the market factor to dominate. Thus, the beta measurement is quite useful for diversified portfolios.

MEASURING RISK-ADJUSTED RETURN

In the preceding section we discussed the characteristic line beta analysis and found that it makes possible the measurement not only of risk and diversification, but also of risk-adjusted return, through the alpha, or intercept, in the analysis. Two additional measurements of risk-adjusted return can be made, using either beta or standard deviation as measurements of risk. This will be explored in terms of the security market line.

The security market line

The security market line relates return and risk. A chart is developed, showing return on one axis and risk on the other (see Exhibit 8–14). The market line connects points representing risk-free securities (such as U.S. Treasury bills) and the

EXHIBIT 8–14
Market security line analysis for period December 1973–December 1978

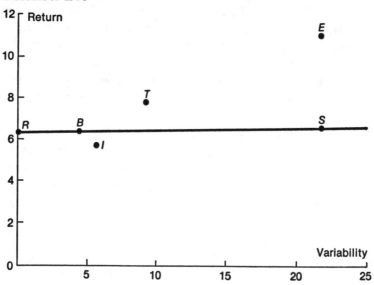

T: Total portfolio.
R: Risk-free rate—U.S. Treasury bills.
I: ML Corporate and Government Master Index.
S: Standard & Poor's 500 Index.
E: Equity portfolio.
B: Bond portfolio.

Source: Merrill Lynch Institutional Computer Services Department.

overall market. The point representing risk-free assets is on the vertical axis, indicating zero risk. The point representing the market is shown as having a greater degree of risk and also, at least in expectation, a higher rate of return. The measurement for risk can be either standard deviation (or a related measure) or beta. The risk and return of an individual portfolio or security can be measured and placed in the market line framework. It is then possible to relate the amount of return achieved to the amount of risk taken. This is normally done by dividing the "excess return" (the return over and above the risk-free rate) by either standard deviation or beta. The former is frequently called a Sharpe measurement, the latter a Treynor ratio.

9

Measuring
risk and return in
fixed income portfolios

*Bonds are strange investments. When you own them you don't even
know whether you want them to go up or down in value.* [1]

Paraphrased from Professor Lawrence Fisher

The measurement of bond portfolios is extremely important to
fund sponsors because of the enormous amount of money they
invest in bonds and because of their increasing concern that
assets be invested prudently and efficiently. Historically, bond
"measurement" has meant measuring the rate of return, and
possibly comparing results with a bond market index or with
other portfolios. Although these analyses are important, they
do not address one of the most significant factors that every
fund sponsor and investment manager should be concerned

---

[1] Bonds would rise in price only if interest rates declined. Although this produces
a capital gain for the investor, it also means that bonds may be "called" and replaced
with lower yielding investments and that the return from the reinvestment of coupon
will be lower.

with—risk. This chapter reviews why bond measurement is important, how risk and return are measured, why fund sponsors should be concerned with risk, and what the sources of risk are in bond portfolios. Finally, the chapter presents a number of methods for measuring risk and return in bond portfolios, using both traditional and new quantitative approaches.

RETURN

In order to begin the measurement process the portfolio's rate of return must first be calculated. For purposes of this analysis, return is the total rate of return on a time-weighted basis. The total rate of return includes income and realized and unrealized capital appreciation, with all assets measured at market value. Total rates of return are used because this makes it possible to perform analyses and make comparisons, and allows time to make changes in the portfolio if the results are not satisfactory. Using book values, whether or not they are amortized, investors cannot do much in the way of analysis, since they are not dealing with the true condition of the portfolio as of any point in time. For the same reason it is not possible to compare the results of one fund to those of another fund or to a market index. Finally, if investors ignore the true value of the portfolio and consider only the book value, they are not likely to recognize problems with the portfolio in time to make changes.

Time-weighted rates of return are calculated in such a way as to distinguish the effects on the portfolio of the timing and magnitude of external cash flows. This places the focus on what the investment manager did with the portfolio rather than on what happened to the fund, and is appropriate for sponsors trying to "manage their investment managers."

RISK

Having described rate of return, we can turn to the measurement of risk. There are many possible definitions of risk. For instance, it is possible to look at risk from loss due to default or change in quality rating, or potential loss if interest rates rise above the current level. Risk is defined here as the uncertainty of return or the uncertainty of the future value of the portfolio. The more uncertainty there is, the more risk the portfolio bears. For instance, we know that a 91-day Treasury bill has no risk for an investor with a three-month time horizon. On the other hand, bonds and stocks have uncertain returns to investors with a three-month horizon, since it is not known what the value of bonds and stocks will be three months hence. Thus, risk can be defined as the amount of uncertainty in the portfolio.

The sponsor of a fixed income portfolio might reasonably ask why it should care about risk. There are three reasons why it should be concerned:

1.   If a fund has an inappropriate risk policy, its chances of meeting its objective are reduced. A good example is a small portfolio owned by a widow on behalf of herself and her children. Her goal is to receive income in order to pay her monthly bills. All of us would agree that the widow's ability to bear risk is very low, that her need for income is high, and that her portfolio should be structured so as to take these factors into consideration. The objectives of pension funds or other tax-exempt funds may not be as dramatically obvious as those of the widow, but nonetheless the investment objective is extremely important. Although it is no easy task to establish a correct policy, nonetheless sponsors must be able to measure the risk of their investments in order to have any hope of establishing one.

2.   A fund may be taking too much risk relative to the return it is achieving. Risk measures make it possible to calculate risk-adjusted returns in order to answer the question "For the risk our investment manager took, did we achieve a high enough return?"

3.   Now that interest rates are higher than they were historically, bonds are more volatile. This is because when interest rates are high, the present value of future cash flows changes more dramatically as interest rates change a given percentage.

The skeptic may ask why he should not ignore risk and instead merely compare his results to any or all of his assumed rate of return, a market index, or other portfolios. Although each of these comparisons is important, none is sufficient. Comparing a fund to its assumed rate of return is not adequate, since in periods when the market declines sharply (such as 1974), almost all portfolios will fail to meet their objectives. Similarly, in a sharply rising market (such as 1975) almost all funds will exceed their assumptions. Thus, the usefulness of this method is limited. It might be suggested that the limitations of comparison to the assumed rate of return can be corrected for by comparing a portfolio's results to a market index or to the results of other portfolios. The drawback of this approach is that the indices or portfolios used as comparative benchmarks may be structured in a way which does not reflect the objectives, needs, or characteristics of the fund in question. Therefore, these comparisons, though certainly useful, are not sufficient.

We have established that return is measured as total, time-weighted return, that risk is uncertainty of return or uncertainty of future value, and that it is vital for a fund sponsor to measure the risk of its portfolio. We will now analyze the sources of risk in bond portfolios.

SOURCES OF RISK IN BOND PORTFOLIOS

The first and foremost risk in bond portfolios is default. If the issuer does not pay interest and principal, the value of the bond is severely diminished. As a practical matter, the vast majority of bond issuers have been able to honor their commitments precisely. Furthermore, most investment managers concentrate in reasonably high-quality bonds, such that the risk of default is more noticeable in the differences in yield between high-quality and lower quality bonds than in the likelihood of real default. However, should the country witness a severe and prolonged depression, the number of bonds defaulting would increase considerably.

For bonds which are not likely to default, two types of risk or uncertainty are of interest: changes in the general level of interest rates and changes in the "spread," or yield differential, between sectors of the bond market. An additional risk is "call" or reinvestment risk, which occurs when interest rates drop sharply and remain down for a long period of time. In this case investors who own bonds with high coupons may find that issuers will sell new bonds at lower rates and use the proceeds to pay off the old bonds which require payment of a higher interest rate. Further, since the new level of interest rates is lower, as cash is received from coupon payments and from maturing bonds this money is reinvested at the new (lower) rates of interest, thus reducing the amount of money received and the return of the investor.

Other risks are introduced by special features of individual bonds. For instance, subordinated bonds place the investor in a position junior to other creditors in the case of default. Convertible bonds, which in many cases are more like equity securities than like fixed income instruments, can be exchanged under certain circumstances for shares of common stock. For these securities the price of the common stock becomes an important determinant of the value of the bond, and consequently introduces a major uncertainty. Another source of risk occurs when bonds are subject to sinking funds. In many cases corporate bonds are offered with a requirement by the borrower to retire a portion of the issue prior to maturity, in order to reduce the amount of liabilities outstanding. Although this activity generally improves the creditworthiness of the bonds, the presence or absence of the issuer repurchasing bonds to meet sinking fund requirements introduces a modest but additional uncertainty in the marketplace.

Inflation risk is present for all assets denominated in money as opposed to materials. That is, since a bond has to be repaid in money it has inflation risk, whereas if a bond were to be repaid in soybeans it would not have such risk.

CHANGES IN THE GENERAL LEVEL OF INTEREST RATES

In looking at the impact of changes in the general level of interest rates, four rules will be established. First, when interest rates change, bond prices also change. Second, the change occurs in the opposite direction. That is, when interest rates decline, bond prices rise, and vice versa. Third, all other things being equal, bonds with longer maturities are more volatile than bonds with shorter maturities.[2] Fourth, bonds with lower coupons are more volatile than bonds with higher coupons.

Exhibit 9–1 shows two bonds with similar coupons and different maturities. When the level of interest rates declines from

EXHIBIT 9–1

When yields decline, longer term bonds rise more sharply than do shorter term bonds.

| | Coupon | Maturity | Level of interest rates | | |
			8 percent price	7 percent price	Percentage change in price
Bond A	8%	One year	100	101	1%
Bond B	8	Two years	100	102	2

If interest rates decline from 8 percent to 7 percent, each bond is worth roughly 1 percent per year more than the prevailing rate. To equalize this change, the one-year bond rises about 1 percent and the two-year bond rises about 2 percent (ignoring call provisions and compounding).

8 percent to 7 percent, both bonds rise in price, as indicated by the first and second rules. According to the third rule, the longer maturity bond rises more than the shorter maturity bond. The reason for this becomes apparent when we consider that a one-year 8 percent bond pays 1 percent more than the going interest rate of 7 percent. Thus, investors in one-year bonds should be indifferent to whether they receive 7 percent interest and pay par or receive 8 percent interest and pay 101 (ignoring compounding, call features, and taxes). Similarly, an investor buying a two-year bond when rates are 7 percent expects to receive roughly 14 percent on his investment over a two-year period. When he purchases a bond with an 8 percent coupon, he receives 16 percent in interest and therefore is willing to lose 2 percent in principal in order to achieve the 7

[2] Technically speaking, it is the duration of a bond rather than its maturity which determines its volatility. Certain (hypothetical) discount bonds of extremely long maturities reach a point at which they become less volatile as maturity increases, since duration at this point is decreasing rather than increasing.

percent per year prevailing rate of return. Consequently, we have verified that bonds with longer term maturities have greater percentage changes in price for a given change in interest rates.

The fourth rule is that lower coupon bonds are more volatile than higher coupon bonds for a given change in interest rates. This behavior can be traced to the fact that a bond returns both interest and a final maturity payment, and that for lower coupon bonds a smaller percentage of the return comes from coupon than is the case with a higher coupon bond. Thus, when rates change, the lower coupon bond must change more in price in order to offset the greater stability of return offered by the higher coupon payments of the high coupon bond. Put another way, since the average time to repayment is farther in the future for lower coupon bonds, there is more impact from discounting their future cash flows.

This principle can be seen from Exhibit 9–2, in which the impact on an 8 percent 20-year bond is compared to the impact

EXHIBIT 9–2

When yields decline, lower coupon bonds rise a greater percentage than do higher coupon bonds.

			Level of interest rates		
			8 percent price	7 percent price	Percentage change in price
	Coupon	Maturity			
Bond A	8%	20	100	110.677	10.7%
Bond B	4	20	60.414	67.967	12.5

on a 4 percent 20-year bond when the level of interest rates changes from 8 percent to 7 percent. Both bonds rise in price according to rules 1 and 2, with the lower coupon bond being more volatile, showing a 12.5 percent increase in price as compared to a 10.7 percent increase in price for the higher coupon bond.

Thus, for a given change in the general level of interest rates the impact is greater for longer maturity bonds and for lower coupon bonds. These impacts can be combined (when quality is unchanged and when the shift in interest rates is uniform for all maturities) into a measure of duration. Duration measures the time it takes for the investor to receive back half of his or her money. In other words, it includes the timing of final maturity *and* the size and timing of coupon payments received in the meantime.

CHANGES IN SPREADS BETWEEN BOND SECTORS

In addition to changes in the general level of interest rates, a major source of volatility in bond portfolios is changes in the spreads between bond sectors. The five types of changes relate to maturity, quality, coupon, issuer type, and coupon area (premium or discount). Exhibit 9–3 shows two bonds with different yields. The difference in yields can be caused by a difference in maturity[3] (with longer term bonds typically having higher yields), quality (with lower quality bonds having higher yields), coupon (with higher coupon bonds typically having higher yields), issuer type (with financial and utility bonds generally having higher yields than industrials), and coupon area (with premium bonds typically having higher yields than discount bonds). The point is that bonds with different characteristics have different yields and that the difference in yield between these bonds can change. For instance, in Exhibit 9–3 bond 1 yields 8.00 percent and bond 2 yields 8.10 percent. We might assume that bond 1 is a AAA bond and bond 2 a AA bond of similar characteristics. There is no reason why this spread relationship must stay at ten basis points; it could become wider or narrower, with either bond rising or declining in yield.[4] Such changes in the relationship between bond sectors can come at any time and be of almost any magnitude.

---

[3] Changes in yield spreads between maturities are typically referred to as changes in the shape of the yield curve.

[4] It is interesting to note that when spreads widen, the investor is better off owning a lower yielding bond, regardless of its other characteristics. If the spread widens because the higher yielding bond rises in yield, this bond will have a decrease in price. If the spread widens because the lower yielding bond drops in yield, this bond will have a capital gain. In either case the investor is better off owning the lower yielding bond. When spreads narrow, the opposite is true.

EXHIBIT 9–3

Changing spreads between different sectors are a source of bond volatility. When the spread between a higher yielding bond and a lower yielding bond widens, the lower yielding bond is the better performer.

Bond 1	Bond 2	Spread
8.00	8.10	−0.10

If the spread widens by Bond 2's yield rising, Bond 2 will sustain a capital loss, making Bond 1, the lower yielding bond, a better performer.

If the spread widens by Bond 1's yield declining, Bond 1 will sustain a capital gain, making it the better performer.

TRADITIONAL RISK MEASURES

Traditional measurements of risk in bonds can be divided into two general categories. The first looks at the underlying strength of the *issuer*, and the second looks at the characteristics of the *bonds* held. The measurements which describe the issuer can be further divided into those which relate the issuer's income or cash flow to the amount of debt service required each year and those which address the amount of debt relative to the amount of assets or equity.

Measurements of the ability to repay include:

1. Earnings before interest and taxes divided by debt service. This measurement views the issuer's net income as an indication of ability to repay debt. Since interest payments are deductible they are included before taxes.
2. Cash flow divided by debt service. Similar to the previous

measurement, this calculation also includes the cash available from noncash charges, such as depreciation.

Measurements relating debt to assets or equity include:

1. Debt as a percentage of total capital. This is perhaps the most traditional measurement of the amount of debt that an issuer can properly handle. These ratios differ considerably from industry to industry and should be considered in that context.
2. Debt as a percentage of equity. This similar measurement relates debt to equity rather than to debt plus equity. Both measurements could define equity as historical book value or market value less debt.

It is also desirable to consider profitability measures, such as profit margins and return on equity or return on total assets, as indications of the long-run ability of the issuer to pay.

In addition to these fundamental measurements, it is possible to use traditional risk measures in the form of maturity, coupon, quality, and issuer type. As discussed earlier, long-term bonds and low-coupon bonds are more volatile than otherwise similar short-term bonds or high-coupon bonds. High-quality bonds are less risky then lower quality bonds. As to issuer type, U.S. government securities are obviously of higher quality and hence less risky than corporate bonds. Among the three corporate sectors—industrial, financial, and utility—no category is inherently more secure than another.

AGGREGATING TRADITIONAL RISK MEASURES OF INDIVIDUAL BONDS INTO PORTFOLIO MEASURES

The measures discussed above are used primarily in analyzing individual bonds for their creditworthiness and their relative value. Fund sponsors are typically less concerned with individual securities and more interested in descriptions of the portfolio in its entirety. It is possible to use traditional measures for the total bond portfolio by measuring each bond and weighting the measurement for the percentage of the portfolio in that security. This can be done for each security, with the sum of the measurements of each security being representative of the portfolio. The aggregate number can then be compared with a similar number for the market as a whole, subsectors thereof, or other portfolios.

QUANTITATIVE TECHNIQUES FOR MEASURING RISK

Although the above measurements certainly provide useful information about a portfolio, they do not indicate its overall risk. At least three measures exist which might do this. First, the standard deviation of the portfolio's returns will be considered, as it was with equities. Second, the beta method for measuring risk in fixed income portfolios will be discussed. Third, a model which measures the sensitivity of a portfolio to changes in the level of interest rates will be considered.

Using standard deviation in market line analysis

The market line is a simple method of measuring risk as well as return in portfolios, as is shown in Exhibit 9–4. The vertical axis shows return and the horizontal axis shows variability as measured by the standard deviation of return. (Since standard deviation is an arithmetic, as opposed to geometric, concept, the returns shown are arithmetic rather than geometric. Although this changes the actual measurement of return somewhat, it does not in any way alter the concept of return.) It can be seen from this framework for measuring risk and return that the most desirable portfolio would be one which is represented by a point at the upper left part of the graph, signifying a low level of risk and a high level of return.

Utilization of the market line begins with measurement of the risk and return of Treasury bills and the overall bond market (index 1). Treasury bills (represented by R) had a return during the period of a little over 6 percent and a variability of zero for a one-quarter time horizon. Similarly, a point is shown which represents the risk and return for the overall bond market, as measured by the Merrill Lynch Corporate and Govern-

EXHIBIT 9–4

Bond portfolio market line analysis for period December 1973 to December 1978

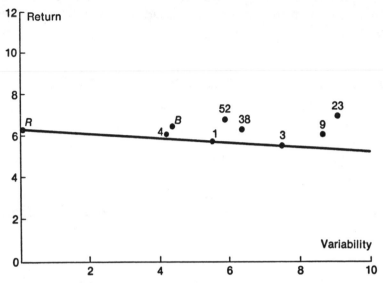

B: Bond portfolio.
R: Risk-free 91-day U.S. Treasury bill.
3: ML 15-year-plus U.S. Treasury bond.
4: ML three–five-year U.S. Treasury bond.
1: ML Corporate and Government Master Index.
9: ML high-quality long-term corporate.
23: ML medium-quality long-term corporate.
38: ML high-quality intermediate-term corporate.
52: ML medium-quality intermediate-term corporate.

Source: Merrill Lynch Institutional Computer Services Department.

ment Master Index. This point shows a return of slightly less than 6 percent, with a variability of about 5 percent. This risk measurement indicates that about two thirds of the time during this period we would have expected the market line to have a return within 5 percent of its average. Put another way, the bond market would have been expected to return between plus 1 percent and plus 11 percent about two thirds of the time. It should be noted that any return is theoretically possible but that a return above or below two standard deviations (plus or minus 10 percent, or outside the range of −4 percent to +16 percent) would only occur 5 percent of the time.

We have thus described two points on the fixed income spectrum, the risk and return of Treasury bills and the risk and return of the overall bond market. We can now draw a market line showing the risk and return of "market" portfolios with a wide variety of risk levels. This is done by connecting the Treasury bill point with the bond market point and indicating that an investor could achieve a portfolio of any risk level and any return shown on that line merely by combining the appropriate proportions of Treasury bills and the bond market. In other words, a point halfway along the line would have a risk of about 2½ percent and a return halfway between that of bills and that of the market. This portfolio can be constructed by allocating half of fund assets at the beginning of the period to bills and the other half to the bond market as represented by the index. Similarly, any other point on the line can be achieved by combining the appropriate amount of bills and bonds. It must be noted that in order to achieve a point to the right of the bond market, the percentage in Treasury bills must be negative; that is, the investor must borrow money, at the risk-free rate, and leverage his portfolio. Although this may not be a legal alternative for most funds, it is at least a theoretical alternative and useful from an analytical point of view.

Having drawn a market line for the period December 1973 to December 1978, we note that during this period the line slants downward. This indicates that during the period there was a slight negative "premium" for bearing risk: the greater the risk that was taken, the worse portfolios tended to do. Although this is contrary to long-run expectations, it is certainly possible during any period, and in fact it is what happened for the five years that ended in December 1978.

Beta analysis

As shown in the equity analysis, the beta measurement presents the relationship between a portfolio's historic rate of return and the market's historic rate of return, with the slope of the line indicating how volatile the portfolio is relative to the market index. Exhibits 9–5 and 9–6 use the beta model to show the relationship between short-term government portfolios and long-term corporate portfolios, both in relation to a broad-based market index. It can easily be seen that the short-term government index has a much flatter slope than that of the

EXHIBIT 9−5

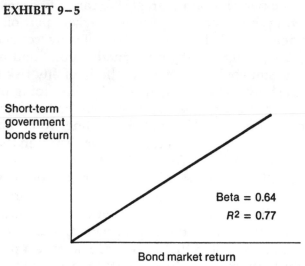

Returns calculated excess of Treasury bills, for period 12/72−12/77.

EXHIBIT 9−6

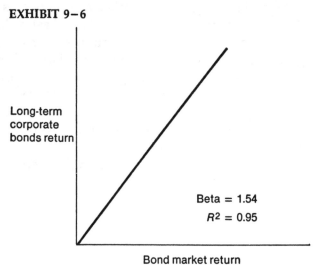

Returns calculated excess of Treasury bills, for period 12/72−12/77.

long-term corporate index, indicating its lesser volatility or risk.

Certain difficulties arise in using the beta measurement for bond portfolios and hoping to make judgments about them. First, the choice of index makes a great deal of difference in the results achieved. Second, the portfolio's characteristics should be stable for the measurement to be highly useful. Since bond portfolios, if no action is taken, are constantly becoming shorter term and hence less risky, this creates difficulties with the measurement. Finally, as will be discussed later, because of these problems it is questionable whether the beta analysis can be expanded beyond risk to measure selection and diversification, as can be done with equity portfolios.

The duration model

In recent years, with the increasing emphasis on measuring fixed income portfolios, considerable importance has been attached to an old idea. This is the idea of duration. Duration measures the average time required for the investor to receive his investment and the interest on it. It is similar to maturity, except that maturity only considers the timing and the amount of the final payment of a bond. Duration, on the other hand, also considers the significant impact on the investor of the timing and magnitude of coupon payments. Consider the bonds shown in Exhibit 9–7. For long maturities the high-coupon bonds have a considerably shorter duration than do the low-coupon bonds. The significance of duration is that the greater the duration, the more volatile a portfolio's return is with respect to changes in the general level of interest rates. In fact, for small changes in rates the relationship is proportional.

EXHIBIT 9–7
Duration of selected bonds at market yield of 6 percent (in years)

Years to maturity	Coupon rates*			
	.02	.04	.06	.08
1	0.995	0.990	0.985	0.981
5	4.756	4.558	4.393	4.254
10	8.891	8.169	7.662	7.286
20	14.981	12.980	11.904	11.232
50	19.452	17.129	16.273	15.829
100	17.567	17.232	17.120	17.064
∞	17.167	17.167	17.167	17.167

* Coupon payments and compounding semiannual.
Source: Fisher and Weil, *Journal of Business*, October 1971, p. 418.

As was noted earlier in the chapter, longer maturity bonds are more volatile than shorter maturity bonds because the time period over which the discounting process takes place is much longer with longer maturity bonds. With low-coupon bonds the percentage of the total return represented by the final payment is much lower, and since the final payment is obviously the longest term payment received, the volatility of the portfolio or bond with respect to changes in interest rates is increased.

The duration measure has several limitations and these should be noted. First, there are risks to portfolios other than those associated with interest rate changes. Second, the precise measurement of the portfolio's volatility with respect to interest rate changes assumes a so-called parallel shift in the yield curve. In other words, if 20-year rates move 1 percent, then a similar change is assumed for 19-year bonds, 10-year bonds, 5-year bonds, and so on. Despite these limitations the duration measure is of considerable use in measuring the risk of fixed income securities.

MEASURING RISK-ADJUSTED RETURN

The rate of return adjusted for the amount of risk taken, also known as the "manager's contribution," can be calculated by using each of the three measurements shown for calculating portfolio risk. Each of these measurements will be discussed below.

Using standard deviation in market line analysis

In the market line analysis a line was drawn representing the risk and return of portfolios consisting of various portions of Treasury bills and the market. This line can be viewed as an unmanaged or "naive" portfolio. In other words, it is possible to suggest that the line represents a market portfolio of a specific risk level, and that the market return for a portfolio of that risk level is the one shown on the vertical axis (see Exhibit 9–4). It is then possible to see whether the return of a specific portfolio is above or below that of the market portfolio of the same risk level. If the return is above the line, it can be stated that the portfolio achieved a risk-adjusted return above that of the market. If the return is below the line, the portfolio did less well than an unmanaged portfolio of the same risk level. As with all measurements comparing actual performance to a market index, it must be considered that the index has no transaction cost and that real portfolios do; consequently, all such measurements are somewhat biased against the investment manager operating in the real world.

Using beta

Just as with equity portfolios, it is possible to use the alpha, or intercept, to measure risk-adjusted returns. However, this procedure is not recommended because of the segmented nature of the bond market; the impact on the portfolio of shifts in the bond yield curve; the varying results which can occur, depending on which index is used to represent the overall bond market; and the changing risk level of the portfolio which occurs as bonds become shorter in maturity and as coupon reinvestment and other funds added to the portfolio change its structure. All of these factors impact the measurement of risk in the portfolio and create the possibility that the alpha is showing a factor representing risk when it is supposedly demonstrating the impact of the manager over and above that indicated by the risk of the portfolio.

Using the duration model

With the duration measurement it is possible to calculate the sensitivity of a portfolio to changes in the general level of interest rates. With this information it becomes possible to attribute the sources of the portfolio's return to the market, the policy effect, the interest rate anticipation effect, the analysis effect, and the trading effect. In the duration model (Exhibit 9–8), the rate of return is shown on the vertical axis and duration on the horizontal axis. This is similar to the market line, except that duration rather than total variability is used as the risk measure. The market effect is the base point, and it represents the return which the market achieved during the period being measured. Moving up the line, the long-term average risk level of the portfolio is shown, the difference between the market return and the return of a market portfolio with the fund's risk policy being the policy effect. If the manager expects rates to change, he will probably shift the duration of the portfolio accordingly. In the example shown (Exhibit 9–8), higher risk

EXHIBIT 9–8
The duration model

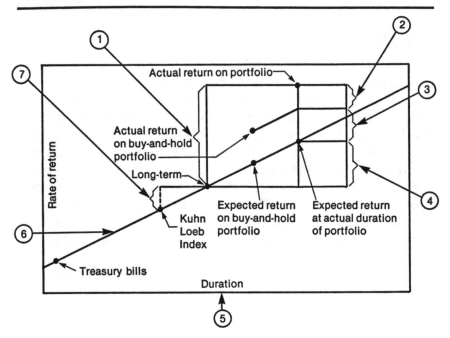

1. The management effect is the improvement in the investment performance of a passive strategy through active bond management. It is the difference between the total bond portfolio return and the expected return at the long-term average duration.
2. The trading effect is the result of the current quarter's trading, either through effective trade desk operation or short-term selection abilities. It is the difference between the total management effect and the effects attributable to analysis and interest rate anticipation.
3. The analysis effect, attributable to the selection of issues with better than average long-term prospects, is the difference between the actual return of the buy-and-hold portfolio at the beginning of the quarter and the expected return of that buy-and-hold portfolio.

4. The interest rate anticipation effect is attributable to changes in portfolio duration resulting from attempts to profit from and ability to predict bond market movements. It is the difference between the expected return at the actual portfolio duration and the expected return at the long-term average duration.
5. Duration, a measure of the average time to the receipt of cash flows from an investment, is a measure of the sensitivity of a bond's price to changes in interest rates. An increase in yields causes a percentage decrease in price equal to the duration times change in yield.
6. The bond market line is a straight line drawn through the return/duration of Treasury bills and the return/duration of the Kuhn Loeb Index.
7. The policy effect is the difference between the long-term duration of a bond portfolio and the duration of a bond market index resulting from long-term investment policy, measured as the return at the long-term average less the return on the Kuhn Loeb Index.

Note: The buy-and-hold portfolio is the composition of the portfolio at the beginning of the quarter. It is used to differentiate between trading gains secured within a quarter and long-term analysis gains.

Source: Wilshire Associates; *Pension World*, June 1977.

was rewarded as the manager increased the duration of the portfolio above the long-run policy average and achieved a higher rate of return in the process. The difference between the return at the actual duration on the market line and the return at the policy duration, also on the line, is the interest rate anticipation effect. If the manager were successful in finding undervalued bonds, his favorable analysis effect would be shown as the difference between the rate of return of the initial portfolio, had it been held for the whole period, and a portfolio of the same duration on the market line. Finally, any difference between the actual rate of return earned and the return on the buy-and-hold portfolio is called the trading effect.

This analysis is extremely interesting, but unfortunately it has limitations. Because measurements are attributed so minutely, it is extremely important that the portfolios be valued precisely and that they be measured whenever any significant cash flow takes place. In other words, the rate of return must be precisely measured for it to be possible to attribute return to the various effects. Also, duration is not a complete measurement of the risk in a portfolio, since it leaves out quality factors. Thus, these factors will be attributed to other areas. In addition, the impact on the portfolio from sinking funds, calls, and redemptions will be attributed to trading, whereas they may be due to fortuitous causes. Naturally, since the market line is based on the return and the duration of the market index, precise measurements of the index must also be available. Finally, it should be noted that there is no generally accepted theory which suggests that a straight-line relationship should exist between return and duration. Although the analysis may be extremely ambitious, nonetheless the results being sought are entirely desirable.

MEASURING THE MANAGER'S CONTRIBUTION

One recently developed approach to bond measurement uses traditional measurements (see Exhibit 9–9). This method compares results to the market and to a buy-and-hold portfolio. The difference between the rate of return on the market and the rate of return on the beginning or buy-and-hold portfolio is considered to be the management differential. The difference between the rate of return on the beginning portfolio and the actual portfolio is called the activity factor. This analysis suggests that the return on a portfolio will equal its beginning yield to maturity if nothing else changes. However, interest rates may change, and this impact is measured by looking at the shift in the government bond yield curve from the beginning to the end of the period. The impact of this shift is called the interest rate effect. To the extent that the portfolio is weighted differently from the market, any changes in the relationship between quality and issuer type will also have an impact on the portfolio. The difference between the total rate of return of the beginning portfolio and the sum of the beginning yield to maturity, the interest rate effect, and the sector/quality effect, is called the residual effect, or "other selection effect." Finally, the difference between the return on the beginning portfolio and the actual return is an activity or swapping factor.

EXHIBIT 9–9
Measuring manager contribution using traditional analysis

Return analysis (beginning portfolio)

	Total return	Adjusted beginning yield to maturity	Interest rate effect	Sector/ quality return	Residual
1. Return of beginning portfolio.........	0.92%	= 2.14% +	(3.84%) +	0.80% +	1.82%
2. Market return.....	(1.25)	= 2.06 +	(4.13) +	0.87 +	(0.05)
3. Management differential........	2.17%	= 0.08% +	0.29% +	(0.07)% +	1.87%

Manager 1's static portfolio performed considerably better (+2.17 percent) than the market portfolio. This better performance was mainly attributable to 1.87 percent from "other selection effects," which occurred on several bonds. Also, about 0.29 percent additional return was experienced because of the shorter maturity of this portfolio (13.5 years) versus the market average maturity of 19.5 years.

Activity factor

Total reported return	vs.	Return on beginning portfolio	=	Activity factor
0.30%		0.92%	=	(0.62%)

Account descriptors

	Market	Manager
Maturity	19.5 years	13.5 years
Coupon	7.9%	8.2%

Source: Russell Fogler and Peter O. Dietz, Frank Russell & Company, Inc.

COMPARISON WITH A BASELINE PORTFOLIO

Some practitioners suggest that it is inappropriate to compare a portfolio's results to a market index or to the results of other funds. Rather, a fund's results should be compared to its objective. The objective is not a simple percentage or dollar amount but a portfolio which meets the needs of the fund sponsor. Assume that a certain fund with assets of $1 million is required to pay $80,000 per year to the sponsor for ten years. In this case the baseline portfolio might be a U.S. government bond with an 8 percent coupon and a ten-year maturity. It is then possible to compare the results of the portfolio in any period to those which would have been achieved by investing in this bond.

This method has considerable appeal, though it is not easy to put into practice. First, it is not easy for most sponsors to articulate their needs as specifically as the method requires. Second, a portfolio must be found which meets these needs. Third, this portfolio must be measured along with the real portfolio. Nonetheless, at least conceptually, there is considerable merit to this approach. If nothing else, the method forces sponsors to investigate and articulate their needs.

10

Measuring
market timing

'Timing is everything''

Old Wall Street saying

Everyone knows in general terms what is meant by market timing—the movement of funds from one asset category, such as equities, to another, such as bonds, in order to maximize returns and minimize losses. However, measuring this phenomenon is extremely difficult since it is desirable to eliminate from the measurement the impact from securities selection, the risk level of the assets owned, and the sensitivities of those assets to the period measured, the average allocation, and the beginning allocation. Various methods for measuring market timing are discussed, along with the pros and cons of each. For purposes of analysis the methods for measuring market timing have been divided into three categories: changes in portfolio value, the use of market indices, and measurement of cash flow movements.

CHANGES IN PORTFOLIO VALUE

This method involves looking at the portfolio at the beginning of the period and calculating the return which would have been achieved had that same portfolio been held throughout the period. That return can then be compared with the actual return achieved to see whether or not the "unmanaged" buy-and-hold portfolio would have performed better than the portfolio with the choices made. Although this information can certainly be of interest, it is really not a satisfactory measurement of market timing. First, this type of measurement is very sensitive to the beginning point chosen. In other words, if the period chosen were one year earlier or one year later, the results might be dramatically different. Also, any aberration in the portfolio's structure at the beginning point impacts the result. More important, this measurement does not distinguish among market timing, the risk level of each asset category, and contributions through selection. Consequently, the measurement has serious deficiencies for sponsors which are trying to determine the contribution made by the manager in timing the market. The impacts of asset category risk level and selection are demonstrated below.

THE USE OF MARKET INDICES

In order to overcome the biases caused by differences in asset category risk level and selection, it is possible to view the portfolio as being invested not in the actual securities held but in market indices. In other words, if the portfolio were 60 percent in equities, 30 percent in bonds, and 10 percent in cash equivalents, we could assume that the portfolio was invested 60 percent in the S&P 500, 30 percent in a bond index, and 10 percent in Treasury bills. This appears to be a quite satisfactory solution to the biases introduced by measuring the actual portfolio owned. Someone might suggest that this is not appropriate, since a manager might go from cash into equities and choose a particular list of stocks which does extremely well, whereas the general market declines. According to general terminology, however, this manager would be deemed to have had especially high success in stock selection but not success in market timing.

Numerous methods can be derived for measuring market timing with the use of indices.

The beginning allocation

It is possible to use the beginning percentage allocation among asset categories in order to see whether the portfolio would have performed better over time had the manager maintained the beginning allocation rather than causing or allowing the allocation to change as it did. Again, this method is very sensitive to the beginning point chosen. It would be possible to repeat this method for each year (or even each quarter or month) of the measurement period. That is to say, we could look at the results from a point starting five years ago, a second point starting four years ago, a third point starting three years ago, and so on. The difficulty with this approach is that the results might be positive for some years and negative for others, without there being an obvious way of averaging the results for the entire period.

Since this method is sensitive to the beginning point chosen, an improvement can be made by making the beginning point less arbitrary. For instance, if the beginning of a market cycle is used as the beginning point and the end of the market cycle as the end point, the period being measured is both rationally determined and the same for all portfolios. In this case the performance in a market cycle would be measured for the two hypothetical portfolios, one with the average allocation during the cycle and the other with the actual allocation. If the portfolio at the average allocation exceeded the portfolio at the beginning allocation, a positive timing score would result. A drawback of this method is that it cannot be utilized unless the portfolio was under the manager's control for at least the full market cycle being measured.

The average allocation

In order to avoid dependence on the beginning point it is possible to use the average allocation during the period rather than the allocation of the beginning point. In other words, if the average percentage in equities, bonds, and cash equivalents is 60/30/10, a comparison can be made of the return which would have been achieved by investing in market indices at the average allocations and comparing it to the return which would have been achieved by investing at the actual quarter-by-quarter allocation which occurred in the portfolio. This method has considerable merit, although, like all of the index methods discussed here, it suffers from two problems: the measurement is "period dependent," and it is sensitive to the level of average allocation. In other words, a manager who behaved exactly the same from 1968 to 1972 as he did from 1973 to 1977 would show different timing results simply because the stock, bond, and cash equivalent markets behaved differently during the two periods. Furthermore, even if we look at only a single period, two funds with significantly different allocations will have different timing measures. This makes it difficult to compare managers over a given period. Such period dependence is the result of a phenomenon which might be called the rebalancing effect, and serious students of performance measurement may wish to study this phenomenon, since it crops up in several different areas of performance measurement.

The measurement technique is looking at the difference between a portfolio which was rebalanced periodically to a certain allocation level and one which was not rebalanced. This means that if the market rises, the percentage in equities increases and the rebalancing occurs by selling sufficient equities to rebalance to the desired level. If the market declines, the percentage in equities also declines, thus making it necessary to rebalance by purchasing additional equities. As long as the market heads in one direction, rebalancing hurts the portfolio. That is, as long as the market is rising, a policy of selling equities obviously hurts the portfolio. Similarly, if the market is declining, a policy of purchasing equities hurts the portfolio. Thus, in periods in which the market goes straight up or straight down, the rebalancing strategy works poorly and the unbalanced portfolio will tend to outperform the rebalanced portfolio. On the other hand, if the market has wide fluctuations but ends up roughly where it started, the rebalancing strategy is effective in increasing returns. This is because the percentage in equities in a rising market is constantly reduced, and at such time as the market declines, the lower level of equities works to the portfolio's benefit. Conversely, in a declining market the policy of rebalancing by purchasing stocks increases the fund's return when the market rebounds to its original position. Thus, the rebalancing effect is different in each period measured due to the differences in what the market did during that period. Consequently, a bias is introduced into all measurements which involve rebalancing. Unfortunately, this includes almost all measurements of timing.

A variation of the measurement of looking at the average percentage in equities versus the actual percentage is to look at the average beta, or market sensitivity, of the total portfolio in comparison to the period-by-period beta. In other words, the expected returns could be calculated for a portfolio with a beta equal to the average beta over the period, and these returns could be compared to the expected returns from the quarter-by-quarter beta of the portfolio. Again, if the average returns exceed the returns quarter by quarter, a negative timing score results.

The trend line allocation

One of the most difficult problems associated with the measurement of market timing is the need to distinguish between the discretionary activity of the manager and the policies dictated by the sponsor. If the sponsor dictates or suggests a change in the percentage in equities, the measurement of market timing must take this change in policy into account. Otherwise, an impact will be attributed to the manager which should be attributed to the sponsor. Similarly, if the manager changes the long-term policy as to percentage in equities, this change cannot easily be distinguished from attempts at timing.

Regrettably, there is no simple way to measure this phenomenon unless the sponsor precisely and before the fact states an investment policy. It is insufficient for him to give general guidelines, and of course there is no way to distinguish between the impact of such policy decisions on a manager and the results of subtle comments by the sponsor, such as "I see you've been doing some buying lately; that surprises me, given the market's outlook." One means for eliminating the impact of these policy decisions involves looking not at the average allocation but at the trend line. That is, if the average, or trend, over time is rising or declining, it is possible to measure the impact of the portfolio's being invested at a higher or lower allocation than that indicated by the trend line. Of course, there is still no way to distinguish between the sponsor's and the manager's impact.

The perfect allocation

It is possible to compare the results of a portfolio at actual allocation with the results of a portfolio which had perfect (or always wrong) allocation. That is, instead of the standard being the beginning point, the average, or the trend line, the standard would be the results obtained from having always been in the highest returning (or the worst returning) asset category. Unfortunately, this measurement is not particularly useful, since it really measures the policy rather than the deviations from the policy which result from the manager's attempts at timing. That is, in a period in which the stock market did well, portfolios with high percentages in equities would show up well under this score even if the manager's activities in deviating from this policy actually hurt the portfolio's results.

All of the measurements using the indices are affected by the frequency with which the percentage in asset categories is measured and by the stability and magnitude of cash flows. If the portfolio's structure is measured only quarterly and there are large, infrequent cash flows, the measurement of the asset allocation would be impacted. For instance, if a portfolio is normally 50 percent each in stocks and bonds, and the annual contribution (equal to 10 percent of the portfolio) is received on March 28 and temporarily put in cash equivalents, the portfolio's allocation as of March 31 will be distorted, even though the distortion lasts only a few days.

MOVEMENT OF CASH

In order to eliminate the problems associated with viewing the percentage allocation, some people feel that it is better to look at the movements of cash. This can be done in two ways:

looking at purchases and sales and looking at the disposition of new cash in the portfolio.

In applying the first method, if the fund's manager in a given quarter purchased $100 in stocks and sold $30, for a net purchase of $70, this would be regarded as an indication of greater commitment to equities, and hence the subsequent performance of equities would be tracked. Although this idea has merit in principle, there are drawbacks. The first is the difficulty of achieving sufficiently detailed information as to when the purchase took place. In other words, if the typical system of using mid-month cash flows is utilized, it is possible that the fund manager purchased securities early or late in the month, when the situation was more favorable than that suggested by use of the mid-month assumption. Even if the exact timing of equity purchases and sales could be shown, there would still be a need to average purchases on the 5th of the month with sales on the 16th in some intelligible fashion. And if this problem could be solved, there would be the question of how long to track the purchases before deciding that the manager did well or poorly by making them. In other words, should we view the change in the market over the next week, month, year, and so on? Another important limitation of this method is that heavy contributions or withdrawals may dictate making purchases or sales at times when the manager would far prefer to be doing just the opposite.

The second method, tracking new cash added to the portfolio, has two limitations. First, if there is no cash flow activity at all, there is no measurement of market timing even though there may have been significant attempts at timing the market. Further, a contribution may be used to purchase stocks, whereas shortly before or after this purchase other, more significant sales of stocks may have been made. Obviously, the disposition of contributions does not provide a satisfactory basis for measuring timing. An effort might be made to look at the allocation of contributions as well as the impact of purchases and sales in order to determine the impact of both. However, it is not clear how this would be done, nor would doing it solve the problems of measuring the timing of purchases and sales and the appropriate period for viewing their results.

DOLLAR-WEIGHTED VERSUS TIME-WEIGHTED
RETURNS FOR ASSET CATEGORIES

For an asset category (but not for the total portfolio) it is possible to look at the difference between dollar-weighted and time-weighted rates of return. The latter assumes that equal amounts were invested in the asset category during the whole period, whereas the former weights returns by the amount of money invested. Thus, if money were moved in and out of the equity portfolio at propitious times, dollar-weighted returns for equities would exceed time-weighted returns. Conversely, if the timing were poor, dollar-weighted returns would be less than time-weighted returns. The measurement could be carried out for each asset sector, though there appears to be no way of combining the results of various sectors unless the portfolio had no external cash flows. If there were no such cash flows, it would be possible to translate the returns into dollars and then combine the dollars in various sectors into a total portfolio measurement. However, if there were external cash flows, there is no obvious way for calculating the average amount of money impacted by the differences between dollar-weighted and time-weighted returns.

DEVIATION FROM "OPTIMUM" AND
PRESCRIBED POLICIES

It is possible to establish a "market line" which shows the risk/return relationship available in the marketplace over any period. A longer period could be broken up into shorter periods, over which risk/return ratios for stocks, bonds, and cash equivalents are each calculated. The investor's bogey would then become, not the actual return of some hypothetical portfolio, but rather the portfolio with the average risk/return characteristics for the period.

Perhaps the only real method of measuring market timing can be made if the sponsor prescribes a policy and deviations from this policy are measured. In other words, if the sponsor says that the policy will be to invest 70 percent in equities at all times, it is possible to look at the return of a portfolio consisting of market indices invested at the 70 percent level and to compare its return with that of a portfolio invested at the actual quarter-by-quarter allocations of the fund. Although this method is quite satisfactory in principle, in practice few sponsors prescribe policies sufficiently to permit such a measurement.

In summary, the measurement of market timing contributions is extremely complex and no bias-free solution appears to exist. Perhaps the only solution, then, is to choose a measurement which is easy to understand and to openly recognize its limitations, so that no one will be misled. With this viewpoint in mind, comparing the return of hypothetical funds invested in market indices at the average with the return of the actual allocations appears to be a satisfactory approach.

11

Controlling
the investment process

This chapter deals with three subjects: establishing a management review process, conducting meetings with investment
managers, and integrating multiple managers. In some respects this chapter is the most important one in the book. Observation indicates that the vast majority of sponsors have not
established standards, either before or after the fact, as to what
constitutes acceptable results. The consequences of this lack of
standards are extremely significant for funds. First, investment
managers operate in the dark since they do not know how they
will be measured. Second, the sponsor's representatives are
frequently uneasy because they do not know whether results
are acceptable or what they should do about them. Third, in
many cases inadequate managers are maintained and in other
cases good managers are terminated. Finally, when a manager
is replaced, the same difficulties arise in dealing with the new
manager, and consequently the change may be of no benefit.

Hopefully, the following discussion will alleviate these problems for many sponsors.

THE MANAGEMENT REVIEW PROCESS

There is no reason why the general techniques for decision making applicable to other management questions cannot be applied to fund measurement. These techniques prescribe that the manager of an organization:

1. Set objectives.
2. Set allowable tolerances around those objectives.
3. Measure results.
4. Establish responses to results below the allowable tolerances.
5. Carry out the responses.
6. Review objectives, tolerances, and responses.
7. Review the allowable tolerances.
8. Review the responses.

The difficulty of invoking this process in dealing with funds lies in the fact that the achievement of a specific objective, such as earning x percent each year, is frequently overwhelmed by the activities of the marketplace. That is, since a portfolio's return in any given year is dominated by the return of the markets for equities or fixed income securities, very frequently a fund does not meet its objective. In other years the objective may be far exceeded, to the point where the specific objective is dwarfed.

A solution to this problem is the use of a relative objective. Results can be viewed not only absolutely but relative to some sort of benchmark, such as a market index or the performance of other funds. Of course, this only partly alleviates the problem, since a fund which outperforms the market may nonetheless be failing to meet its objective, with disastrous consequences for those relying on the fund.

Since both relative and absolute decisions are important to the control process, it is advisable to have both relative and absolute standards. We will thus analyze both relative and absolute measures and attempt to combine the two into a workable format.

Setting objectives

Absolute measures are aimed primarily at ensuring that the portfolio provides sufficient assets to meet the fund's needs. Let us assume that the fund has a 6 percent actuarial assumption, meaning that the fund's assets must grow by 6 percent per year in order to meet future fund needs. This assumed rate of return would be an appropriate absolute measurement. A slightly different tack can be taken by measuring the number of dollars that is required to meet benefits and then measuring whether the fund has increased by a sufficient number of dollars to meet the fund's needs.

Relative objectives might be established such that the fund's performance is equal to some market average, or the typical portfolio in a universe of funds, or some measure of risk-adjusted return.

Setting allowable tolerances

In determining allowable tolerances, two factors must be considered: the size of the tolerances and the time frame in which it develops. Unfortunately, these two factors are intertwined, since tolerances which might be acceptable over a three-year period might be unacceptable over a six-month or six-year period. The first thing to be done is to decide on the "normal" time horizon, the frequency of measurement, and the allowable tolerances for a normal period. Then tolerances should be established for periods shorter than the normal period.

The normal time horizon. The decision on the time horizon over which to judge a manager can be stated as the following question: "How long must we observe a manager so that we do not allow him to injure the fund excessively during the short run while we attempt to be sure that we do not discharge him for poor short-term performance when he might be a top performer over the long run?" Sometimes the question raised is how long should a manager be retained before it is "fair" to discharge him, but this is really not the issue. The real issue is the interest of the fund, not whether the manager's feelings are being hurt or whether business is being taken away from the manager unjustly.

The most common answer to the question of time horizon is a market cycle. This period is presumably chosen because it allows for differences in risk postures and investment styles. It does not seem to make sense to fire an aggressive equity manager for having poor results over a six-month period if during that period the stock market declined sharply. Continuing with the manager over a complete cycle would allow his selection ability to show up in both good times and bad. As to different investment styles, some equity managers prefer growth stocks, others income stocks; some prefer large companies, others small; and so on. Similarly, bond managers have different styles with respect to coupon and maturity structures. No one would expect the market to favor all of these groups at the same time. Instead, there is a group rotation in each cycle during which different types of stocks and bonds successively take their turns as good or bad performers. Thus, there is considerable merit to the idea of measuring a manager over at least a market cycle.

The second most frequent measurement period is three to five years. However, most of the sponsors which use this time horizon relate it to the length of market cycles. Virtually all sponsors agree that periods of one month, one quarter, or even one year are inadequate measurement periods unless calamitous results befall the portfolio.

The frequency of measurement. The most common frequency of measurement is quarterly, followed by monthly and annual frequencies. Virtually all corporate sponsors review their results quarterly, and some jointly trusteed or endowment funds review their results only annually. Given the logic of the market cycle as a time horizon, quarterly reviews seem appropriate, since this frequency is sufficient to spot disastrous results in time. Monthly reviews seem to be overkill for a sponsor which uses the market cycle measurement period, since the typical market cycle of 53 months would imply reviewing results 53 times before making a decision on the manager.

An interesting anomaly results for sponsors and managers after the manager has been retained for the normal time horizon. At this time the horizon appears to shrink to the period of measurement. Let us assume that the normal time horizon is three years, that the frequency of measurement is quarterly, and that the manager has been employed by the sponsor for three years. In this case the measurement period presumably is moved ahead every quarter to encompass the most recent three years, after which the manager's three-year results are reviewed. Since the results of the quarter to be dropped from the earlier period are known in advance, the only unknown factor in the three-year measurement horizon is the current quarter. Consequently, to some extent the manager who has been employed for the sponsor's time horizon becomes subject to discharge after each quarter's results are measured.

Allowable tolerances within the normal time horizon. For *absolute* measures the sponsor should determine how much damage the fund can tolerate before the sponsor's goals are placed in jeopardy. For instance, the sponsor might decide that if the fund lost 15 percent per year for three years, or if it lost x dollars, the sponsor would be seriously injured. This factor would then be considered in establishing the fund's investment policy, and the allowable tolerance might be set at a loss of 5 percent per year for two years, after which the asset allocation policies and the investment manager's activities would be closely scrutinized. Assuming that the investment manager was aware of this criterion two years earlier, he should have adopted portfolio policies which would have had a high probability of avoiding such losses.

Relative measures could be established such that the fund does as well as the market index or that it is the top two thirds of the funds in an appropriate comparative universe. A custom or tailored market index could be established reflecting the fund's policies. Thus, if a fund has a long-term goal of being 60 percent in equities and 40 percent in bonds, the appropriate market index would be 60 percent of the return of an equity index plus 40 percent of the return of a fixed income index. The difficulty of using market indices is that they sometimes act very differently from the average portfolio. It would be difficult to justify discharging a manager for failing to equal the market index in a period such as the five years ended 1977, when approximately 85 percent of equity fund managers failed to meet this objective.

A combined relative and absolute measure is probably the most logical approach. It does not seem appropriate to fire a manager who is performing better than most other managers, even though market conditions are so bad that the fund falls far short of its objective. Conversely, if a fund greatly exceeds its objective in a favorable market environment, but the manager ranks near the bottom in performance as compared to other managers, his position should be reviewed. The approach favored here is to combine absolute and relative measures, as follows.

Absolute measures should be used in determining the fund's policy. That is, the maximum damage which the fund can tolerate should be calculated, and an investment or risk policy chosen which makes it highly unlikely that the damage will be incurred. Each year both the estimate of the maximum allowable damage and the investment policy for avoiding this result should be recalculated. If the fund's asset base has changed sufficiently, or if the sponsor's needs have changed enough, the risk policy should be adjusted.

Relative objectives are appropriate for measuring the manager as opposed to the policy. That is, it is probably desirable to view the market as being substantially unpredictable, and consequently the broad swings which impact fund results so dramatically should be viewed as beyond the manager's control. This makes it difficult to hold the manager responsible for absolute results. Hence the investment policy was established with absolute results in mind. However, it is entirely plausible to measure the results of the manager against those of other managers to judge whether the performance of the manager is adequate to justify continuing the use of his services. Chapter 7 provides appropriate measurements for comparing investment performance. Thus, we must only decide here how bad the manager's performance must be in order to justify discontinuing his services. Although everyone would like a manager to perform in the top percentiles, it must be recognized that the odds are against a manager's being above average for a long period. However, it is also unlikely that a qualified manager will remain in the bottom third of comparable managers for a full measurement horizon, so logically performance below the 60th or 70th percentile can be viewed as inadequate to justify continuing with a manager unless contrary reasons prevail.

The distinction between using absolute and relative objectives, respectively, for evaluating policies and managers appears to be quite appropriate, with one exception. That exception is the manager who views himself as being able to time the market. Such a manager will want broad latitude both in establishing policies and in selecting securities. Fortunately, this does not present a problem for the sponsor. If the manager is a successful market timer, he will do well relative to other funds and he will also have excellent absolute results, never coming anywhere near the poor results which would dictate a change in investment policy. On the other hand, if the manager were extremely unsuccessful at market timing, he would show up poorly in both relative and absolute terms. In utilizing such a manager, the sponsor must exercise care, since the fund will lack safeguards (i.e., an investment policy which limits asset allocation) to protect it when markets move adversely. Consequently, the sponsor should be especially careful in monitoring the manager's activities during bear markets.

Responses during time periods shorter than the normal time horizon. Measurements should be made more frequently than the normal measurement horizon when the sponsor has to be alert to a management organization which has been delivering extremely poor results. Absolute results which should push the sponsor toward a serious review of the manager's activities before the normal time horizon would include absolute declines twice that of the allowable rate. That is, if it were allowable to lose 10 percent per year for two years, certainly losing 20 percent in one year should be of concern. For relative results, performance below the 80th percentile for a one-year period should encourage the sponsor to investigate any changes in the manager's structure or style, as well as the reasons for having chosen the particular manager.

Responding to results below allowable tolerances

When *absolute* results fall below the standard established in advance, it is necessary to decide whether the unsatisfactory results are due to market conditions or to the activity of the investment manager, since the action to be taken differs in each case. This distinction can be made by seeing what returns the fund would have achieved if it had invested in the market or if it had invested with the average manager at the fund's policy allocations and then comparing those results with the results actually received. Assume that the risk policy is to be 60 percent in equities and 40 percent in bonds. Further assume that during this period the average equity fund returned −30 percent and the average bond fund returned −2.5 percent. As can be seen in Exhibit 11–1, a fund achieving average results in equities and bonds and having our policy mix of 60 percent equities would have returned −19 percent. It is now possible to analyze the three cases where actual results could be below

EXHIBIT 11–1

Deciding whether unacceptably low returns are due to the manager or the risk policy.

Equity/bond risk policy: 60/40
Return of average equity fund: −30 percent
Return of average bond fund: −2.5 percent
Return of the total portfolio which had average returns in both equities and bonds and had our risk policy:

$$0.6 \times -30\% = -18\%$$
$$0.4 \times -2.5\% = - \ 1\%$$
$$-19\%$$

The three cases where actual results are below acceptable are:

A.

5% total shortfall

$\left\{\begin{array}{l}\text{Minimum acceptable return} \\ \text{"Average" fund with our} \\ \quad \text{policy} \\ \text{Actual results}\end{array}\right.$

−15% } 4% shortfall due to policy

−19%] 1% shortfall due to
−20% } manager

B.

4% shortfall due to policy

$\left\{\begin{array}{l}\text{Minimum acceptable return} \\ \text{Actual results} \\ \text{"Average" fund with our} \\ \quad \text{policy}\end{array}\right.$

−15%] 3% total
−18% } shortfall

−19% } 1% gain due to manager

C.

3% shortfall due to manager

$\left\{\begin{array}{l}\text{"Average" fund with our} \\ \quad \text{policy} \\ \text{Minimum acceptable return} \\ \text{Actual results}\end{array}\right.$

−19% } 1% gain due to policy

−20%] 2% total
−22% } shortfall

minimum acceptable returns and attribute the arising shortfall to either the policy or the manager.

If actual results fall below the "average" fund with our policy, the manager has subtracted from performance. This is because the manager must have underperformed the "average" fund in equities or bonds, or in market timing, in order for the fund to have underperformed the "average." If the results of the "average" fund with our policy fall below minimum acceptable returns, then the policy is a reason for the shortfall. This is because we assume that, if we have chosen the policy properly, average managers using our policy will not fall below minimum acceptable returns.

In case A, actual results were below the minimum acceptable return of −15 percent, leading to a total shortfall of 5 percentage points. Since "average" results were below the minimum acceptable return, a shortfall exists due to policy, in this instance 4 percentage points. Since actual results were below "average" results, the manager provided an additional shortfall, one percentage point.

A similar analysis can be made for case B and case C, where actual results also fell below minimum acceptable results.

If the problem is with the policy, then reassessment must be made of the choice of policy and of any changes in the structure of the marketplace. If it is assumed that no change occurred in the structure of the investment marketplace, then a decision must be reached as to whether the impairment of the fund's assets has been so great that it is no longer prudent to employ a policy whose risks are as high as those which led to the unsuccessful results. This procedure is not without its risks, however, for two reasons. First, when the market is low, it is easy to become discouraged and to view the future with pessimism. This might cause a conservative policy to be chosen at the worst time in the market cycle. It is not easy to determine whether a structural change has occurred within the market, such that the return or risk expectations which were used to create the original policy must now be rejected in favor of less optimistic ones. During bear markets there is always a tendency to assume that what is being witnessed is something new, whereas bear markets have occurred every 3 or 4 years for the last 50. Nonetheless, the procedure described above is the relevant procedure for making a decision.

Although not totally satisfying, that procedure is at least a rational way of reviewing investment results, and since it has a defensible methodology it is likely to achieve better results than those currently employed by many fund sponsors. Nonetheless, the sponsor is not relieved of the difficult assignment of determining whether it is appropriate to become more conservative on a long-term basis after having witnessed a severe decline in assets, despite being fully aware that the decline may be reversed dramatically in the ensuing six months to two years.

If the manager fails to meet *relative* standards of performance, or if the preceding analysis indicates that the manager rather than the policy is the source of the fund's unsatisfactory results, then the manager rather than the policy should be reviewed in detail. Through the performance measurement techniques described in Chapters 6 through 10, it will be possible to determine whether the shortfall is within the equities or fixed income area and whether it arose from poor security selection or timing or from asset volatility. Although difficulties with the results of a manager can presumably be addressed by replacing the manager, this can be an expensive and fruitless process. Thus, it is helpful to consider ways in which such difficulties can be corrected while still retaining the manager.

If securities selection is at fault, it is possible to achieve enhanced results by minimizing selection through increasing diversification. That is, the more securities the fund owns, the less chance there is of making serious errors in choosing them. If market timing is leading to poor results, this can be corrected by attempting to keep the portfolio near the guideline asset allocations. Thus, if the policy is to be 60 percent in equities, the portfolio can be "rebalanced" each quarter or month to keep within close tolerance of this goal. If the volatility of each asset category is causing unacceptable results (presumably because of an aggressive policy during a declining market), this can be the result of either the sponsor's or the investment manager's choice. It is possible that a choice for the asset category of assets with a volatility significantly different from that of the market may be frustrating the overall asset allocation policy. That is, if the fund intends to be 60 percent in equities, it is important to know whether the equities owned are to be extremely aggressive or extremely conservative. This factor should be incorporated into the overall policy decision, and it should be treated in the same way as the policy determining the allocation between stocks and bonds.

Carrying out responses

In all phases of the review process a practice of openness with the investment manager is urgently required. Because of his familiarity with investment markets he may be able to make important contributions to any adjustments of the risk policy. Also, if performance results are inadequate, the manager should be apprised periodically of the sponsor's awareness of the shortcoming (if the guidelines have been sufficiently well communicated to the manager, he will already be fully aware that there has been a shortfall).

Reviewing objectives, tolerances, and responses

As with any management process, it is necessary to review investment procedures and criteria periodically to ensure that they are still relevant. This process should be carried out at least annually, should receive endorsement from the highest level in the organization, and should be communicated to all parties having an impact on the success of the fund.

CONDUCTING THE REVIEW MEETING

Since most of the contact between the sponsor and the manager will occur during periodic review meetings, it is vital to the control process that these meetings be as informative as possible. Typically, this is not the case.

Most meetings between sponsors and investment managers consist of a review of economic and market forecasts and comments on the purchases and sales made in the portfolio since the last meeting. These meetings are almost always controlled by the investment manager, with the sponsor's representatives listening attentively and occasionally asking questions. Too frequently the meetings, though pleasant and perhaps interesting, are unsatisfying and insubstantive. With relatively little effort on the part of the sponsor, significant increases in the usefulness of the meetings can be achieved.

The portfolio structure versus the investment policy. The first point of business at each meeting between the client and an investment manager should be to review how the portfolio is structured in relation to the client's needs, how those needs may have changed, and anything which the investment manager sees as indicating that either the client's needs or the portfolio's structure in response to those needs may have changed. In other words, the fund's basic investment policies should be discussed at each meeting, with all of the investment policies described at the end of Chapter 3 being at least touched on. The manager should describe any changes in this structure that have taken place since the last meeting.

The portfolio structure versus economic and market forecasts. After the proper structuring of the portfolio relative to the client's long-term objective has been ensured, the next major question is to what extent the portfolio is consistent with the investment manager's economic and market observations. This area is fairly tangible, and sponsors should press hard to be sure that the portfolio manager's activities "make sense." It is surprising how frequently there can be an inconsistency between the way in which a portfolio is structured and the manager's view of the future market environment. The most classic example would be a manager who was bearish on stocks or bonds but was adding them to his portfolio. A sponsor should not tolerate such apparent inconsistencies without evidence that some other factor is making it appropriate for the manager to act opposite to his forecasts. For instance, a manager might indicate that his economic and stock market forecasts suggest that the stock market will be noticeably lower 12 months hence, but that he is buying a particular issue because it is extremely undervalued relative to new developments which have occurred. In view of his forecasts this manager might want to consider selling other, less undervalued stocks in order to maintain an appropriate percentage in equities without missing the opportunity presented by the especially undervalued stock.

Also deserving of attention is a situation in which the manager has been increasing his risk exposure in bonds, for instance by extending maturities, while decreasing his percentage in equities. In recent years inflation and interest rates have dominated the environment for both stocks and bonds, so normally one would expect an investment manager to be bearish or bullish on both at the same time. However, these two markets need not be moving in tandem, and it is possible for one to be relatively undervalued with respect to the other. In any event, the sponsor should inquire into the activities of the manager if this policy has been pursued.

The manager's measurement standards for determining his policy. The sponsor should be familiar with the variables that the manager is using to make decisions on the investment outlook. For instance, if the manager says that "long-term bonds will continue to do poorly," the sponsor should be aware of what category of long-term bonds the manager is talking about—all bonds, ten-year maturities, governments, corporates? A sponsor should also receive from the manager or from other sources information on historical yields, so that it can monitor the trend which is important to the investment manager. In no sense should the sponsor second-guess the manager, but if the manager is saying that the trend of interest rates is down and the sponsor's data show them to be up, then there is a need for further communication.

The manager's basis for changing his policy. The investment manager should be pursuing a policy, but he should also have a predetermined standard for determining when that policy is wrong. In other words, if he is strongly bullish on the stock market, there must be some reason for this bullishness and some criteria which would indicate that this view was wrong. This is perhaps the area in which managers are the weakest and fund sponsors are most in the dark. A manager who was bearish because interest rates were rising, and consequently had a large cash position, should have some idea of what would be required to reverse his bearishness. It is easy for a manager to be lulled into a mistaken sense of security by having been right for a long period of time, only to find that the marketplace reverses itself, thus leaving the fund inappropriately structured for the coming market move. If, for instance, the manager has been bearish because of rising interest rates, a sponsor should be aware of the manager's criteria for changing this view. These criteria might include the volume of business loans (since a slackening of loan demand typically leads to lower interest rates), short-term interest rates (which typically lead long-term rates), Federal Reserve policy, and so on.

Measuring the manager's previous estimates.   It is advisable for the sponsor to keep a record of the manager's predictions in order to measure his record, understand his thought processes, and see how those thought processes evolve. Certainly no one expects an investment manager to be a perfect predictor of the future, yet it does not seem to make much sense to have one who is excessively imperfect. The sponsor must try not to emphasize all of the manager's errors, of which there will be many in the area of forecasting. Of particular interest is the process by which a manager adjusts portfolios as new information suggests that past forecasts were in error. In many respects this is the acid test of an investor.

Although it is extremely important to follow the approach listed above, second-guessing must be avoided and the manager must be convinced that, though you are following his analysis, you are not expecting him to defend his previous forecasts. Rather, you are expecting him to make rational decisions in a rational way and to communicate those decisions to you. The worst thing that can happen is for a manager to feel that he must stay with a previous policy, even though he now thinks it is wrong, because he will come under more fire from the sponsor for changing his mind than for losing money with a bad policy. Although the sponsor must understand what the manager is doing, the sponsor must also make it clear to the manager that the main responsibility is with the manager and that it is perfectly appropriate to change one's mind when new facts become available.

Setting objectives to be accomplished by the next meeting.   As with any continuing process, at the end of the review meeting a summary should be made of what the meeting accomplished and of the objective to be accomplished prior to the next meeting. Further, specific responsibilities should be assigned, so that there is no doubt in anyone's mind as to what is to be done, who is to do it, and when it is to be done. As a final step, an approximate date for the next meeting should be established, so that the review process continues in an orderly fashion rather than languishing.

INTEGRATING MULTIPLE INVESTMENT MANAGERS

Controlling the investment management process is considerably more difficult for sponsors which have multiple investment managers. Further, it is more expensive to have multiple managers than to have a single manager. This is because virtually all investment managers charge a declining fee based on asset size. In addition, operating costs tend to be higher with multiple managers because multiple accounting and custodial systems are necessary and because the sponsor must deal with several groups rather than one. Thus, it is extremely important that sponsors carefully choose their managers and structure the way in which the managers are integrated and controlled. This chapter reviews the reasons for having multiple managers, when to consider adding a second manager, how to account for split portfolios, the criteria for deciding how to allocate new money among managers, the monitoring of multiple managers, and ways for keeping the activities of one manager from offsetting those of other managers.

Reasons for having multiple managers. Three reasons for having multiple managers can be identified—for specialization, in order to diversify styles, and for diversification. Clearly, some managers have *special skills* which other managers do not have. For instance, some managers specialize in stocks, whereas others specialize in bonds. Increasingly, sponsors have come to feel that they are unlikely to find the best bond manager and the best stock manager within the same firm, so they seek organizations which specialize in one asset category or another.

Diversification of styles is a second goal sought by sponsors which use multiple managers. Assume for a moment that half of all stocks are low yielding growth companies, whereas the balance are high yielding concerns with slow growth. A sponsor might wish to have representation in the entire market, but to own the best growth stocks and the best income stocks, and consequently it chooses one manager in each category.

The third goal, *pure diversification,* is indicated by the case in which managers are chosen for no particular reason other than that they are "good" managers, and it is desirable to have more than one manager in case a manager makes a large error.

When sponsor should consider multiple managers. There is very little tangible basis for deciding at what point, if any, a fund is better off being split among multiple managers instead of continuing to be invested solely with one manager. The most distinguishable factor is the desire for specialized talent, and this relates to the abilities of the current manager. In other words, if the current manager is unsuccessful in stocks but successful in bonds, the sponsor will tend to look to a specialty stock manager. Beyond such individual factors, most sponsors make decisions of this kind intuitively, based on the preferences of trustees or administrators. It is rare for an investment manager to indicate to a sponsor that a fund's assets have grown so large that the manager would prefer to have some of them diverted to other managers, though extremely large sponsors sometimes find small managers who will accept only relatively small amounts of money. At the other end of the spectrum, some managers are unwilling to accept accounts which are below certain minimum sizes. Although the acceptable minimum varies greatly it seems to be increasing, and it is frequently in the $5 million to $10 million range for all but the smallest investment managers. If a manager is willing to use commingled funds, almost no size is too small to be acceptable to the manager. Of course, this presumes that a commingled fund is available to the investment manager, which is true for most banks and not true for independent investment advisers.

Criteria for allocating new money among multiple managers. Just as there is no firm basis for deciding when to have multiple managers, so there is no prescribed formula for deciding how to allocate new contributions among existing managers. Such allocations may be made equally, proportionally, according to performance, in order to maintain a risk policy, by funding a new manager, intuitively, to the most undervalued portfolio, and so on. Perhaps the simplest way to allocate new money is to give each manager an *equal* amount. However, this changes the proportions allocated among the managers (which may or may not be desirable). In order to keep the *proportions* the same each manager can be given his pro rata share. It is also possible to divide new money by *performance*. Here there are two theories: give the money to the manager who has performed best or give it to the manager who has performed worst. The former theory suggests that the manager who has done a good job will continue to do well, or at least that the sponsors odds are better if it sticks with the manager who has done well than if it goes with the manager who has done poorly. The contrary view is that the market moves in cycles and that the manager who has done well recently probably owes his success to the fact that the recent market cycle favored his investment philosophy. Since market cycles change, it is advisable to give the money to the manager who has done worst, since his poor performance was due to his participation in an unfavored sector of the market, though, hopefully, this sector will be more favored in the coming months. New money can also be allocated *to maintain a risk policy*, such as the percentage in equities. If the policy is to be 60 percent in stocks and 40 percent in bonds, it makes sense to allocate 60 percent of new money to equity managers and 40 percent to fixed income managers. Further, it is possible to allocate contributions to a *new manager*. Sponsors willing to make market judgements can find the manager whose portfolio *style or asset category is most undervalued*. The last basis—*intuitive*—suggests that a number of factors should be weighed and that in an informal way it should be decided where to place the new money. This is probably the way most new money is moved among managers.

The reverse process, finding a source for liquidating securities when the sponsor needs money from the fund, also presents problems. The criteria for allocating new money are also applicable to removing money. One caution is in order. During declining markets it is tempting to remove cash from the manager with the largest cash position. This may, in effect, penalize the manager who has been most successful in predicting the market's decline, and it may damage the fund by reducing the importance of the most successful manager.

Accounting for multiple managers. The use of multiple managers creates difficulties in accounting for assets and transactions. Although this problem is simple conceptually, the lack of uniform reporting can be a source of great frustration to a sponsor which is relying on this information for decision-making purposes. Difficulties arise in five areas: the information included in reports, the periods covered, comparisons, definitions, and the timing of the receipt of reports. It is important that the *information included* be *consistent*, so that, for instance, all managers are reporting on equity and bond results as well as total portfolio returns. The *period covered* should also be consistent. If one manager is reporting on a moving one-year basis, whereas another manager is reporting on a "year-to-date" method, it is not possible to compare the managers. The third area, *comparisons*, can also be a source of frustration. There should be uniformity in the market indices utilized and uniform comparative universes. If one manager uses the Dow Jones average and another manager uses the S&P, or if one manager uses commingled fund comparisons and another manager uses separately managed funds, the sponsor's analytical task will be complicated. It is also necessary that consistent *definitions* of terms be utilized by all managers or that adjustments in definitions be made. For instance, the measurement of fixed income performance should include or exclude accrued interest consistently, and convertible securities should be consistently defined as equities, bonds, or a separate category. Also, calculation formulas should be uniform, particularly for time-weighted returns, betas, volatility, and so on. Finally, it is helpful for the *timing* of *reports* to be such that information on all fund managers is received at approximately the same time in order to simplify analysis.

There are three possible solutions to the problem of consistent accounting for multiple managers. The first, and the simplest, is to ask each manager to supply a summary page in a predetermined format. In this way the sponsor can determine what information is provided, the period being measured, and, to a certain extent, the comparisons, the definitions, and the timing. In addition, this enables the sponsor to determine the format rather than have an outside party make this decision. A sample format is given in Exhibit 11–2. The second alternative is to use outside consultant or monitoring firms which have an established format for use on all managers. Finally, a number of master trust custodial organizations provide uniform accounting facilities for multiply managed portfolios.

Monitoring multiple managers. Sponsors with multiple managers will probably want to measure each individual investment manager as well as the portfolio as a whole. As with

EXHIBIT 11-2
Sample format for summary sheet to be completed by each investment manager

Rates of return

	Quarter ending 12/78		Year ending 12/78		Cumulative period 12/73–12/78		
	Return	*Rank*	*Return*	*Rank*	*Cumulative return*	*Annual equivalent return*	*Rank*
Total portfolio ...	0.1	2	6.9	15	1.6	0.3	95
Equities	−5.0	51	5.6	68	−12.1	−2.5	93
S&P 500	−4.9	49	6.6	58	23.8	4.4	28
Bonds	2.2	1	7.8	1	40.4	7.0	12
ML Bond Index	−1.4	51	1.2	44	31.9	5.7	56
U.S. Treasury bills	2.2		7.6		36.8	6.5	

Asset allocation (as of 12/78)

	Value ($000)	Percentage of portfolio	Rank
Equities	4,433	28.2	85
Bonds	10,038	63.8	5
Cash and equivalents	1,267	8.0	63
Other assets.........................	0	0.0	
Total portfolio value	15,738	100.0	

Courtesy of Merrill Lynch.

the measurement of an individual portfolio, the key factors to be considered are the rates of return, risk, diversification, and the manager's contribution. Each of these factors can be looked at separately and in comparison to the market or other portfolios. The principal risk measurement that should be considered is the percentage in equities. For the overall fund this amount will depend not only on how each manager raises or lowers his exposure to the stock market but also on what the market does. Since stocks are more volatile than bonds, a rise in the stock market increases the percentage in equities. The risk level of individual sectors, such as the beta of the equity portfolio, should also be considered. Since diversification is an important reason why many sponsors have multiple managers, it makes sense to measure the diversification levels of the individual parts of the portfolio as well as the diversification level of the portfolio as a whole. Finally, the contribution that each manager makes to the portfolio through securities selection and timing should be considered.

It would be useful to be able to determine each manager's contribution to the portfolio rate of return. However, this is not possible because of movements of cash both within sectors and from outside the portfolio. An alternative might be to perform a regression analysis (see Chapter 9 and Appendix B) of the rates of return of each investment manager's portfolio against those of the composite portfolio for the entire fund. In this way it would be possible to see which managers were above or below the fund average in various measurements. However, though this is not conceptually difficult, it requires a fair amount of special effort. Most of this information can be obtained by looking at how the fund and each investment manager's section performed against the market rather than against the composite portfolio.

Interrelationships among multiple managers. One of the most frustrating aspects of having multiple managers is the knowledge that their activities tend to be offsetting. That is, manager A is increasing the percentage in equities while manager B is decreasing it, or manager C may even be buying General Motors stock while manager D is selling it. Frustrating as this may be, it is not clear what should be done about it. Sponsors do not want to see managers B and D offsetting managers A and C, except that if B and D happen to be right, this is beneficial to the portfolio. Since there is no way of knowing which manager is correct, the sponsor cannot interfere to halt the incorrect trade. Sponsors which are concerned about this problem can do a number of things: use specialists, have mutually exclusive security lists, require the managers to work as a team, and consider market inventory funds. If A manages equities and B manages bonds, it does not seem likely that the actions of these managers will offset each other. Similarly, if growth stocks are being managed by one manager and income stocks by another, the portfolios of these managers will tend to be independent. Carrying this idea to an extreme, the managers could be assigned mutually exclusive security lists. For example, one manager could be limited to stocks A through L and another manager to stocks M through Z. Or, more logically, the two managers might themselves divide up the universe of stocks somehow, say by each taking half of the stocks in each industry or half of the industries. In all of these cases it is necessary for some control to be imposed as to the percentage in equities, or this policy decision will end up being made as a residual or leftover decision rather than through conscious choice.

At least one fund sponsor has decided that its managers should work as a team rather than as individuals working independently or even competitively. In this case the managers meet with the sponsor, discuss policies, and establish strategies which are presumably in the interest of the sponsor and the fund. A key to the success of this method is the adoption of a payment procedure which does not penalize a manager for suggesting that his particular area of specialty is currently overvalued and that assets should therefore be taken away from him. Another problem with this method is suggested by the fact that few investment committees seem to have demonstrated greater investment ability than have individuals operating on their own. Due to the unfortunate tendency toward the herd instinct in all human affairs, including investing, this caution must be taken seriously.

One imaginative solution to the problem is the market inventory fund (see Chapter 5). The MIF recognizes the problem of offsetting transactions and attempts to save the transaction costs associated with them. This is accomplished by establishing an index, or market, fund which trades at no cost with the investment managers. If the operator of the inventory fund feels that it can accommodate an additional 1,000 shares of XYZ without overweighting in this industry or that company, it purchases the 1,000 shares from a manager who has expressed a desire to sell the 1,000 shares. Clearly, this saves the transaction costs, though a question arises as to the benefit received by the fund, regardless of whether XYZ shares rise or fall.

Some investors have suggested, perhaps tongue in check, that there is one area in which it would be advisable to have managers offset one another's actions. In this argument it is claimed that most managers find it easier to buy securities than to sell them. Therefore, a sponsor would do well to have one investment manager making purchase decisions and another making sell decisions. It is claimed that investors have become emotionally involved with the securities which they have recommended and purchased on behalf of their clients and that they have tended to fall in love with them or they have become so used to defending them to clients that they find it impossible to sell them. This difficulty can be avoided by having a completely independent organization review the reasons for purchasing securities and giving it full discretion to sell them. Although most sponsors would find this an impractical method of operation, it is nonetheless an interesting way of trying to deal with the frequently discussed but seldom solved problem of how to get investment managers to sell securities at the proper time.

In summary, the control process utilized by a sponsor has significant impact on the fund's success in supporting the organization. By carefully managing the review process, conducting meetings with investment managers, and integrating multiple managers, the control process can be made both comprehensive and simple. In this way the likelihood of the fund's success is greatly enhanced and all of the parties concerned will be much more comfortable about the way in which the fund is being administered.

12

Prudence in managing the manager:
Fraud, speculation, and breach of fiduciary responsibility

"It is always easier to believe than to deny.
Our minds are naturally affirmative." [1]

The sponsor must always keep in mind that it has control over an enormous amount of money, in the form of the fund, which, peculiarly, it has responsibility for but which does not belong to it. To make matters worse, the sponsor may not be technically qualified to make the decisions about the fund which practical necessity requires it to make, and there is substantial liability to the sponsor and some of its key employees for failure to conform properly. Therefore, it is necessary that the sponsor understand and recognize the forces which might unnecessarily "separate" the fund from its assets. These forces are fraud, speculation, and breach of fiduciary responsibility.

---

[1] John Burroughs, "The Light of Day," from *The Modern Skeptic*.

FRAUD

The available evidence indicates that it is relatively rare for pension funds to be defrauded. However, it is desirable to consider the possibilities of fraud, so that the sponsor can be aware of them. Perhaps the greatest potential losses might come from the massive misappropriation of securities. Since most funds do not physically hold securities, this problem exists more for the custodian than for the fund, but if securities were stolen from a custodian which did not have sufficient assets or insurance to cover the loss, obviously the fund could lose money. Increasingly, as securities exist only as electronic bookkeeping entries, the opportunity for physically stealing securities becomes almost nonexistent. However, the potential for computer fraud involving the misappropriation of securities may be as great as the previous potential for stealing securities.

A second area of potential fraud is the investment of fund assets at inflated prices or sale at below market value in non-arm's-length transactions. At least two instances of this type of fraud can be cited. One labor union fund invested in real estate mortgages which were based on overvaluation of the underlying asset. Thus, in the case of bankruptcy there was insufficient equity in the real estate to protect the fund. In another case stocks were bought at prices slightly in excess of the prevailing market price, with the differential illegally shared between brokerage firm and the securities trader at the institution managing the pension funds.

A third potential area of fraud is the deployment of brokerage commissions to brokers who may provide services to representatives of the investment manager or the fund sponsor rather than the fund. Given that commission rates are now negotiated, additional surveillance is needed by the sponsor in order to ensure that commission dollars are spent appropriately.

A final potential area of abuse is the purchase of unnecessary services or excessively priced useful services. Again, though there have been extremely few instances of abuse, it is only sensible for the sponsor to be aware of ways in which people might take unfair advantage of the fund.

SPECULATION

For every dollar that is lost to pension funds through fraud, perhaps $10,000 will be lost through speculation. Speculation is probably as old as investing itself, and it is undoubtedly rooted in certain aspects of the human psyche which cause people to do what everyone else is doing and to seek something for nothing. Famous speculative binges of the past include the tulip bulb boom in Holland and the South Sea bubble in England. In the decade prior to 1929 there was tremendous speculation in commodity prices, stock prices, and Florida land prices. One measure of speculation in the stock market is the level of price/earnings ratios. Exhibit 12–1 shows this relationship for Standard & Poor's Industrials from 1929 to 1979. It can be seen that whenever price/earnings ratios rose above 20, the odds of a market decline increased greatly. Conversely, when price/earnings ratios declined below ten, the odds favored a market rise. Exhibit 12–2 shows median price/earnings ratios for companies on the more speculative American Stock Ex-

EXHIBIT 12–1

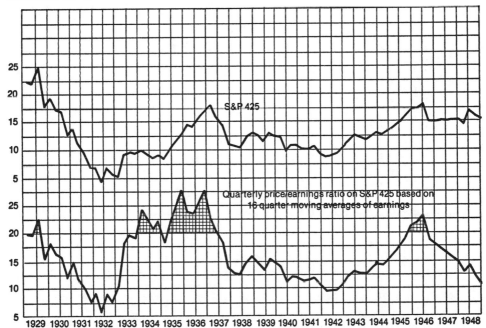

EXHIBIT 12–1 (*continued*)

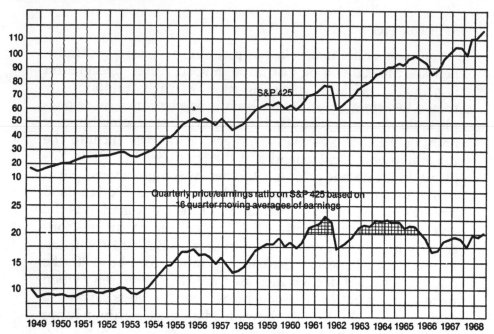

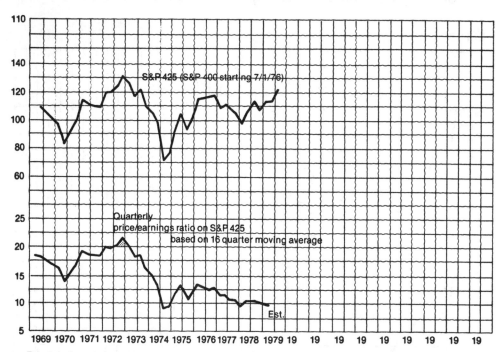

Price/earnings ratios prior to 1940 based on yearly earnings and quarterly price index.
Source: Merrill Lynch.

EXHIBIT 12–2

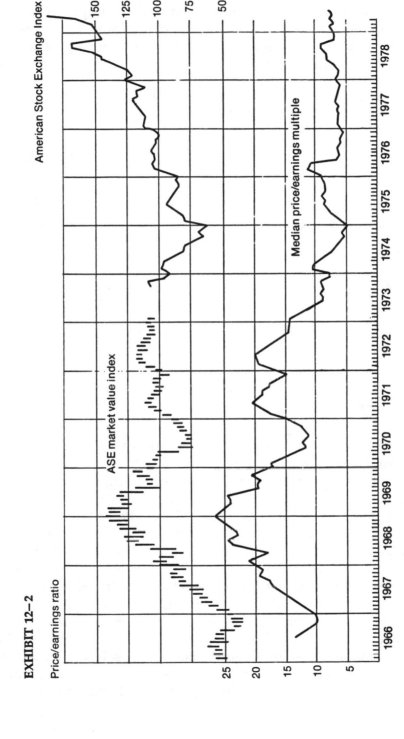

change. It can be seen that price/earnings multiples rose from 10 in 1966 to over 25 in 1968, to be followed by a six-year decline to 5. This represented a very substantial boom-and-bust to investors. Exhibit 12–3 is a price index of six companies

EXHIBIT 12–3
Price index of six gambling stocks

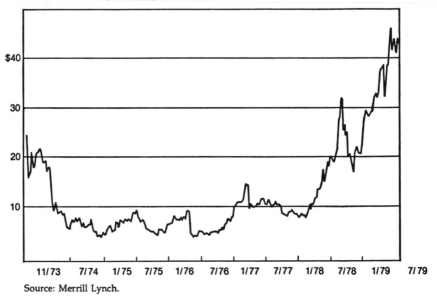

Source: Merrill Lynch.

with interests or prospective interests in gambling casinos. This group rose in price almost tenfold from 1976 to 1979.

Speculation can occur in high-quality securities as well as in more aggressive securities. It is difficult to believe the results one sees in Exhibit 12–4, which shows the Standard & Poor's Utility Index from 1926 to the present. This index exceeded the value of 80 in the 1929 boom, and it has not reached this point since. From the level of 10 in the early 1940s it rose again to about 75, only to decline to the level of 30 in 1974.

Although speculation in individual securities is an everyday occurrence, it is fascinating to look at the case of sugar, a commodity which moved far above any historical or rational value and then declined to its previous level. This is seen in Exhibit 12–5, where the price of sugar presents one of the greatest examples in recent years of a speculative boom-and-bust.

EXHIBIT 12–4

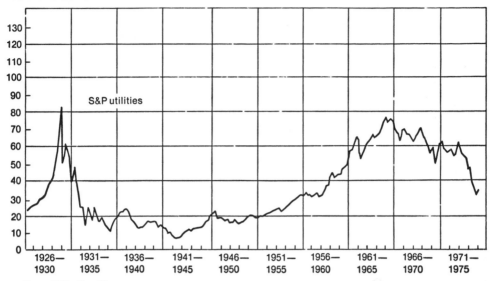

S&P utilities

Base: 1941–43 = 10.
Source: Standard & Poor's Corporation.

It is admittedly difficult to distinguish between speculation and investment. Some cynics would suggest that an investment was a speculation if the investor lost but an investment if he succeeded. Presumably the courts look at the reasoning process which went into recommending the investment rather than the results. Given sound business judgment behind the investment decision, no conflicts of interest, an adequately diversified portfolio, and appropriately addressed liquidity needs, the investor can feel confident that he is in fact investing rather than speculating.

Protection against speculation requires exercising common sense, which is perhaps the most valuable asset that any investor or any investment manager can have. The sponsor watching over investment managers must attempt to understand what its managers are doing and to view those activities as objectively as possible. He must constantly ask the question "Does this make sense?" Relative valuation yardsticks should be kept of such broad investment factors as stock market levels, price/earnings ratios (see Exhibits 12–1 and 12–2) and interest rate

EXHIBIT 12–5
Average price of raw cane sugar
Cents per pound

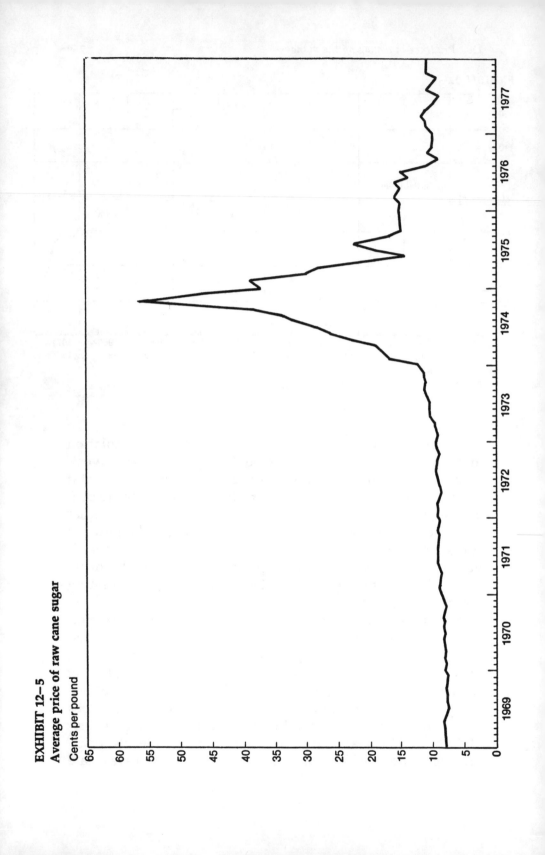

EXHIBIT 12–6
Long-term bond yields: Quarterly averages
Percent per annum

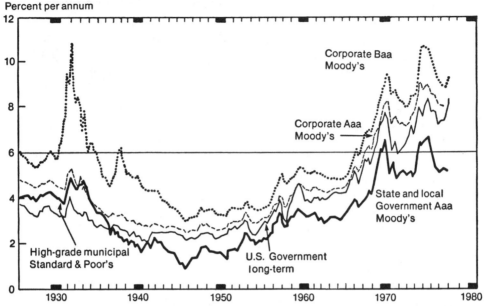

levels (Exhibit 12–6). It is unrealistic to expect the future to be exactly like the past, but clearly there is something to be learned from studying past trends.

BREACH OF FIDUCIARY RESPONSIBILITY

In order to understand where abuses of fiduciary responsibility may arise and how the government views them, it is interesting to note the suits that have been filed by private individuals and by the government, principally the secretary of labor. Two areas of particular interest are imprudence in investing that results from poor judgment and from conflicts of interest. A brief review of cases on these topics appears below.

Imprudent investment that resulted from poor judgment

Inadequate diversification and speculation. A number of court cases have provided insight into the important but imprecisely defined section of ERISA which requires trustees to act in the interest of participants and beneficiaries "with the care, skill, prudence, and diligence" of a prudent, knowledgeable man and "by diversifying the investments of the plan so as to minimize the risk of large losses, unless under the circumstances it is clearly prudent not to do so." [Section 404(B).]

The case of *Ray Marshall, Secretary of the U.S. Department of Labor* v. *Teamsters Local 282 Pension Trust Fund* is of interest because it provides some authority on two areas, speculation and lack of diversification. In this case the secretary of labor brought action to stop the trustees of a pension fund from making a proposed loan. The fund had intended to lend $20 million under a construction-permanent mortgage to finance a hotel and gambling casino in Las Vegas. The fund had assets of $55 million, which was less than its actuarial liabilities. Further, its current contributions were less than its current actuarial costs. The loan could not be made because the court ruled that the project was excessively risky, that the proposed mortgage rate of 9¾ percent was only fractionally above that carried by "Ginnie Mae" securities guaranteed by the U.S. government, and that the loan represented too large a portion of the fund's assets.

Expected return inadequate relative to risk. In *Marshall* v. *Fitzsimmons et al.*, the secretary of labor sued various trustees and related parties of the Central States Teamsters' Pension Fund for, among other things, making a $30 million loan secured by a casino in Las Vegas. The interest rate was deemed inadequate relative to the risk taken.

Failure to collect loans in default. In *Marshall* v. *Wilson et al.* and *Marshall* v. *Fitzsimmons et al.*, the secretary of labor filed suit under ERISA, claiming that the trustees had not taken action to collect loans in default.

The case of *Marshall* v. *Fitzsimmons et al.* contains other charges which might be viewed as representing poor judgment in the investment area. These include:

Failure to obtain an independent and reliable appraisal of properties prior to making a loan.

Failure to obtain sufficient reliable information regarding the financial condition of the borrower before the loan was made and before granting a moratorium on payments following a delinquency in receipt of interest.

Failure to enforce the right of the plan to the assignment of rents when interest payments were delinquent.

Failure to monitor the borrower's performance adequately under the terms of the loan agreement.

Failure to cease making loans when the value of the security and the likelihood of repayment were such that further disbursements were imprudent.

Making a loan to a cable TV company without adequately assessing the economic feasibility of the operation.

Failure to pursue the guarantor of the defaulted loan.

Imprudent investment that resulted from conflicts of interest

Usery (Secretary of Labor) *v.* Penn.   In this case the buyer of a company had been made the trustee of its profit-sharing plan, at which time he immediately used the assets of the plan to purchase 97 percent of the shares outstanding from the company's former owner.

O'Neil *v.* Marriott Corp.   The trustees of a plan were officers and major shareholders of the sponsor, and the major asset of the plan was shares of the sponsor. The plaintiffs charged that the trustees of the plan were in a position of conflict of interest since they were insiders to the activities of the company and were also major company shareholders themselves. For both of these reasons the trustees were said to be inhibited from acting in the sole interest of the plan participants.

Marshall (Secretary of Labor) *v.* Snyder et al.   In this case the officers of the union controlled the pension plans and the firm which was the administrative agent of the plan. The complaint alleged that the plan trustees permitted the unwarranted expenditure of plan assets, including a $1 million loan to one defendant, a $380,000 outlay to refurbish the union headquarters, and $300,000 to purchase stock from the administrative agent. These other interesting points of law were noted in this case:

1. Just because a previous consent order established maximum compensation to be paid to parties of interest, these amounts were not necessarily reasonable. The trustees still had a fiduciary responsibility to see that only reasonable fees were paid for services rendered.
2. The burden of proof as to the appropriateness of a transaction between a party in interest and the fund is on the person involved in a transaction, not on the person challenging it.
3. A fiduciary who serves as an employee, agent, or other representative of a party in interest, still remains subject to the party in interest prohibitions of ERISA.
4. It is not necessarily sufficient for a fiduciary who breaches his duties to make good the losses resulting from the breach. Other remedies may also be appropriate. In this case a receiver was appointed to take over responsibility from the trustees who were charged with breach of duty.

Additional cases showing conflicts of interest. In the case of *Marshall* v. *Deep South Electric et al.* the preponderance of the fund's assets was in receivables, of which over 90 percent were based on loans made to the plan sponsor, with the remainder attributable to loans to a company owned by the plan trustee. Interestingly, since the loans had been negotiated before the effective date of ERISA, the Labor Department acknowledged that there was no duty under ERISA to see that they were adequately secured. However, the Labor Department felt that the trustees had a fiduciary responsibility to seek repayment of the loans once they were in default and ERISA had taken effect.

One of the most unusual cases brought by the Labor Department was *Marshall* v. *Conser et al.*, in which the plaintiff was alleged to have failed to act in the best interests of the plan participants because the fiduciary attempted to resign without appointing a successor trustee. The court recognized the severity of the problem, but instead of stopping the trustee from resigning, it approved a new trustee to serve the plan.

Conflicts of interest arise because of the ERISA requirement that employee benefit plans be operated "solely in the interest of participants and beneficiaries, and for the exclusive purpose of providing benefits to participants and beneficiaries and defraying reasonable expenses of plan administration."

The case against the Central States Teamsters contains a number of accusations of breach of fiduciary responsibility which serve aptly to demonstrate various problem areas. This is demonstrated in the following sentence:

7. Defendants, during their respective tenure as plan fiduciaries, breached their fiduciary obligations by failing to discharge their duties with respect to the plan solely in the interest of its participants and beneficiaries, and for the exclusive purpose of providing benefits to participants and beneficiaries and defraying reasonable expenses of plan administration, and with the care, skill, prudence and diligence under the circumstances then prevailing that a prudent man acting in a like capacity and familiar with such matters would use in the conduct of an enterprise of a like character and with like aims, in violation of ERISA §§404(a)(1)(A) and (B), 29 U.S.C. §§1104(a)(1)(A) and (B), by, among other things:

a. failing to adhere to procedures designed to and which would in fact ensure that adequate information was available to them for consideration in connection with decisions concerning the management of plan assets;

b. failing to employ, retain and consult with an adequate staff of persons whose professional background, skill and experience would enable them to make appropriate recommendations with respect to the management of plan assets;

c. entering into commitments to disburse and disbursing plan assets for ventures as to which they had, at the time of such action, insufficient information to make a prudent judgment as to the economic feasibility of such ventures, the degree of risk thereof, and the probable security of plan assets devoted thereto;

d. entering into commitments to disburse and disbursing plan assets in transactions which were imprudent because the plan's expected return in or as a result of such transactions was not commensurate with the plan's risk of loss therein;

e. failing to enforce the plan's right to compliance, by persons who were borrowers of plan assets, with the terms of loan agreements, security agreements and other undertakings, when compliance with such undertakings by the borrowers would have tended to benefit the plan;

f. surrendering rights, security interests and other assets of the plan in exchange for no consideration or inadequate consideration to the plan;

g. granting modifications of agreements controlling the obligations of borrowers of plan assets, granting moratoria on the payment of principal and interest required by such original agreements, making new extensions of credit and otherwise restructuring the terms of such agreements to the advantage of borrowers and the disadvantage of the plan, when such modifications were not calculated to increase the likelihood of repayment, the value of the plan's security or the return on its investment;

h. failing to monitor the use of loan proceeds by borrowers of plan assets, when loan agreements required that such use be limited to specific purposes related to improvements on property in which the plan held security interests;

i. failing to act diligently and promptly to secure protection of the plan's tangible property from damage, enforce the plan's right to have borrowers obtain insurance for and pay taxes relating to property held as collateral, and record mortgage instruments on property held as collateral for loans;

j. failing to exercise the plan's options to demand payment of loans from borrowers, to cease making advances to borrowers in default on their obligations, and to demand payment from guarantors;

k. causing the payment of plan assets to persons and on behalf of persons having no claims against the plan and without consideration to the plan; and

l. failing to pursue claims of restitution on behalf of the plan against persons who have diverted plan assets or otherwise unlawfully derived benefit from the plan to the plan's detriment.[2]

APPENDIX: CHECKLIST OF FIDUCIARY RESPONSIBILITY

In order to ensure that a fund is being properly managed and to help satisfy fiduciary obligations, the sponsors should ask themselves whether they have exercised prudence in:

1. Analyzing what it is that the organization wants from the fund. Yes _____ No _____
2. Assigning responsibility for the fund to a person or group within the organization, including de-

---

[2] U.S. Department of Labor Complaint against Teamsters Central States Pension Fund, Civil Action 78C342; quoted from *BNA Pension Fund Reporter* Bureau of National Affairs, Inc., February 6, 1978, no. 174, p. R-1.

grees of responsibility and authority. Yes _____ No _____

3. Analyzing the fund's needs and
stating an investment policy. Yes _____ No _____

4. Periodically reviewing those
needs and the policy (at least annually). Yes _____ No _____

5. Hiring investment managers,
including an analysis of how the
investment managers' particular
skills are applicable to the fund's
specific needs. Yes _____ No _____

6. Delegating investment responsibility to the investment managers
and securing their acknowledg-
ment that they are fiduciaries
under ERISA. Yes _____ No _____

7. Continuing the use of investment
managers, including an analysis
of whether the fund has met its
financial goals and of how the
fund's performance compares to
appropriate indices and universes
on an absolute basis and on a risk-
adjusted basis. Yes _____ No _____

8. Reviewing fund assets to be sure
that the portfolio is adequately
diversified. Yes _____ No _____

9. Providing adequate information
for the investment manager about
the fund's policies, objectives,
and measurement standards. Yes _____ No _____

10. Establishing procedures of communication between the invest-
ment manager and the sponsor. Yes _____ No _____

11. Being sure that all interested parties (sponsor's representative,
investment manager, actuary,
lawyer, accountant, etc.) are
operating with the same guidelines. Yes _____ No _____

12. When making direct loans of the
fund's assets, establishing and

continuing to monitor the economic feasibility of the venture, the adequacy of the security, the record of the borrower as to past success, and the financial condition of the borrower.   Yes _____ No _____

13. Being aware of the activities of co-fiduciaries and of any potential conflicts of interest or other breaches.   Yes _____ No _____

14. Taking action when this is warranted by conditions.   Yes _____ No _____

15. Documenting all activities, so that a historical record indicates adequate analysis and prudence for all decisions.   Yes _____ No _____

13

Managing
the custodial process

ANALYSIS

Although the choice of the investment manager has a far
greater impact on the fund than the choice of the custodian, the
fund sponsor's daily life will be much simpler if the custodian
is operating efficiently. Consequently, it is advisable that great
care be exercised in choosing a custodian. The key factors in an
organization's ability to provide effective custodial service are:

1. The financial stability of the organization
2. The adequacy of security procedures.
3. The accuracy of record keeping.
4. The scope of record keeping/analysis.
5. Timeliness.
6. Consulting and other special services.
7. Cost.

Financial stability.   Since the cash in the sponsor's portfolio
is commingled with that of other customers of the custodian, as

well as with the funds of the custodial organization itself, it is obviously essential that the custodial organization have sufficient capital, antifraud safety procedures, management controls, and insurance to provide safety for the sponsor's assets. Although it is hoped that the appropriate regulatory authorities will take adequate care in overseeing custodial organizations, nonetheless the sponsor should consider these factors before choosing a custodian.

The adequacy of security procedures. The safekeeping of the physical securities owned by trusts has become less important with the growth of the Depository Trust Company. The DTC holds vast amounts of securities and issues electronic records against them, much as a bank issues statements against a checking account. The development of the DTC offers tremendous possibilities for eliminating wasteful and costly effort and minimizing security risks. Presumably, at some point in the future, virtually no physical securities will exist and all transactions in securities will be carried out without physically transferring the securities. Nevertheless, the sponsor should consider the adequacy of security procedures in choosing a custodian.

The accuracy of record keeping. No matter how complete and timely, the records provided by the custodian to the fund sponsor have little value unless they are credible to all parties. Therefore, it is extremely important that the custodial organization provide accurate information. Sponsors can take two steps in order to gain confidence that accurate information will be provided, though typically they only use a third method. The third method is to ask the custodial organization whether its process produces accurate information. A more reliable method is to discuss the custodial organization's error-checking procedures with its representative. Details should be obtained regarding the manual checks made and regarding the checks built into the computer programs which produce the custodial reports, including the exception reports which are printed when unusual results occur. Finally, existing customers can be questioned as to the success of the custodian in this all-important area of accurate reporting.

The scope of record keeping/analysis. This area can be further broken down into basic record keeping, regulatory information, analysis, and comparison. The basic record-keeping information required is periodic positions and transaction statements. A beginning balance of cash and securities in the account is shown as the initial position. Following that, every transaction which affects the cash balance or the securities held is reported in the cash or transaction statements. Finally, an ending position is shown.

Items affecting cash are the receipt of income, purchases and sales, and contributions and withdrawals. Factors affecting the balance of securities, in addition to purchases and sales, are stock splits and stock dividends and contributions and withdrawals of securities "in kind." Position statements can be provided at book value or at both book value and at market value. Position statements at book value permit reconciling all positions through changes in book value that arise from purchases and sales. Market valuations permit assessment of the fund based on the true value of its assets as of a point in time. The usefulness of such valuations may be affected by the sources of the prices used to arrive at them. Although this is typically not a problem with common stocks, it is a problem with corporate bonds, which, unlike stocks, are not traded in a central marketplace. Even more difficult to price are private placements and mortgages, for which there are generally no public markets. Some care should be used in noting the sources of valuations, especially if the custodian also serves as the investment manager. Summaries of the information provided in the transaction statements can be very helpful. Such summaries might include listings of all dividends received, all interest received, all common stock purchases, and so on. This information is required in order to make performance calculations and other analyses, and the extent to which it is provided *and* broken down determines the level of analysis that is possible.

Regarding regulatory information, reporting requirements for both endowment funds and ERISA funds have been established by regulatory authorities, and the custodian is in an excellent position to provide this information at relatively little cost. Among the information of an analytical nature which the custodian might provide to the fund sponsor are performance measurement (both time-weighted and dollar-weighted rates

of return), risk analysis, beta, alpha, and R^2. The custodian
might also furnish comparisons of the fund's performance with
stock and bond market indices and the performance of commingled and separately managed funds. Since this information
is analyzed in detail in the chapters discussing performance
measurement, no further analysis of them will be made here.

Timeliness. Obviously, the usefulness of any record-
keeping or analytical tool is partly a function of the time lapse
between the period reported on and the receipt of the report by
the appropriate official. Although it might seem that statements should be available a day or two after the close of an
accounting period, there are valid reasons why it usually takes
one to three weeks to supply them. First, if the custodian is not
the investment manager for the complete portfolio, time must
be allowed for any transactions made near month-end to be
reported to the custodian and inputted into the custodian's accounting system. Second, if the sponsor's portfolio holds
commingled funds as part of its assets, the commingled funds
must be valued before the final valuation can be provided on
the portfolio. Since most funds now invest in short-term instruments through commingled portfolios, this delay is likely
to impact a high percentage of all accounts. Third, depending
on the periods covered and on the policies of the custodian and
the sponsor, there may be a need to audit the statements prior
to their issuance. Finally, assuming that the custodian is valu-
ing the positions, information regarding the prices of the secu-
ritied held must be received and inputted. All of these factors
tend to delay the preparation of custodial reports beyond the
processing and mailing times which are inherent to any reporting system. In years to come this information will undoubtedly
be made available to the sponsor through an electronic medium such as a CRT, a typewriter terminal, or a minicomputer.
This will eliminate the delays associated with mailing, but the
other delays will still be present.

Consulting and other special services. It is almost imperative that a custodial organization which supplies information
beyond basic record keeping also offer interpretation of the
analytical information provided. Since custodians have not traditionally supplied analytical information, it is not surprising
that they do not have the staffs available to provide the consult-

ing services. However, this is likely to change in the relatively near future.

Cost. As with the services offered by custodians, large variations exist among the costs charged for those services. Needless to say, the cost of each custodial component and the cost of the total custodial package must be carefully analyzed.

MONITORING

A number of firms have developed in-depth services for monitoring the effectiveness of the custodial process. Typical factors monitored are the accuracy and timeliness with which dividend and interest income is credited, the correctness of calculations of accrued interest on the purchase and sale of bonds, the efficiency with which free cash balances are invested in short-term securities, stock execution prices outside the reported daily highs and lows, and so on. Since audits by certified public accountants typically do not go into great detail in these areas, such analyses of each transaction within a portfolio can be quite useful. In addition, since all transaction information is captured in the monitoring audit, the data obtained in this way can be used for ERISA reporting (such as the reporting of parties in interest transactions) and for analyses of individual transactions or portfolio components.

14

The art of
being a good client

One of the difficult things about managing money is that clients tend to have absolute objectives in bear markets and relative objectives in bull markets.

Previous chapters have discussed the investment and administrative process from the sponsor's point of view. This chapter, like the others, attempts to provide insight for the sponsor, only this time by presenting the point of view of those who provide services to the sponsor. If the sponsor's representatives have a better understanding of the problems encountered by the people who serve them, they will be in a better position to derive the maximum benefit from those people. As the chapter title implies, there is no precise method of achieving this goal. Being a good client is more an art than a science, with empathy and common sense being important factors.

BEING A GOOD CLIENT OF AN INVESTMENT MANAGER

The do's and don'ts of being a good client of an investment manager are as follows:

1. *State your goals.* If the investment manager is going to help you achieve your goals, he must know what they are. (This, of course, assumes that you do, which point has been addressed elsewhere in this book.)

2. *State your goals precisely.* Everyone wants high returns with no risk. Try to be as specific as possible.

3. *Don't change your goals too frequently.* It is important to monitor the progress of the fund in terms of its goals and in terms of how the sponsor's needs change over time. However, investing is a fairly long-term process, requiring a time horizon of several years, and the investment manager cannot be expected to shift the portfolio back and forth within shorter periods. Also, goals cannot be shifted between relative and absolute standards. As the quotation under the chapter title indicates, most sponsors would like to meet their assumed rate of return when the market falls apart and to rank number one when the market is rising sharply. These goals are inconsistent. If your objective is to meet your assumed rate of return, you can't complain if you are up 10 percent when the market is up 50 percent. On the other hand, if you want to be up 50 percent when the market is up 50 percent, you have to be prepared to be down 20 percent when it is down 20 percent.

4. *Don't compare yourself to others with different goals.* If you decide that you can meet your plan's needs by investing in long-term U.S. government bonds, don't be shocked that an equity-oriented fund outperformed yours in a rising stock market.

5. *Provide your manager with cash flow projections.* Give him as much information as possible about the plan's liquidity requirements in future years. This will help him establish both cash flow and risk objectives.

6. *Don't make surprise contributions or withdrawals.* This greatly frustrates the investment manager, who may have put considerable effort into establishing an appropriate portfolio only to have it become inappropriate because of the fund's new cash situation.

7. *Confide in your manager about internal preferences, utilities, and politics.* If your plan has very little ability to bear risk but the chief executive of the organization is a crapshooter, the investment manager should know this. He may want to spend more time educating the chief executive; he may try to walk the fine line between the two extremes; or he may simply resign the account.

8. *Don't fall for every fad.* One investment strategy pursued consistently and successfully will probably produce better results than ten different strategies pursued in succession. The manager should be hired to perform a specific function and should be left pretty much alone to carry it out.

9. *Don't believe the performance figures of every person who walks in the door.* Some investment managers feel that their biggest threat is not their inability to meet client needs but their inability to outperform the standards set by the marketing representatives of other investment management organizations.

10. *Don't expect miracles.* If the market is not completely efficient, it sure comes pretty close. It is not realistic to expect an investment manager to consistently outperform peers who are working with substantially the same tools that he uses. If your investment manager achieves at least average performance, takes the time to understand you and your organization, is responsive to requests and even anticipates them, you are probably deriving about as much as you can expect from your relationship with him.

BEING A GOOD CLIENT OF A CUSTODIAN

An organization providing custodial services would appreciate the following:

1. Regarding the timeliness of reports, please recognize that if you own commingled funds, they must be valued before your portfolio can be valued, and that both your fund and the commingled funds are frequently audited before the custodian's final valuations are issued. These factors delay the submission of reports.

2. Your custodial organization does its best to assure accuracy, but mistakes do happen. Therefore, please try to re-

view reports as soon as you receive them rather than waiting until the day before the board of directors meeting.

BEING A GOOD CLIENT OF A PERFORMANCE MEASUREMENT CONSULTANT

1. Your consultant's reports cannot be produced until statements are received from the bank custodian. Please recognize this, and in addition, please use your influence to see that the custodian's statements are produced and mailed promptly.
2. In order to compare your results with those of other funds, it is necessary that those funds be measured first. Obviously, this delays the processing of your report.
3. Measuring performance is different from creating accounting reports. If your accounting procedures are inadequate, you should correct that problem instead of expecting your consultant to do so.

Appendixes

This book was organized in the order in which problems would be faced and decisions made by the governing body of an organization. The appendixes, on the other hand, serve to provide further information on specific subjects. Included are:

Appendix A.   Tax consequences of the timing of contributions.

Appendix B.   Mathematics refresher.

A

Tax consequences of the timing of contributions

For sponsors which are taxable entities, such as corporations, some thought should be given to the tax implications surrounding the timing of contributions. For purposes of this analysis it is assumed that corporations pay taxes at a 40 percent rate and that the corporation in question is considering whether to make its annual contribution on January 1 of the current year or December 31. It is further assumed that short-term interest rates are 10 percent. If the contribution is made on December 31, the corporation will invest the funds. Two examples will be shown. In the first, the corporation will invest the amount to be contributed in short-term investments, as would the fund. In the second, the corporation has other investment opportunities such that the amount to be contributed will be invested at this higher rate, in this case 20 percent.

261

Investment in short-term securities

In this case the corporation is better off making the contribution on January 1 because the fund pays no taxes on the profits it makes from interest, whereas the corporation does. This can be seen from the example in Table A–1.

TABLE A–1

Contribution made on January 1st

Fund receives $100 × .10 = $10 interest
Taxes   0
After tax benefit $10

Contribution made on December 31st

Corporation receives $100 × .10 = $10 interest
Taxes = $10 × .4   = 4
After tax benefit $ 6

Combined entity better off making contribution on January 1st by amount equal to short term investment rate multiplied by tax rate.

Investment paying 20 percent pretax per year

In this case the corporation is better off by $2 after taxes, or 20 percent of the contribution at year-end. This can be seen from the following:

The company makes 20 percent pretax (12 percent after tax) on the $100, or $12. This exceeds the $10 "after tax" that the fund makes, and hence it is superior.

The company will be better off making the contribution on December 31 if its pretax return times 100 percent minus the tax rate is greater than the short-term interest rate.

B

Mathematics refresher

There is no need for representatives of fund sponsors to be statisticians or mathematical wizards. On the other hand, the trend toward increasing the measurement of all business activities is strong, and this trend will continue. Thus, it is desirable for sponsors' representatives to become more familiar with quantitative techniques than has traditionally been the case. This appendix is directed at people who would like to go beyond the measured results to determine how they are calculated, or who want to be able to make their own calculations. Three areas of measurement will be discussed: measures of central tendency (averages), measures of dispersion around the average (variabilities), and measures which show the relationship between two or more variables (correlations). In addition, the appendix will discuss calculations of dollar-weighted rates of return, time-weighted rates of return, and the "linking" of returns from one period to another.

Measures of central tendency

Two measures of central tendency are used in the investment area. The *arithmetic mean* is the traditional average, and it is calculated by adding up all the numbers and dividing the total by the number of observations. The *median* is the number midway between the high point and the low. Columns A and B below show two series of numbers and their respective means and medians. It is worth noting that the mean and median for a series can be the same, but they need not be, and that either can be greater than the other. In series A the mean is smaller than the median because the number 1 is not as close to the median as is the number 6. In distribution B the mean and the median are equal. Distributions in which the mean and median are close to each other are considered to be "normal" distributions. A distribution in which the mean is different from the median is considered to be "skewed" to either the right or the left.

	A	B
	6	6
	5	5
	1	4
Total	12	15
Mean	4	5
Median	5	5

Additional measures of central tendency include the *mode* (the number which appears the most times) and the *geometric mean* (which is calculated by multiplying all numbers in the series together and taking the nth root of the product).

Measures of dispersion

Just as it is frequently desirable to know something about the "average" of a series, it is also useful to know how the results are distributed around the mean. For instance, 10 is the average of 11 and 9 and it is also the average of 0 and 20. The quality control inspector in a pharmaceutical plant would want to know not only the average amount of medication in each capsule but also whether or not there was a wide dispersion around the average. If 10 grains were the desired average, 9 or

11 might be tolerable, but certainly 0 and 20 would not be. Measurements of dispersion to be discussed are range, mean absolute deviation, standard deviation, variance, and semivariance. In order to show examples of each calculation, the series in column C will be used.

Measures of Dispersion

C

30
26
20
15
12
7
2

$$\text{Mean} = \frac{\Sigma 2 \ldots 30}{7} = \frac{112}{7} = 16$$

Median = Halfway point between high and low = 15

Range = High − Low = 30 − 2 = 28

Mean absolute

deviation = Average of the absolute difference between each observation and the average of all observations ("absolute" means without regard to sign; 3 and −3 both have the absolute value of 3; the sign for absolute value is $\|$, such that $\|-3 = \|3$

$= \|(30 - 16) + \|(26 - 16) + \|(20 - 16) + \|(15 - 16) + \|(12 - 16) + \|(7 - 16) + \|(2 - 16)$

$= 14 + 10 + 4 + 1 + 4 + 9 + 14 = 56$

$56 \div 7 = 8$

Variance = Sum of the squares of the differences between each observation and the average, divided by the number of observations

$= 14^2 + 10^2 + 4^2 + 1^2 + 4^2 + 9^2 + 14^2$

$= 196 + 100 + 16 + 1 + 16 + 81 + 196 = 606$

$$\frac{606}{7} = 86.6$$

Standard

deviation = Square root of variance = $\sqrt{86.6} = 9.3$

Semivariance = Sum of the squares of the differences between the mean and each observation that is
smaller than the mean, divided by the
number of observations that are smaller than
the mean.
$$= 1 + 16 + 81 + 196 = 294 \div 4 = 73.5$$

Range. The range shows the difference between the high and the low of the series and thus gives a rough idea of how representative of the distribution the mean is.

Mean absolute deviation. Whereas the range looks only at the two extreme points, the mean absolute deviation considers every observation and its relation to the average. "Absolute" deviations are shown (i.e., minus signs are ignored), since otherwise pluses and minuses would cancel out, thus showing no deviation.

Variance. The variance is a true measure of the width of the distribution. Like the mean absolute deviation, the variance relates each observation to the average. Unlike the mean absolute deviation, which solves the problem of minus signs by ignoring them, the variance solves this problem by squaring each number (multiplying a negative number by itself produces a positive number).

Standard deviation. This measure, also referred to by the Greek letter sigma (σ), is the square root of the variance. The standard deviation is a useful and widely used measure because it has the interesting characteristic that, for a normal, or bell-shaped, distribution, 68 percent of the observations fall within ± 1 standard deviation and 95 percent fall within two standard deviations. Since it is usually reasonable to suggest that distributions in finance are normal, a good estimate of the dispersion of a distribution around its average is provided by the standard deviation measure.

Semivariance. This measure considers only downside dispersion. Since measures of dispersion are frequently used to measure risk in securities and portfolios, the amount of uncertainty as to future value is one definition of risk. Some investors find this definition difficult to accept because they feel that only below-average expectations represent risk. If an investor expects a stock to rise from 10 to 12, and it actually goes to 13, the extra point is not risk (though it is clearly uncertainty).

Thus, these investors are more comfortable with the semi-variance measure. However, as a practical matter, both variance and semivariance lead to very similar results.

Measures relating two or more variables

By far the most common technique for determining the statistical relationship between two variables is regression analysis (also called correlation analysis). This procedure was described in considerable detail in Chapter 8 as the beta analysis for measuring equity portfolios. In more general terms, the simple regression analysis attempts to measure the relationship between any two variables. It takes the form of the equation:

$$y = a + bx + c$$

Here, y is the variable to be predicted based on knowledge of the current value of x plus the historical relationship between x and y. The term b is key because it tells us how many x's equal one y. If b is 0.5, for every increase by one unit of x, y increases by one-half unit. The term a is a constant, and c represents an error term. That is, if a and b do not completely account for the movement of y, then some additional factor has to be considered, and this is represented by c. The following example illustrates the use of this technique in estimating the total costs of production in a widget factory. (In Greek "a" is alpha and "b" is beta, hence the terms used in Modern Portfolio Theory.) If overhead, such as rent, heat, light, and the boss's salary, costs $10,000 per month, and it costs $1 to produce each widget, the total costs of producing the widgets will equal $10,000 plus $1 times the number of widgets produced. If in a certain month 20,000 widgets were produced, the total costs would be as follows:

Total costs = Fixed costs + Number of units produced
× Variable costs + Unforeseen costs
y = $10,000 + 20,000 × $1 + c$
y = $30,000 + c$

The preceding is an example of a "simple" "linear" regression. The regression is "simple" in that only one independent variable, x, was used. It is possible to utilize more complex equations in which more than one independent variable helps explain the y term. For instance, in the preceding example it would have been possible to consider additional costs which impact the total costs. The experience level of employees, number of new employees to be trained, absentee rate, changes in material costs, and so on, all could have been related to the total costs.

The relationship is called "linear" because the line drawn on a scatter diagram relating the variables is straight. This can be seen in chart A. Chart B shows an exponential relationship,

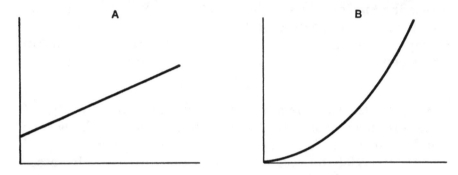

such that y equals x^2. In this case the line curves sharply upward. Other more complex measurement techniques permit the consideration of relationships which are nonlinear.

Time-weighted, dollar-weighted, and linked rates of return

There are several ways of computing the total rate of return on a portfolio. Each means something slightly different. We will examine three such ways.

The time-weighted rate of return. The time-weighted rate of return is the most effective way to compare the returns of different portfolios. It counts each period equally, and thus it assumes no control over the size and timing of cash flows by the portfolio manager. It requires a knowledge of the value of the portfolio at the time of each cash flow. Assume three time periods. At each we have a known value for the portfolio.

Time beginning of	Value before cash flow	Cash flow
1974 = T_0	100 = V_0	10 = C_0
1975 = T_1	130 = V_1	5 = C_1
1976 = T_2	150 = V_2	

For the return between T_0 and T_1 (during 1974),

$$r_1 = [V_1/(V_0 + C_0) - 1] \times 100$$
$$r_1 = [(130/110) - 1] \times 100, \text{ or } 18.2\%$$

For the return between T_1 and T_2 (during 1975),

$$r_2 = [V_2/V_1 + C_1) - 1] \times 100$$
$$r_2 = [(150/135) - 1] \times 100, \text{ or } 11.1\%$$

To find the time-weighted rate for the total period (1974 and 1975) we link r_1 and r_2:

$$1 + r_T = (1 + r_1)(1 + r_2)$$

This is what we mean by linking. Therefore, the total rate

$$r_T = [(1.182)(1.111) - 1] \times 100$$
$$= 31.32\% \text{ for two years}$$

Note that each interval of the same time period has the same impact on the total, no matter how much is in the portfolio during that period. Therefore, the annual rate is computed by $\sqrt{1 + r_T} - 1, = 14.6\%$, the annual time-weighted rate of return. This is the amount which, when linked with itself, yields 31.3 percent.

Note also that in most cases in which the cash flows as a percentage of the portfolio value are small, the time-weighted and the dollar-weighted rates are similar (14.6 compared to 14.5). However, if the cash flows are large or if the number of periods being measured is great, the differences can be significant.

The dollar-weighted rate of return. This rate is often called the internal rate of return or the discounted cash flow. It assigns more importance to the cumulative rate of return of periods when the portfolio is worth more. It may be a meaningful measure of a manager's performance if he has complete control of cash flows. It does not require knowledge of the value of the portfolio at each cash flow, but only at the beginning and ending of the measurement period. The essential form in an n-period model of the rate of return is reflected in the formula:

$$V_n = V_0(1 + r)^{T_0} + C_0(1 + r)^{T_1} + C_1(1 + r)T_2$$
$$+ \cdots C_n(1 + r)^{T_n}$$

where r is the internal rate of return.

In our 1974 to 1976 sample

$$V_2 + V_0(1 + r)^2 + C_0(1 + r)^2 + C_1(1 + r),$$
$$\text{or } 150 = 100(1 + r)^2 + 10(1 + r)^2 + 5(1 + r)$$

Note that this becomes a quadratic equation. We can solve it by using the quadratic formula or by using different values of r (trial and error, or "iteration"), and we find that $r = 14.5$ is the annual dollar-weighted rate of return.

The linked internal rate of return. The linked internal method is an approximation of the time-weighted return and a hybrid of the dollar-weighted and time-weighted rates. The internal rate is used to find returns for shorter intervals within a larger period of time, and these internal rates are linked together to find the time-weighted rate of return for the entire period. For instance, the internal rate may be used to find quarterly rates of return which are then linked together to find the annual rate. If the quarterly returns are called $r_1, r_2, r_3,$ and $r_4,$ then the annual return is found by the formula $(1 + r) = (1 + r_1)$ $(1 + r_2)(1 + r_3)(1 + r_4)$. From the resultant $1 + r$ we subtract 1 and multiply by 100 to find the percentage return for the full period.

Assume that the dollar-weighted rates per quarter were 5 percent, −10 percent, 20 percent, and 4 percent, respectively. Then the linked annual rate would be:

$$[(1 + 0.05)(1 - 0.10)(1 + 0.20)(1 + 0.04)] - 1 \times 100 = 17.9\%$$

This method is used to approximate the time-weighted rate when more frequent valuations are not available.

Bibliography

Lawrence Fisher and James H. Lorie. *A Half Century of Return on Stocks and Bonds: Rates of Return on Investments in Common Stocks and U.S. Treasury Securities, 1926–1976.* Chicago: University of Chicago Graduate School of Business, 1977.

The authors were pioneers in the establishment of the Center for Research in Security Prices (CRSP), which established an enormous stock price data file to permit basic research into security price movements. This book, which updates an earlier study, shows returns on stocks both by weighting each stock equally and by weighting each stock according to the market value of the company.

Measuring the Investment Performance of Pension Funds for the Purpose of Inter-Fund Comparison. Park Ridge, Ill.: Bank Administration Institute, 1968.

The BAI is a not-for-profit corporation designed to assist bank administrators in achieving high levels of professional expertise. In about 1965 it assembled a group of practitioners and academicians to study questions regarding the measuring of pension fund performance. After considerable study the group concluded that:

1. Performance should be measured in terms of both rate of return *and* risk.
2. The rates of return should be total, that is, they should include income and changes in market value.
3. The measurements should be based on calendar quarters in order to facilitate comparison, but no great importance should be attributed to comparisons for periods as brief as three months.
4. Although there is no obviously best way to measure risk, the variability of time-weighted return is recommended, with mean absolute deviation as the measure of variability.
5. Comparisons should distinguish between funds which are discretionary and those which are not.
6. Measurements of the total portfolio can be usefully supplemented by similar measurements for common stocks and warrants, convertible securities, cash and temporary investments, fixed income assets, assets purchased or held at the direction of the sponsor, and other assets.
7. Comparative data should be pooled to increase the size of the relevant universe.
8. Further research should be conducted.

The study goes on to discuss the results of tests on actual portfolios. It also provides formulas for those wishing to implement specific calculation techniques.

Sidney Homer and Martin L. Leibowitz. *Inside the Yield Book: New Tools for Bond Market Strategy*. Prentice-Hall, Englewood Cliffs, N.J., and New York Institute of Finance, New York, N.Y., 1972.

This landmark text on bond investing presents with considerable precision the factors influencing the investment return on fixed income securities. Among the topics it discusses are interest on interest, the volatility of bond prices, and bond swaps. The concept of "realized compound yield" is presented to derive the total return of a bond investment from the three main sources: coupon interest, interest on coupon interest, and principal value at sale or maturity. Of particular interest to fixed income investors are the discussion of the sources of volatility in bond portfolios and the analysis of how various kinds of bonds swaps can add to investment return.

Jack Clark Francis II. *Investments: Analysis and Management*. 2d ed. New York: McGraw-Hill 1976.

This comprehensive textbook describes securities, securities markets, and bond and stock valuation and provides a broad discussion of topics relating to quantitative approaches to investing. It includes discussions of risk, diversification, portfolio theory, and random walk and market efficiency. The book is a useful reference tool on a broad variety of financial subjects, providing a considerable depth of analysis. A combination of straightforward organization, ample graphics and layperson's language (supported by statistics) enhances its readability.

Jerome B. Cohen, Edward D. Zinbarg, and Arthur Zeikel. *Investment Analysis and Portfolio Management*. 3d ed. Homewood, Ill.: Richard D. Irwin, 1977.

This comprehensive text, now in its third edition, describes the structure of the investment community, methods of security evaluations, investment timing, and portfolio management. It stresses traditional methods of investment analysis, while also describing and integrating the ways in which modern portfolio techniques can be used by investors.

Harvey E. Bines. *The Law of Investment Management*. Boston: Warren, Gorham & Lamont, 1978.

This broadly based and highly documented work describes the law of investment management as well as the history and logic behind it. Fundamental principles describing the duties of reasonable care (prudence) and loyalty to the client are traced for both trust and agency (advisory) relationships through the common law and statutes. Federal laws and the various regulatory authorities, such as the Securities and Exchange Commission, the Federal Reserve Board, and the comptroller of the currency, are also discussed.

Particular attention is paid to the impact of Modern Portfolio Theory, ERISA, and the Securities Acts Amendments of 1975, all of which are of major importance to fund sponsors and investment managers. The book also contains an excellent discussion of the law surrounding the use of brokerage commissions for the purchase of brokerage and research services.

The Pension Reform Act of 1974: Law and Explanation. Chicago: Commerce Clearing House 1974.

This volume provides the complete text of the Pension Reform Act and of the report of the joint House and Senate committees which conferred to unite the two versions of the Act. It also explains many sections of the Act.

Peter O. Dietz. *Pension Funds: Measuring Investment Performance*. New York: Free Press, 1966.

Based on a Columbia University doctoral dissertation, this book was among the first discussions of how to measure the returns on pension funds and why this information is necessary. Dietz analyzes a three-part model in which portfolio management is broken down into strategic decisions (the choice of a risk policy to produce the desired balance of liquidity, return, and risk), tactics (specific security selection), and timing (changes in the investment policy based on changing market conditions).

Portfolios are then measured and ranked against each other as follows. Strategic decisions are measured by calculating the annual time-weighted rate of return and the variability, or standard deviation, of annual returns, with the portfolios then being ranked based on their risk and return success. Tactical decisions relating to the common stock sector or the fixed income sector are calculated by looking at the sector's rate of return over many time periods and assigning a point score to each fund based on the number of periods in which it ranked first, second, third, and so on. To measure timing, which he defines as the movement of assets between common stocks and fixed income securities, Dietz looks at purchases as a percentage of total purchases and sales—he also looks at the dollar value of stock purchases relative to the dollar value of the total portfolio—and relates this percentage to the historical percentage in stocks.

In conclusion Dietz presents results on each of the six portfolios for which he had actual data.

William J. Chadwick.   *Regulation of Employee Benefits: ERISA and the Other Federal Laws.* International Foundation of Employee Benefit Plans, Brookfield, Wisconsin.

This book summarizes the impact on employee benefit plans of ERISA, tax laws, labor laws, securities laws, equal employment laws, and banking laws, and it also shows what departments and agencies are involved in the administration of these laws. It analyzes the relevant statutes and important case law relating to employee benefit plans. Although somewhat difficult to use because of an inadequate table of contents and inadequate section headings (the index partly overcomes this problem), this is a useful reference.

Harry M. Markowitz.   *Portfolio Selection: Efficient Diversification of Investments.* a Cowles Foundation monograph New Haven: Yale University Press, 1959.

This historic publication marked the beginning of Modern Portfolio Theory by showing that a portfolio can have characteristics which are quite different from those of the securities in the portfolio (and that investors should therefore be more concerned with the portfolio as a whole than with its component securities). This phenomenon derives from the fact that although a portfolio's return is entirely dependent on the return of the securities it contains, the risk of the portfolio is dependent on the risk of the securities held *and* on the interrelationship between the risk or movement of each security and the risk or movement of each other security. For example, a conservative portfolio could be constructed from two risky securities if the comovement of the two securities were such that when one security was up, the other was down, and vice versa. Thus, an investor would estimate, for the securities in which he was considering investing, the expected return, the risk or uncertainty of return, and covariance of return for each pair of securities. From this information can be calculated a set of "efficient" portfolios, each of which has the characteristic that for a given level of risk no other portfolio has a higher level of return, or that for a given level of return no other portfolio has a lower level of risk. Once the investor has established the set of efficient portfolios, his next step is to choose the portfolio with the highest level of return for the level of risk that he is willing to endure, or the portfolio with the lowest risk for the level of return that he requires. This choice involves the investor's "utility," or his estimate of the value *to him* of each level of risk and return.

Roger G. Ibbotson and Rex A. Sinquefield. *Stocks, Bonds, Bills, and Inflation: The Past (1926–1976) and the Future (1977–2000)* Charlottesville, Virginia. Financial Analysts Research Foundation, 1977.

Ibbotson and Sinquefield review the historical rates of return on common stocks, long-term government bonds, and Treasury bills. They also show the trend in inflation, and simulate future returns of stocks, bonds, and Treasury bills based on the historic relationship between inflation, the "real" interest rate, and risk premiums.

James H. Lorie and Mary T. Hamilton. *The Stock Market: Theories and Evidence.* Homewood, Ill.: Richard D. Irwin, 1973.

This book, written by the renowned Professor Lorie of the Center for Research in Security Prices at the Graduate School of Business, University of Chicago, and his counterpart at Loyola University, surveys the theoretical and empirical studies that have been made on a wide range of aspects of the stock market. The book contains sections on the behavior of the market, the evaluation of securities, and portfolio management. It also includes a glossary of modern portfolio theory terms and a list of complementary readings. Among the topics that receive special attention are the efficient market hypothesis, stock valuation models, the capital asset pricing model, and measuring risk and evaluating performance in portfolios.

Peter F. Drucker. *The Unseen Revolution: How Pension Fund Socialism Came to America.* New York: Harper & Row, 1976.

This extremely thought-provoking book makes two main points:

> An enormous change is occurring in American capitalism as pension funds become the owners of most of the equity in American corporations. The control of these corporations is thus shifting, at least indirectly, from a very small number of extremely wealthy people to a very large number of workers.

> The post–World War II population boom is creating a considerable change in the attitudes of the population as people born after the war move from college age to retirement age, with the movement to retirement being the more important.

Drucker indicates that in 1975 corporate pension funds owned about 25 percent of the equity capital of American business, and he predicts that by 1985 these funds will own 50–60 percent of equity capital. Moreover, the largest employee funds—the 1,000–1,300 largest companies plus the 35 largest unions—already control (own at least one third of) practically all of the 1,000 largest companies. He goes on to say that, "aside from farming, a larger sector of the American economy is owned today by the American worker through his investment agent, pension funds," than that owned by the governments of Chile under Allende, Cuba under Castro, or Hungary or Poland under Stalin.

Equally fascinating is Drucker's discussion of demographic trends. He cites the 1591 census of Zara in Italy, according to which only 1 person out of 40 was over 50 years old. This compares to the ratio in developed countries in which one out of four people are over 50 and about one out of ten are over 65. The population structure in Europe continued, by Drucker's estimates, to be similar to that of the Zara census for several hundred years. When social security came into being in 1935, there was only about one American over 65 alive for every nine or ten people in the labor force, as compared to the current one-in-four ratio.

Drucker goes on to describe the implications of these changes from political and economic points of view. Although this book has been in print for several years, the title of its first chapter, "The Revolution No One Noticed," is still very appropriate, though it is difficult to imagine that this revolution will remain "unseen" for many years longer.

Howard E. Winklevoss. *Pension Mathematics: With Numerical Illustrations.* Homewood, Ill.: Richard D. Irwin for Pension Research Council, Wharton School, University of Pennsylvania, 1977.

Sponsors wishing to learn more about actuarial science will find this work extremely useful. It is fairly brief, straightforward, and well written. Its only shortcoming is that it does not tie the terminology it uses to describe actuarial cost methods with the customary terminology. Nonetheless, it is a very useful book for those who want to learn more about the work of the actuary. Some of its major topics are briefly described below.

The need for actuarial fund estimates arises because sponsors, either by choice or by law, are required to measure the cost of providing benefits. This "cost" can be interpreted to mean either the amount to be recognized from an accounting point of view as the liability established by the plan's provisions, or the funding necessary to provide adequate assets to permit the payment of benefits at some distant future time. Making reasonable estimates of this cost is complex since so many variables must be considered. The assumptions underlying these estimates are as follows:

1. *Salary assumption.* Since most pension funds provide for benefits based on future salary (such as that of the final five years of employment), it is necessary to estimate employees' future salaries.
2. *Benefit assumption.* Each plan provides for specific payments, and these must be calculated for the employees. For instance, a plan might provide a pension of 1 percent of the employee's final salary for each year worked.
3. *Probability of receipt.* Since employees may die, retire early, terminate employment, or become disabled, there is a significant chance that an employee will not collect his normal retirement benefit.
4. *Interest assumption.* Since money is being funded currently to provide for future needs, some estimate must be made as to the rate of return that is to be achieved on this investment. Alternatively, it is possible to estimate the current value or "cost" of the benefit by considering the amount to be paid in some future year and discounting it to the present by a rate established in the interest rate assumption.

After decisions have been made as to the benefits to be paid and the probability that participants will be eligible, a method must be chosen to calculate the precise amount of the sponsor's annual contributions. This is the most confusing area of actuarial work. In general, two broad methods are used, each of which has a number of variations. The *accrued benefit cost method* (a version of which is sometimes called the unit credit cost method) looks to the benefits accruing in the current year and the benefits which have accrued cumulatively. The *projected benefit cost method* (versions of which are sometimes called the entry age normal method, the individual level premium method, and the attained age normal method) looks to the future benefit to be paid and apportions the cost of that benefit to the current year.

Although the work of the actuary is difficult to understand, it is by no means impossible to understand. Some effort is required to learn the actuarial terminology and actuarial notations (the particular symbols defining certain terms or conditions), which appear to be more difficult than the underlying concepts. The effort will prove rewarding, particularly for people who have a good background in mathematics.

Index